HONEY
from
the
ROCK

James Robson's new book on Deuteronomy is an excellent, stimulating and thoughtful guide that will be suitable for students and preachers alike. Robson discusses the major issues and theology of the book in an engaging way. *Honey from the Rock* is far from merely academic as he seeks to encourage readers still to hear the voice of God through Deuteronomy, as well as to use the book in ministry. Robson succeeds in whetting the appetite for reading and applying Deuteronomy.

Paul Barker, lecturer in Old Testament at Seminari Theoloji, Malaysia and Adjunct Professor of Old Testament at Myanmar Evangelical Graduate School of Theology

In what ways can the Old Testament be Scripture for the church? James Robson's *Honey from the Rock* is an excellent and timely answer. In Deuteronomy, he addresses a book that is of profound significance for biblical religion, demonstrating the rich possibilities of biblical law for the Christian life, exposing misconceptions about law in relation to the New Testament, and offering wise guidance about some of the commonly experienced difficulties in its use. Literate, engaging and erudite, this is a must-read for teachers of the Bible.

Gordon McConville, Professor of Old Testament Theology, University of Gloucestershire

HONEY
from
the
ROCK

· ·

Deuteronomy for
the People of God

JAMES ROBSON

APOLLOS (an imprint of Inter-Varsity Press)
Norton Street, Nottingham NG7 3HR, England
Email: ivp@ivpbooks.com
Website: www.ivpbooks.com

First published 2013

British Library Cataloguing in Publication Data
A catalogue record for this book is available from the British Library.

ISBN: 978-1-84474-625-5

Set in Monotype Garamond 11/13pt
Typeset in Great Britain by Servis Filmsetting Ltd, Stockport, Cheshire
Printed and bound in Great Britain by Ashford Colour Press Ltd, Gosport,
Hampshire

Inter-Varsity Press publishes Christian books that are true to the Bible and that
communicate the gospel, develop discipleship and strengthen the church for its
mission in the world.

Inter-Varsity Press is closely linked with the Universities and Colleges Christian
Fellowship, a student movement connecting Christian Unions in universities and
colleges throughout Great Britain, and a member movement of the International
Fellowship of Evangelical Students. Website: www.uccf.org.uk.

CONTENTS

PREFACE

Honey from the Rock seemed particularly appropriate as a title for this book. It is a quotation directly from Deuteronomy, from the song of Moses in chapter 32 (v. 13). There Moses illustrates God's faithfulness to his recalcitrant people with the striking image of Yahweh's suckling his people with honey from a rocky crag.

Honey speaks of sweet nourishment. In the Old Testament milk and honey are the enticing fare of the Promised Land. But honey as sweet nourishment extends to Yahweh's words. Yahweh taught Israel in the wilderness that people live not just on bread alone but on every word that comes from Yahweh's mouth (Deut. 8:3). The psalmist celebrates God's word as 'sweeter than honey' (Pss 19:10; 119:103). As we shall see, Deuteronomy is a book filled with Yahweh's words.

That this honey comes from the 'rock' is fitting in two ways. Most straightforwardly, a rock is hardly the most promising place to find nourishment, and perhaps for many readers Deuteronomy may seem equally unpromising. Alongside this is the picture in the song of Moses of Yahweh as the rock. Yahweh the rock stands resplendent at the start of chapter 32 (32:4), and the metaphor is repeated six more times in the chapter (32:13, 15, 18, 30, 31, 37). Our nourishment comes not just from Deuteronomy, but from God himself. Although the rock as the source of honey is a different word from Yahweh as rock elsewhere (*selaʿ* vs. *ṣûr*), yet the intimate image of 'suckling' and the use of this same image in Psalm 81:16 with the rock there as *ṣûr* suggest that the honey is from God the rock. In short, 'honey from the rock' indicates that

Deuteronomy, though perhaps an unlikely place, supplies sweet nourishment from God.

Deuteronomy often emphasizes one generation teaching the next. Some of my first classes in Old Testament as a theological student at Wycliffe Hall in Oxford were taught by Gordon McConville. As I have come to teach and now to write on the book of Deuteronomy, I find myself as Tutor in Old Testament back at Wycliffe Hall, and it has been to his work that I have often turned. A short article of his, 'Deuteronomy: Torah for the Church of Christ', provided some of the seeds from which the following chapters have grown. I and many others owe a great deal to his thoughtful engagement with the Scriptures for the sake of the church. I trust that in turn this book will be of benefit to, among others, my own students past, present and future. It has been and remains my privilege to serve each one.

ABBREVIATIONS

AB	Anchor Bible
ABD	*Anchor Bible Dictionary*, ed. David Noel Freedman, 6 vols. (New York: Doubleday, 1992)
AGJU	Arbeiten zur Geschichte des antiken Judentums und des Urchristentums
ANF	*The Ante-Nicene Fathers: Translations of the Writings of the Fathers Down to A.D. 325*, ed. A. Roberts and J. Donaldson, 10 vols. (Peabody, Mass.: Hendrickson, repr. 1994)
Ant.	*Antiquities of the Jews* (Josephus)
AOTC	Apollos Old Testament Commentary
BBR	*Bulletin for Biblical Research*
BDB	F. Brown, S. R. Driver and C. A. Briggs, *A Hebrew and English Lexicon of the Old Testament* (Oxford: Clarendon, 1907; repr. Peabody: Hendrickson, 2005)
BEATAJ	Beiträge zur Erforschung des alten Testaments und des antiken Judentums
BECNT	Baker Exegetical Commentary on the New Testament
BETL	Bibliotheca ephemeridum theologicarum lovaniensium
BHQ	*Biblia Hebraica Quinta*, Deuteronomy, Fascicle 5, ed. Carmel McCarthy (Stuttgart: Deutsche Bibelgesellschaft, 2007)
Bib	*Biblica*

BSac	*Bibliotheca sacra*
BZAW	Beihefte zur Zeitschrift für die alttestamentliche Wissenschaft
c.	circa
CBQ	*Catholic Biblical Quarterly*
CBR	*Currents in Biblical Research*
esp.	especially
ESV	English Standard Version
EuroJTh	*European Journal of Theology*
ExpTim	*Expository Times*
FAT	Forschungen zum Alten Testament
HALOT	L. Koehler and W. Baumgartner, *The Hebrew and Aramaic Lexicon of the Old Testament*, tr. and ed. under the supervision of M. E. J. Richardson, 5 vols. (Leiden: Brill, 1994–2000)
HBT	*Horizons in Biblical Theology*
Heb.	Hebrew
HS	*Hebrew Studies*
HSM	Harvard Semitic Monographs
ICC	International Critical Commentary
Int	*Interpretation*
ITC	International Theological Commentary
JBL	*Journal of Biblical Literature*
JBQ	*Jewish Bible Quarterly*
JETS	*Journal of the Evangelical Theological Society*
JJS	*Journal of Jewish Studies*
JM	Paul Joüon and Takamitsu Muraoka, *A Grammar of Biblical Hebrew*, rev. ed., Subsidia biblica 27 (Rome: Pontificio Istituto Biblico, 2006)
JPS	Jewish Publication Society translation
JSJSup	Journal for the Study of Judaism Supplements
JSOT	*Journal for the Study of the Old Testament*
JSOTSup	Journal for the Study of the Old Testament, Supplement Series
JTISup	Journal of Theological Interpretation Supplements
LCC	Library of Christian Classics
LHBOTS	Library of Hebrew Bible / Old Testament Studies
lit.	literally

LNTS	Library of New Testament Studies
LXX	Septuagint
MT	Masoretic Text
NAB	New American Bible
NASB	New American Standard Bible
NCBC	New Century Bible Commentary
NIBC	New International Biblical Commentary
NICNT	New International Commentary on the New Testament
NICOT	New International Commentary on the Old Testament
NIV	New International Version
NRSV	New Revised Standard Version
NSBT	New Studies in Biblical Theology
OBT	Overtures to Biblical Theology
OTG	Old Testament Guides
OTL	Old Testament Library
OTS	Old Testament Studies
Proof	*Prooftexts: A Journal of Jewish Literary History*
PBM	Paternoster Biblical Monographs
pl.	plural
PTMS	Pittsburgh Theological Monograph Series
SBLDS	Society of Biblical Literature Dissertation Series
SBLMS	Society of Biblical Literature Monograph Series
SBLSS	SBL Semeia Studies
sg.	singular
SHS	Scripture and Hermeneutics Series
SNTSMS	Society for New Testament Studies Monograph Series
SSN	Studia semitica neerlandica
tr.	translation, translated by
TUGAL	Texte und Untersuchungen zur Geschichte der Altchristlichen Literatur
TynB	*Tyndale Bulletin*
VT	*Vetus Testamentum*
WBC	Word Biblical Commentary
WMANT	Wissenschaftliche Monographien zum Alten und Neuen Testament

WUNT   Wissenschaftliche Untersuchungen zum Neuen
            Testament
ZABR   *Zeitschrift für altorientalische und biblische Rechtsgeschichte*

1. INTRODUCTION

James Michener's novel *The Source* traces the development of Jewish history through successive layers of an archaeological dig. Michener's patience and painstaking attention to detail match that of any archaeologist. Each of the layers of the dig at the archaeological site of Tell Makor gives a window into the life and times of the Jewish people. At one point in the novel the following conversation occurs between two archaeologists, the American chief protagonist Dr Cullinane and the erudite Israeli Dr Eliav.[1] Cullinane, keen to understand the Jews better, wants to know what to read. At first Eliav highlights a number of modern scholars with whom Cullinane is already familiar. Then he mentions Maimonides, the medieval Jewish scholar. Again Cullinane has read his work. Eliav continues:

Eliav: There's one better.
Cullinane: What?
Eliav: Read Deuteronomy five times.

---

1. James A. Michener, *The Source* (London: Mandarin, 1993), p. 184.

Cullinane: Are you kidding?

Eliav: No. Deuteronomy. Five times.

Cullinane: What's your thought?

Eliav: It's the greatest central book of the Jews and if you master it you'll understand us.

Cullinane: But is it worth five readings?

Eliav: Yes . . .

This fictional conversation raises in striking ways some of the important questions this opening chapter and the ensuing ones will deal with. At the most foundational level it asks of Deuteronomy, 'Is it worth five readings?' Why would anyone choose to invest concentrated time and energy on a book written so long ago? Beyond that, it raises questions of why different readers read Deuteronomy and what they (can) hope to get out of it. In the novel it was an inquisitive archaeologist as the reader. And why should he read it? Dr Eliav holds out the tantalizing possibility of *mastering* the book – and not just any book, but 'the greatest central book of the Jews' – and, with it, the possibility of understanding the most enigmatic of people, the Jews. But what of contemporary readers? Why might they choose to read it, and what might they hope to get out of the book as they read it? What might be achievable? What might contemporary readers come to understand or appreciate?

Naturally there is a sense in which these questions interlock. Readers read books for different purposes. And this is true not just of Deuteronomy, but also of this work. In the remainder of the opening chapter there will be some introductory comments on Deuteronomy followed by a general orientation regarding the chapters that follow. This will, I trust, whet the reader's appetite both for the rest of the book and, more importantly, for Deuteronomy itself.

Orientation to Deuteronomy

Where it fits and what it is about
Deuteronomy is the fifth book of the Christian Old Testament and the Jewish Tanakh. As such, it is the final book of the Christian

Pentateuch and the Jewish Torah. The death of Moses, the human figure dominating the Pentateuch as leader and lawgiver, marks the end of Deuteronomy and the end of the Pentateuch. Since the birth of Moses at the start of Exodus, the action-packed narrative of God's rescuing his people from slavery in Egypt has provided the context for the giving of the law. In that lawgiving, as we encounter his address to Moses, we have heard the voice of Yahweh unmediated. Deuteronomy is different. We hardly hear the voice of Yahweh other than mediated through Moses; there is almost no action or spatial movement in the book, for the people are no closer to the Promised Land at the end than at the start. Instead of action, the book is chiefly made up of the words of Moses as he addresses Israel in the plains of Moab. They are on the edge of the land. Moses must die outside the land (Num. 20:12), and they must cross the Jordan and take possession of it without him.

After the prologue in 1:1–5, Moses' first speech runs from 1:6 to 4:40. In it he outlines recent history and calls them to obedience. His next speech begins in 5:1 and continues until the end of chapter 26. After spelling out the basic 'commandment' of love and loyalty, he gives more detailed stipulations. Chapter 27:1–10 breaks the flow, as others speak alongside him (elders, v. 1; Levitical priests, v. 9). Moses speaks again on his own from 27:12, continuing until the end of chapter 28, outlining blessings for obedience and curses for disobedience. Moses' final speech starts in 29:2 and continues until the end of chapter 30, as he spells out the covenant in the plains of Moab. In chapter 31 Moses' words are embedded within a narratival context. Deuteronomy 32:1–43 gives Moses' song, and is followed by his brief exhortation to take all his words seriously (32:46–47). Chapter 33 consists of the blessings of Moses, his final words recorded in the book, and chapter 34 narrates his death.

Given that the vast majority of Deuteronomy consists of the words of Moses, it is an appropriate question to ask what all his talk is trying to achieve. As the Israelites stand in the plains of Moab on the verge of entering the Promised Land, Moses outlines God's agenda for the future and summons them 'today' to decision, to 'choose life' (30:19). Life is obedience, blessing and possession of the land. This call to decision is rooted in two realities.

First, their 'today' is linked to the past. The critical point is this. Moses speaks to them as if they had been in Egypt or at Horeb, though they had not! For example, he urges them to remember, sometimes explicitly through using the word 'remember', sometimes simply through rehearsing the events of the exodus: they are to recall what God *did* in rescuing them from Egypt (e.g. 7:18–19) and what God *said* at Horeb (e.g. 5:4; 5:22). Yet in Moses' first speech those who have made it to Moab (with the exception of Moses, Joshua and Caleb) were not actually present because the entire generation of adults had died on the way (2:14; also 1:35). That does not stop the sense of solidarity and continuity. In 1:26 Moses claims that his listeners share the responsibility for the earlier rebellion: 'Yet *you* were not willing to go up, but rebelled against the command of Yahweh your God';[2] in the plains of Moab forty years on they now have the chance to put things right. The same picture is to be found in 4:9–10 and most explicitly in 5:3. There, with a breathless cascade of hearer-embracing terms, Moses declares, 'Not with our fathers did Yahweh make this covenant, but *with us, we, these, here, today, all of us, alive*' (my word-for-word 'translation'). The covenant was not simply a one-off event with those who were at Horeb but is also for those in the plains of Moab. In fact, if the rhetoric of 5:3 is taken too literally, the covenant was not with those at Horeb at all. In other words the events at Horeb have a contemporary force for those on the edge of the Promised Land in the plains of Moab. 'The past is brought into the present with compelling power. Action in the present is conditioned by what is remembered.'[3]

Secondly, their 'today' is linked to the future. In 4:25 Moses looks into the distant future (cf. 'children's children'), to life in the land, and anticipates future rebellion and deportation. It is striking how 'the Israel of the future can also be taken into the "you" form

---

2. Unless stated otherwise, translations are my own.

3. J. Gary Millar, *Now Choose Life: Theology and Ethics in Deuteronomy*, NSBT 6 (Leicester: Apollos, 1998), p. 79.

of address, and be supposed to have stood in principle at Horeb'.[4] This same future perspective is evident in 29:14–15, where the covenant is also with those who are 'not here with us today'. The past and the future are compressed into the moment of 'today' in the plains of Moab as Moses addresses all Israel. He 'is calling Israel to *an act of corporate, imaginative remembrance* as the insights of the past are brought to bear on the decisions of the present and future'.[5]

Moses thus proclaims for Deuteronomy a relevance that endures down the generations, into the future. That is confirmed by his writing it down and giving instructions for its preservation and proclamation in the future (31:9–13). 'Today' is the moment of decision, the moment of covenant, the moment of demand. And this 'today' is ever present. Events in the past, at Horeb and in the wilderness, and events in the future, entry into the land and life in the land, are all compressed into this 'today' in Moab. Every day is a plains-of-Moab day, a 'choose life' day, wherever they find themselves. The way to enter the land is the way to live in the land. That was true of Israel and it is true of the Christian. The way *in* is the way *on* (cf. Col. 2:6). Christians are to deny themselves, take up their cross and follow 'daily' (Luke 9:23), and exhort one another not to be hardened by sin's deceitfulness 'as long as it is called "today"' (Heb. 3:13; cf. Ps. 95).

Who wrote it, when and why?

These questions have been the subject of huge scholarly discussion. In short, no one knows for certain. I have discussed this elsewhere.[6] In my view, although there is a complex prehistory, the ultimate context for the book is Israel in exile, confronted a second time with the chance to 'enter' the land. Moses' words are

---

4. J. Gordon McConville, *Deuteronomy*, AOTC 5 (Leicester: Apollos, 2002), p. 109.

5. Millar, *Now Choose Life*, p. 77 (emphasis original).

6. James E. Robson, 'The Literary Composition of Deuteronomy', in Philip S. Johnston and David G. Firth (eds.), *Interpreting Deuteronomy: Issues and Approaches* (Nottingham: Apollos, 2012), pp. 19–59.

're-presented' for this new context. Some of the reasons and the background for this conclusion will emerge in what follows.

Is it worth five readings?

This was Dr Cullinane's question. How to frame this answer depends in large measure on who the reader is. For some modern readers Deuteronomy is a book to be repudiated, at least in some measure. Recently, Professor Richard Dawkins, the author of *The God Delusion* and a militant atheist, refused to debate in Oxford with the American Christian philosopher and apologist William Lane Craig. In an article in the *Guardian* newspaper defending this refusal, Dawkins highlighted what he termed the 'call to genocide' of Deuteronomy 20:13–17. He went on to excoriate Craig as a 'deplorable apologist for genocide' for his apparent acceptance of such verses.[7] From within the world of Old Testament scholarship a similar view may be found, albeit expressed in more measured fashion:

> the very assumption that Israel could be the beneficiary of a divinely given entitlement to conquer, repress, and exterminate an entire population in order to gain possession of their land undermines the many richer ethical and spiritual insights the book contains.[8]

To these points we shall return. In reality, readers can think Deuteronomy worth reading without necessarily either endorsing or repudiating it. This is because of its central importance in (at least) three areas.

First, Deuteronomy is often regarded as the centre of the Old

---

7. Richard Dawkins, 'Why I Refuse to Debate with William Lane Craig', *Guardian*, 20 Oct. 2011. Two days later Deuteronomy again featured, as another 'sceptic', Daniel Came, took issue with Dawkins's refusal ('Richard Dawkins's Refusal to Debate Is Cynical and Anti-Intellectualist', *Guardian*, 22 Oct. 2011).
8. Ronald E. Clements, 'The Book of Deuteronomy: Introduction, Commentary, and Reflections', in Leander E. Keck (ed.), *The New Interpreter's Bible* (Nashville: Abingdon, 1998), p. 285.

Testament and of Old Testament theology. This is partly because
it closes the Pentateuch. In the Pentateuch the definitive saving
event for Israel has happened in the exodus, the definitive revela-
tory event has happened at Sinai, and the definitive formational
event, of the people of Israel constituted as Yahweh's people,
has happened in and through the exodus and the covenant made
there. In that sense the five books can be regarded as the 'Gospels'
of the Old Testament. Moses, the figure astride the majority of
the Pentateuch, dies as Deuteronomy ends. Deuteronomy not
only ends the Pentateuch but also provides the framework and
the lenses through which to read the subsequent historical books
from Joshua to the end of 2 Kings. Deuteronomy is central to the
Old Testament because its language, thought forms and theology are to be found in many other parts of the Old Testament. It
has many echoes in the wisdom literature, with the call to 'fear'
Yahweh, the choice of life and death, and the importance of a
theology of retribution. Deuteronomic language is to be found in
the prophetic literature of the northern kingdom, Israel (Hosea),
and the southern kingdom, Judah (Jeremiah and Ezekiel). Further,
it has clearly shaped the post-exilic community (cf. Ezra 9; Neh.
1; 8). Given such prominence within the Old Testament, it is no
surprise that it was highly influential at Qumran and in the development of Judaism.[9]

A second way in which Deuteronomy is pivotal is in the role
it has played in critical scholarship since the beginning of the
nineteenth century. Ever since de Wette (1805), Deuteronomy
has proved a battleground for scholars endeavouring to date and
document the production of Old Testament literature. De Wette
not only linked the kernel of Deuteronomy (Deut. 12 – 26) with
the reforms of Josiah, the young king of Judah (2 Kgs 22 – 23),
but also regarded it as written just before its discovery and as being
separate from Genesis–Numbers. It is the work of two other
scholars, building on these insights, that illustrates Deuteronomy's
central role in critical scholarship.

---

9. See esp. David Lincicum, *Paul and the Early Jewish Encounter with
Deuteronomy*, WUNT 2.284 (Tübingen: Mohr Siebeck, 2010).

First, there is the hypothesis stated articulately by Julius Wellhausen.[10] For Wellhausen Josiah's reforms (622 BC) provide an anchor point by which other parts of the Pentateuch and historical writings are to be dated and evaluated. Works are either pre- or post-Deuteronomic. In particular, parts of the Pentateuch believed to be written by the Yahwist (J) and the Elohist (E) are said to pre-date Deuteronomy (D), while parts believed to be written by the Priestly writer (P) are said to post-date Deuteronomy. The latter point was Wellhausen's most distinctive contribution. This view of the composition of the Pentateuch, the Documentary Hypothesis, held sway over the vast majority of scholars for more than a hundred years. Although the scholarly consensus on the Documentary Hypothesis has evaporated, with many scholars thinking that material assigned to J and E dates from (much) later than the tenth–ninth century BC, the dating of D has emerged largely unscathed.

The second scholar is Martin Noth.[11] Noth turned his attention to what followed Deuteronomy rather than what preceded it. He argued that an existing law code (12 – 26) and its introduction (5 – 11) together were prefaced by a historical narrative (1 – 3 [4]). This historical narrative served not as an introduction to chapters 5–26 so much as to the books subsequent to it. Together the code and narrative prologue introduced and shaped the portrayal of theology and history in the books of Joshua to 2 Kings. The resultant work, designated the Deuteronomistic History, served the purpose of explaining why the exile happened. The work of these two scholars has been the springboard for innumerable articles and books on Deuteronomy and its significance.

A third way in which Deuteronomy is pivotal is in its New Testament significance. It is one of three books quoted more than any other Old Testament books (the others being Isaiah

---

10. Julius Wellhausen, *Prolegomena to the History of Ancient Israel: With a Reprint of the Article 'Israel' from the Encyclopaedia Britannica* (Gloucester, Mass.: Peter Smith, 1983 [German original 1878]).

11. Martin Noth, *The Deuteronomistic History*, tr. D. Orton, JSOTSup 15 (Sheffield: JSOT Press, 1981, 2nd ed. [German original 1957]).

and Psalms).[12] Jesus himself quoted from Deuteronomy more
than from any other Old Testament book. Its influence, without
any direct citation, can be seen in innumerable ways in John's
Gospel (e.g. in the linking of love and obedience, and Jesus as the
prophet like Moses). It clearly shaped Paul's reading of the events
surrounding the death and resurrection of Christ and the circumcision of the heart (Rom. 2:29; 10);[13] it also shaped Paul's ethics.[14]
It formed a significant backdrop for the book of Hebrews.[15] The
first and greatest commandment Jesus cites, the Shema, comes
from Deuteronomy: 'Hear . . .' (Deut. 6:4).[16]

Deuteronomy, then, is central within the Old Testament and
within subsequent Judaism, within Old Testament scholarship,
and because of its significance for the New Testament. For different readers Deuteronomy is worth reading because of its
pivotal importance. But beyond these reasons, many will read
Deuteronomy because they recognize that in it is to be found
'honey from the rock', the sweet nourishment of God's words.

---

12. The same three books also have the greatest representation at Qumran,
    in terms of number of copies in Hebrew/Aramaic found. See James C.
    VanderKam, *The Dead Sea Scrolls Today*, 2nd ed. (Grand Rapids: Eerdmans,
    2010), p. 48.

13. David Lincicum, 'Paul's Engagement with Deuteronomy: Snapshots and
    Signposts', *CBR* 7 (2008), pp. 37–67; Lincicum, *Paul*.

14. 'When Paul regulates conduct in the churches, he is dependent on the
    Scriptures in general and on Deuteronomy, it appears, in particular'
    (Brian S. Rosner, *Paul, Scripture and Ethics: A Study of 1 Corinthians 5–7*,
    AGJU 22 [Leiden: Brill, 1994], p. 178).

15. See esp. David M. Allen, *Deuteronomy and Exhortation in Hebrews: A Study in
    Narrative Re-Presentation*, WUNT 238.2 (Tübingen: Mohr Siebeck, 2008).

16. See further Steve Moyise and Maarten J. J. Menken (eds.), *Deuteronomy in
    the New Testament: The New Testament and the Scriptures of Israel*, LNTS 358
    (London: T. & T. Clark International, 2007); and, more generally, D. A.
    Carson and Greg K. Beale (eds.), *Commentary on the New Testament Use of
    the Old Testament: An Exploration of Old Testament Quotations, Allusions, and
    Echoes Occurring from Matthew Through Revelation* (Grand Rapids: Baker;
    Nottingham: Apollos, 2007).

And rather than read it in order to 'master' it, as Eliav puts it, mastering Deuteronomy is neither possible nor desirable, for it is God's Word. Instead, we should desire it to master us.[17]

Orientation to this book

What the book is and who it is for

This is a book *about* Deuteronomy, or, rather, a book about reading Deuteronomy. It is not meant to be a substitute for reading it, but a guide in doing so. It is self-consciously not a commentary. Commentaries are valuable and there are many excellent ones on Deuteronomy. Sometimes, though, it is possible to lose the wood for the trees in a commentary. Neither is it a monograph or treatment of the book from a particular angle. Again these books are illuminating, allowing one to read the book through one set of lenses, such as Deuteronomy's ethics or the death of Moses,[18] or focusing on particular passages.[19] But they are different from the chapters below. Neither is this an eclectic work, collecting different essays by one (or more) author(s) without a necessary connection between the essays.

Rather, my aim is to orient readers to Deuteronomy before and after reading: before, to guide them in what to expect and to help them interpret what they find; after, to help them think through the wider significance of what they have read. As we saw a moment ago, Deuteronomy is pivotal in more than one way. So there will be many legitimate reasons for reading it or regarding it as worth reading. This book is meant for those coming to read Deuteronomy for a definite set of reasons.

It is written for those who are convinced that the future to which Deuteronomy pointed has become a reality in Jesus Christ.

---

17. A point highlighted by a former student, Paul Kerry.

18. Millar, *Now Choose Life*; Dennis T. Olson, *Deuteronomy and the Death of Moses: A Theological Reading*, OBT (Minneapolis: Fortress, 1994).

19. E.g. Paul A. Barker, *The Triumph of Grace in Deuteronomy: Faithless Israel, Faithful Yahweh in Deuteronomy*, PBM (Carlisle: Paternoster, 2004).

The centrality of Deuteronomy for the Old Testament and for Old Testament theology means that attention to Deuteronomy's place within that world is critical. At the same time such attention will not exhaust our focus, nor will it be our exclusive focus. This study is for those interested in understanding Deuteronomy's role within a *Christian* biblical theology.

It is also written for those convinced that when Deuteronomy is read, God's voice is heard. It is written for those who take Deuteronomy's inspiration seriously. Its focus, then, will not be on the scholarly debates of the last two hundred years or so. Although many readers may now breathe a sigh of relief, it is the conviction of this author that these scholarly debates are not simply an unwelcome distraction from the real task of interpretation. This work is rooted in and grows out of such scholarship, but the latter will not be our focus. Here Deuteronomy is the object of study not as a historical artefact, but as the living word of God. It is not concerned about the history of its influence over a people, such as Dr Eliav suggests. Rather, it is for the pastor, the (theological) student, the congregation member who wants to get a window into Deuteronomy. This may be with a view to preaching or teaching it, but it need not be.[20]

Finally, it is written for those who (need to) recognize that the Old Testament is not a repository of sound bites or an encyclopedia of promises, advice and commands I need to marshal to live my life. Rather, I need a paradigm shift whereby I enter its world rather than bring it to mine, where the centre is not me and my life but God and his action in history. Bonhoeffer puts it brilliantly as he extols the value of consecutive public Bible reading:

> Consecutive reading of Biblical books forces everyone who wants to hear to put himself, or to allow himself to be found, where God has

---

20. Those readers looking for a more typical scholarly introduction to Deuteronomy may refer to Ronald E. Clements, *Deuteronomy*, OTG (Sheffield: JSOT Press, 1989); Alexander Rofé, *Deuteronomy: Issues and Interpretation*, OTS (Edinburgh: T. & T. Clark, 2002); Philip S. Johnston and David G. Firth (eds.), *Interpreting Deuteronomy: Issues and Approaches* (Nottingham: Apollos, 2012).

acted once and for all for the salvation of men. We become part of what once took place for our salvation. Forgetting and losing ourselves, we, too, pass through the Red Sea, through the desert, across the Jordan into the promised land. With Israel we fall into doubt and unbelief and through punishment and repentance experience again God's help and faithfulness. All this is not mere reverie but holy, godly reality. We are torn out of our own existence and set down in the midst of the holy history of God on earth. There God dealt with us, and there He still deals with us, our needs and our sins, in judgment and grace. It is not that God is the spectator and sharer of our present life, howsoever important that is; but rather that we are the reverent listeners and participants in God's action in the sacred story, the history of the Christ on earth. And only in so far as we are *there*, is God with us today also.

A complete reversal occurs. It is not in our life that God's help and presence must still be proved, but rather God's presence and help have been demonstrated for us in the life of Jesus Christ.[21]

Method

In the pages below I work with a narratival, synchronic reading of Deuteronomy as a discrete book. This is worth unpacking because each statement could be contested. By narratival and synchronic I indicate that I am working with the text as we have it, rather than focusing on different sources or redactional layers.[22] This is not to deny that Deuteronomy has a compositional history, but it is to say that, alongside the greater value a Christian would place upon reading the text in its final (canonical) form, there is also great value *as a scholar* in working with the book as it is.

---

21. Dietrich Bonhoeffer, *Life Together*, tr. John W. Doberstein (London: SCM, 1954), p. 38 (emphasis original).
22. By talking of 'the text as we have it' I am conscious of oversimplification. Questions include the following: Hebrew or Greek? Which Hebrew? How should we handle textual variants? The position I adopt is to work principally with (English translations of) the Hebrew Masoretic Text (MT), while being willing in principle to countenance emending that text. These questions are of great importance in 32:8, 43.

It needs to be said that the world behind the text, the world of authors, events, text production, is an important one for the Christian and not just for the scholar. This is, after all, the world in which God has acted and that can help us understand who produced Deuteronomy and why. However, a diachronic approach, one that focuses on the depth dimension of the text or its compositional history, too often means that the final form of the book is untouched. To use the image of an enthusiastic DIY car mechanic, the car lies in bits and pieces all over the garage, and is never put back together, let alone driven. So a Christian regarding Deuteronomy as an inspired authoritative text understandably is keen to focus on the book as a whole.

But for a scholar too there is value in focusing on the book as it is. Some scholarship does so because it is concerned to look at the world within the text and to read the Bible as literature.[23] But it seems to me that there is value for the scholar concerned for history to focus on the final form of Deuteronomy.[24] That is because there are historical questions that revolve around the book as we have it. Why is it the shape it is? What was the author trying to do in producing the book?

The second part that needs unpacking is 'Deuteronomy as a discrete book'. This is important because most scholars see in the book of Deuteronomy the flowering of Deuteronomic movement and a deuteronomic theology that is by no means restricted to Deuteronomy itself, but is to be found elsewhere, both in the subsequent historical books from Joshua to Kings, and, to a debatable degree, in the books that precede. In other words those who produced Deuteronomy in the form we have it incorporated it into a larger work, and their distinctive theological outlook is to be found not just in Deuteronomy, but in other works too. There is

---

23. E.g. Robert Polzin, 'Deuteronomy', in Robert Alter and Frank Kermode (eds.), *The Literary Guide to the Bible* (London: Fontana, 1987), pp. 92–101.

24. This is one enduring legacy of Brevard Childs, with his insistence that attention to the canonical form is an appropriate matter for scholarship and not a flight to pre-critical reading of the Bible. See esp. his *Introduction to the Old Testament as Scripture* (London: SCM, 1979).

then an argument that the focus should not be on Deuteronomy, but on Deuteronomic theology.[25]

Without denying Deuteronomy's place within other works, there *is* something discrete about the book. It stands both with and apart from what precedes and what follows.[26] With Noth, it stands with Joshua–Kings in terms of what follows in the portrayal of history. Yet in certain senses it stands apart. As Deuteronomy ends and Moses dies, there is no single 'heir' to Moses in all his roles. Responsibility is now devolved (16:18 – 18:22) and Joshua, though like Moses (31:7–8; cf. Josh. 1:5; 4:14), is not a lawgiver but is to be obedient to the law Moses gave. Moses is unique and normative. Deuteronomy is the benchmark by which subsequent history is judged.

With von Rad and others it stands with what precedes, forming part of the narrative of taking possession of the land. That narrative climaxes not with Moses' death or with Israel on the edge of the land looking in, but with the promises fulfilled and the land possessed (cf. Josh. 21:45). Closure comes with possession, with allocation, with covenant (Josh. 24) and with the burial of Joseph's bones (Josh. 24:32; cf. Gen. 50:25; Exod. 13:19).

Yet there *is* something distinctive about Deuteronomy itself. As Rendtorff comments, 'it is obvious that Deuteronomy is a separate book. It is clearly framed by a new beginning and a definite end; it has its own style, its own topics, and its own theology.'[27]

---

25. See esp. the insightful analysis of J. Gordon McConville, *Grace in the End: A Study in Deuteronomic Theology*, Studies in Old Testament Biblical Theology (Carlisle: Paternoster, 1993). Some also see a distinction between Deuteronomic and Deuteronomistic theology. That is to say, the Deuteronomistic Historian (or more than one) worked with existing Deuteronomic material and fashioned a new work with overlapping but not identical emphases and convictions.

26. See further Robson, 'Literary Composition'.

27. Rolf Rendtorff, 'Is It Possible to Read Leviticus as a Separate Book?', in John F. A. Sawyer (ed.), *Reading Leviticus: A Conversation with Mary Douglas*, JSOTSup 227 (Sheffield: Sheffield Academic Press, 1996), p. 24.

Outline

My book has two parts. Part 1 focuses on the storyline Deuteronomy tells and to which it contributes. Chapter 2 takes seriously the fact that Deuteronomy as a book tells its own story. The title of the book, derived from the Greek words *deuteros* and *nomos* (second law), based on Deuteronomy 17:18, can give the impression that it is principally 'law'. In similar vein the decision of those who translated the Hebrew Old Testament into Greek to render *tôrâ*, 'instruction', as *nomos*, 'law', has also given the impression that it is essentially 'law' in the juridical sense. It is true that the central section of Deuteronomy, chapters 12–26, comprises laws, but Deuteronomy itself is more than that (though it is not less than that). It gives a narrative, a storyline of events from Horeb (or Sinai) through into the future. Chapter 2 will explore that story. Chapter 3 explores how Deuteronomy as a book forms part of a wider story. The story starts with the opening chapters of Genesis; it has various complications and resolutions, and climaxes with the person and work of Jesus Christ. There is a sense in which Deuteronomy's story governs and shapes the story that follows, yet there is ever something new, something fresh about subsequent events and their telling.

Part 2 looks at Deuteronomy's enduring function as an authoritative word for the Christian and the church, and focuses particularly on Deuteronomy's laws. Chapter 4 sets out Deuteronomy's vision for Israel and what Israel should be. At every point this vision is rooted in what Yahweh has done for them. Chapter 5 outlines five common ways of interpreting Deuteronomy's laws, which, although popular, are in reality dead ends. Chapter 6 explores some of the challenges for the Christian who wants to recognize and heed Deuteronomy's demands. Finally, chapter 7 sets out more positively some of the key principles in interpreting Deuteronomy's laws and works through one example by way of illustration. Although there is a flow and thread to this book, it is possible to read the parts and even the chapters as discrete entities.

PART I

A WORD WITH AND IN A
STORY

2. A WORD WITH A STORY

One of the features we noticed in the first chapter is that Deuteronomy is dominated by Moses' speeches. In them Moses 'concertinas' past and future events into the 'today' of the plains of Moab. Alongside this compression into the existential 'now' there is a strong sense of unfolding history, a storyline that reaches back into the past, and will reach into the future. Again this is told for the sake of the present, but that storyline needs unpacking. Moses tells it in speech and song, and when he turns from the past to the future, there is an intriguing interplay between what Israel *should* do and what they *will* do, between what *could* happen and what *will* happen. Such an interplay takes us to the heart of Deuteronomy's ongoing significance. This chapter will outline that history, first through *tôrâ*, then through song. The distinctive presentation found in the Song of Moses (Deut. 32:1–43) demands a separate treatment.

Story in *tôrâ*

God's promises to Abraham

Although there are brief glimpses of events before Abraham, such as mention of creation of the world in 4:32, it is the promises God made to Abraham that stand resplendent behind Moses' words, just as they do over the Pentateuch as a whole.[1] For a book dominated by God's words it is fitting that the first landmark event recalled is God's word of promise to Abraham and the other patriarchs. The promises first appear in Genesis 12:1–3, and develop further over subsequent chapters. In Genesis 12 there are six promises split into two groups of three. The notion of 'blessing' dominates, occurring five times. The first group focuses on greatness of name and nation: 'I will make you into a great nation, and I will bless you, and make your name great.' The second group builds on the result of the first set: that Abraham will 'be a blessing'.[2] They focus on Yahweh's response to those who engage with Abraham: 'I will bless those who bless you, while the one who curses you I will curse; and in you all the families of the earth shall be blessed.' Abraham will be so great that blessing will extend to others.[3] In Genesis 15 and 17 God incorporates these

---

1. See esp. David J. A. Clines, *The Theme of the Pentateuch*, 2nd ed., JSOTSup 10 (Sheffield: Sheffield Academic Press, 1997); and, for Deuteronomy, pp. 43–47, 57–65.

2. Note that this phrase means Abraham's name will be used as a byword or model for blessing ('may I/you/he be like Abraham') rather than that Abraham will be a vehicle or source of blessing (cf. Jer. 29:21–23; 24:8–9; Zech. 8:13). See R. W. L. Moberly, *The Theology of the Book of Genesis*, Old Testament Theology (Cambridge: Cambridge University Press, 2009), pp. 152, 157. The notion of a name as a byword for blessing rather than as a vehicle of blessing is perhaps clearer when we think of the antonym 'be a curse' (cf. 2 Kgs 22:19; Jer. 42:18; 44:8, 12, 22; 49:13); in these instances it does not mean others will be cursed through them; rather, they will serve as a byword for what it means to be cursed when others utter curses.

3. For a recent defence of the traditional passive translation 'be blessed', as opposed to seeing this final promise as a repetition of 12:2d, that

promises more formally within a covenantal context. How to sum-
marize these promises is not straightforward, because elements
may be subordinate rather than primary. Clines speaks of three
('descendants', 'relationship', 'land'), while Wenham gives four
('land', 'numerous descendants ("a great nation")', 'blessing, that is
protection and success', 'blessing of the nations').[4]

At the outset of Deuteronomy Moses draws on these promises.
In 1:8 he recalls Yahweh's words at Horeb, 'See, I have set the land
before you; go in and take possession of the land that I swore to
your ancestors, to Abraham, to Isaac, and to Jacob, to give to them
and to their descendants after them.' The 'sweeping scope' of the
'boundaries' resonates with Genesis 15:18–21.[5] The promise of
land in 1:8 is matched by clear echoes of the promise of *offspring* in
1:10–11. Unlike many leaders for whom the problems of growth
foster grumbling, Moses celebrates the fact that 'Yahweh your
God has multiplied you, so that today you are as numerous as the
stars of heaven' by praying for further increase (v. 11) despite the
problems (v. 9). Language of being as numerous as the stars of
heaven has been used before only in God's promises to Abraham
(Gen. 15:5–6; 22:17; 26:4; cf. Exod. 32:13). Moses' language of
'Yahweh your God has multiplied you' further reinforces the sense
in which the population explosion is nothing other than God's
faithful outworking of his promise.

The promise of numerous offspring is not prominent through
the rest of Deuteronomy. There are further explicit references in
10:22, and in the covenant curses as a height from which they will
fall because of disobedience (28:62). Moses reminds them in 7:6–8
that God did not choose them because they were many – indeed,

Abraham's name will be a model or byword for blessing, see Benjamin J.
Noonan, 'Abraham, Blessing, and the Nations: A Reexamination of the
Niphal and Hitpael of ברך in the Patriarchal Narratives', *HS* 51 (2010),
pp. 84–88.

4. Clines, *Theme of the Pentateuch*, pp. 30–47; Gordon J. Wenham, *Exploring
the Old Testament*, vol. 1: *The Pentateuch* (London: SPCK, 2003), p. 40.

5. Walter Brueggemann, *Deuteronomy*, Abingdon Old Testament
Commentaries (Nashville: Abingdon, 2001), p. 27.

they were 'the fewest of all peoples' (7:7); finally, there is a hint in 4:6, when Israel is put together with other 'great' nations, though there perhaps notions of greatness are being recast. Greatness is not about number or about military power, but about having right-eous laws and God near them.

The relative paucity of references to numerous descendants is in striking contrast to the myriad references to the land. The land is one that Yahweh has promised (e.g. 6:3) or sworn to their ancestors (e.g. 6:23; 8:1; 9:5),[6] it is one that Yahweh is giving (more than sixty times) and that they are entering to possess (more than twenty times). 'Deuteronomy, therefore, is oriented to the land that yet remains to be entered, and regards the entry into the land as essentially a fulfilment of the patriarchal promises.'[7]

That foundational event, the promises to Abraham, provides the main impetus for possession of the land as they stand in Moab. But the significance of the promises is not restricted to the 'today' of the plains of Moab. Restoration, the other side of a bleak future of exile for failure to keep the covenant made at Horeb, Moses

----

6. Thomas C. Römer ('Deuteronomy in Search of Origins', in Gary N. Knoppers and J. Gordon McConville (eds.), *Reconsidering Israel and Judah: Recent Studies on the Deuteronomistic History*, Sources for Biblical and Theological Study [Winona Lake, Ind.: Eisenbrauns, 2000], vol. 8, pp. 112–138), believes that 'the fathers' in the oldest parts of Deuteronomy refer to the exodus generation, and only when Deuteronomy became the conclusion to the Pentateuch rather than the start of the Deuteronomistic History does the phrase refer to Abraham and the other patriarchs (Deut. 1:8; 6:10; 9:5, 27; 29:13; 30:20; 34:4). There *is* some fluidity in the referent. In some contexts it is the patriarchs (e.g. 1:8); in others, it is the generation that stood at Horeb (e.g. 5:3); in others, it is those who enjoyed possession of the land (e.g. 30:5, 9). In a recent monograph Jerry Hwang (*The Rhetoric of Remembrance: An Investigation of the 'Fathers' in Deuteronomy*, Siphrut: Literature and Theology of the Hebrew Scriptures 8 [Winona Lake, Ind.: Eisenbrauns, 2012]) interprets the change in referent not through redaction-critical lenses that discern layers, but through rhetorical-critical lenses that see it as an intentional literary device to reinforce solidarity.

7. Clines, *Theme of the Pentateuch*, p. 63.

knows is a possibility. Like Joseph he knows that Yahweh will
bring them from a land not their own to the land he has promised
(cf. Gen. 50:24). His confidence about the future is rooted in his
experience of Yahweh and his response to intercession in the past.
When Israel rebelled in the incident with the golden calf, it was
to God's servants the patriarchs that Moses successfully appealed
when destruction seemed imminent (9:27). So in exile Yahweh in
his mercy will neither abandon nor destroy them, nor will he forget
the covenant he made with their fathers (4:31). Standing behind
the covenant at Horeb lie the promises God made to Abraham.
They provide the grounds for ongoing preservation and for entry
into the land, whether initially or after the judgment of exile.

Exodus

The second major element in Israel's history that Moses highlights
is the exodus. If the promises to Abraham focus on God's words
(and their partial fulfilment), the exodus displays God's action.
The picture Moses paints in different parts of Deuteronomy has
characteristic elements. Egypt was the place of slavery in which
they languished (e.g. 6:12; 15:15); Yahweh with a mighty hand
and an outstretched arm brought them out with great signs and
wonders (e.g. 6:22; 11:3). When they were helpless slaves, God
acted to redeem them. Strikingly, for Israel in the plains of Moab,
these events of Israel's history are the root both of profound
theology and of moral obligation.

First, Israel's identity and election arise out of the events of
the exodus. 'Israel is in a special relationship with God which it
cannot evade, because it has been brought about by historical
circumstances.'[8] This is seen particularly in 4:20, where Moses
declares, 'But Yahweh has taken you and brought you out of the
iron-smelter, out of Egypt, to become a people of his very own
inheritance, as you are now.' Their identity as the people of God,
a people belonging to God as his possession, is rooted in their
experience of redemption and rescue. They, and only they, have

---

8. Ronald E. Clements, *God's Chosen People: A Theological Interpretation of the
Book of Deuteronomy* (London: SCM, 1968), p. 33.

experienced a redemption like this (4:32–34). They are a people with a shared history, which constitutes who they are. Further, their self-understanding as a people chosen and loved by God without warrant arises from that same experience (Deut. 7:7–8).

Secondly, Israel's knowledge of and loyalty to their God is rooted in their experience of Yahweh's redemption. Their knowledge of God was supremely shaped by God's actions on their behalf in history. Although Deuteronomy emphasizes words, they are words that capture the reality of a profound experience of God in history, in event. They were to acknowledge Yahweh alone and that there is no other, not as an abstract point of dogma, but as a result of their experience of God in delivering them from slavery in Egypt (Deut. 4:32–35). No other god had done such for any other people, so he alone was God, and he alone was their God. Whether monotheism in its theoretical sense is in view here is beside the point. Israel were to recognize that Yahweh was and is the only God. 'YHWH appears in a class of his own'; we should speak of Yahweh's 'transcendent uniqueness'.[9] This knowledge was to shape them in war and in worship (Deut. 7:18; 5:7).

Thirdly, Moses rooted Israel's ethics in their experience of slavery and redemption. As they were confronted with dehumanizing social deprivation, their past was to shape their present.[10] This was true in the central legal section (chs. 12–26): they were to release the slave with generous provision (15:12–15); they were to involve the whole community in their worshipping life without distinction, because as a whole community they had been delivered (16:11–12); and they should ensure justice, right treatment and adequate provision for those who were helpless (24:17–18, 21–22).

---

9. Richard J. Bauckham, 'Biblical Theology and the Problems of Monotheism', in Craig Bartholomew, Mary Healy, Karl Möller and Robin Parry (eds.), *Out of Egypt: Biblical Theology and Biblical Interpretation*, SHS 5 (Bletchley, UK: Paternoster, 2004), pp. 196, 210.

10. Cf. Georg Braulik, 'Deuteronomy and Human Rights', in Ulrika Lindblad (tr.), *The Theology of Deuteronomy: Collected Essays of Georg Braulik, O.S.B.*, BIBAL Collected Essays 2 (N. Richland Hills, Tex.: BIBAL, 1994), pp. 135–136.

Beyond these particular references, though, the Decalogue as a whole is rooted in Yahweh's declaration of deliverance from slavery in Egypt. Before they received any obligations, Yahweh reminded them of who he was and what he had done: 'I am Yahweh your God, who brought you out of the land of Egypt, out of the house of slavery.' 'The God who commands is the God who delivers.'[11] Redemption precedes obligation as much in the Old Testament as in the New. It is a profound misunderstanding of the Old Testament to think otherwise. It was out of loyalty to Yahweh who had redeemed them from slavery, who had brought them out of Egypt with such great power, that they were to worship and obey him. This opening 'reference to the Exodus suggests that the theological intention of the Ten Commandments is to institutionalize the Exodus: to establish perspectives, procedures, policies, and institutions that will generate Exodus-like social relationships'.[12] Slavery (Heb. root *'bd*) to Pharaoh is to give rise to serving (*'bd*) Yahweh (6:13). There is continuity, for humanity has to serve somebody (as Bob Dylan sang); and there is discontinuity, for serving Yahweh is very different from serving Pharaoh. The sabbath captures this profoundly. Six days they shall labour (*'bd*); the seventh day is a day of rest from labour, akin to redemption from slavery, and it is to include everyone, including the slave. Worship expressed by the keeping of the sabbath was inclusive, social, joyful and costly (the slaves were not serving). Every week it dramatized and enshrined the once-for-all exodus event.

Horeb

The third major landmark within Deuteronomy's story is the encounter with Yahweh and the giving of the law at Horeb. Moses recounts the events there with three main purposes beyond simple rehearsal.

First, it is the root of profound theology and anthropology: the events illuminate the character of Yahweh and Israel. The most

---

11. Walter Brueggemann, *Theology of the Old Testament: Testimony, Dispute, Advocacy* (Minneapolis: Fortress, 1997), p. 184.

12. Ibid.

significant characteristic for theology is that God revealed himself
through voice and word, not through a form (4:12, 15). There
were awesome accompanying phenomena, including fire, cloud
and deep darkness (4:11; 5:22). These were terrifying (5:5), but,
strikingly, not as terrifying as hearing the voice of God (5:25–26).
That the revelation of God was through word not through form
meant that a visual representation of him was idolatrous (4:15–20;
5:8–10). The shape and nature of Israel's religion as aniconic
stemmed from their experience of Yahweh at Horeb.

Israel's response to this revelation gives an insight into their
true character. At the very moment Moses was up the mountain
receiving the Ten Commandments the people were constructing
a golden calf at the foot of the mountain. There is something
profoundly depressing about Yahweh's 'quickly' (9:12). It is not
as if Israel's turning away from Yahweh was the product of a
long process of heart-searching and agonizing. The very opposite
is true. Everyone, including Moses' mouthpiece, Aaron, rushed
headlong into corruption. Israel's idolatrous, uncircumcised heart,
even at this stage, was plain for all to see (cf. Deut. 10:16). A place
of great privilege did not guarantee an appropriate response in
those days, it did not do so in Jesus' time, nor does it do so now.
The complaint 'If only I'd been there' as an excuse in any age for
not responding to God reveals a profound lack of self-awareness.

In turn, Moses spells out Yahweh's reaction to this rebellion
(chs. 9–10). Yahweh burns with anger, ready to destroy the errant
people. It is only Moses' forthright hurling down of the tablets, his
intercession for the people and for Aaron, and his annihilation of
the golden calf that spares them from destruction (9:15–21). At a
general level this revelation of Yahweh as fully personal in speaking and acting provides the impetus for the right way for Israel to
respond (10:12–13). At a more specific level God's anger at Israel's
idolatry casts a dark shadow over the future, while his willingness
to relent in response to intercession shines brightly.

The second main purpose for his recounting of the events at
Horeb is to highlight both the unique and the paradigmatic nature
of the events there. They are unique in the sense that they are unre-
peatable. The giving of the tablets and the revelation of Yahweh
was a once-for-all event, which they 'saw with their eyes' and will

never see again.[13] There will be no new Horeb, no new lawgiving. At the same time it is a paradigmatic event. It is one in which they representatively stood (5:2–3) and in which every future generation stands (29:14–15). They are to teach it to their children, who in turn are to teach their children (4:9). Whenever the people of God gather 'before Yahweh' to hear the word of God, they are re-enacting that great day of the assembly (or 'gathering', *qhl*; 9:10; 10:4) at the mountain of God. This is precisely the logic of 4:10. The sequence runs, 'gather (*qhl*) . . . that I may let them hear . . . that they may learn to revere . . . and (that) they may teach their children'. That was the pattern at Horeb, but it is an enduring pattern.[14] This makes Horeb a present reality for each generation; they are to gather as the people of God for God to speak to them the words he spoke. They are to respond to the teaching (*lmd*) by learning (*lmd*) to fear Yahweh and, in turn, to pass that same word on (cf. Heb. 12:18–29).

The third main purpose of revisiting Horeb is to connect the giving of the statutes and commandments (chs. 12–26) in the plains of Moab with the giving of the law at Horeb. In particular, Moses shows why these words given in Moab come with the same authority and relevance as those at Horeb. Chapter 5 is the key chapter. Moses starts with an exhortation to Israel to listen to what he is commanding them 'today' (in the plains of Moab). But why should they listen? The rest of the chapter makes it clear. The covenant at Horeb was not just with their forefathers, but with them (vv. 2–3; though they were not there!). Then Moses retells the Ten Commandments with a clear purpose. Moses says (vv. 23–31):

> We all heard these words – definitive, authoritative, unique; you were
> so scared at having heard the voice of Yahweh that you asked me to

---

13. Though in fact they were not there, and did not see (except for any who were children at the time). See Moshe Weinfeld, *Deuteronomy 1–11*, AB 5 (New York: Doubleday, 1991), p. 203.
14. Hearing 'before Yahweh' in 4:10 at Horeb continues in Moab (29:14–15) and into the festivals (31:11). Cf. J. Gordon McConville, 'Deuteronomy: Torah for the Church of Christ', *EuroJTh* 9 (2000), p. 37.

mediate for you. For once, Yahweh said you'd spoken rightly (!), and told me to tell you to return to your tents. I had the job of mediating and now, today, in the plains of Moab, I am telling you what Yahweh commanded me. If you are wondering why you should listen to me, it is because you asked me to mediate. I am only giving you today in Moab what you asked for back then at Horeb! Don't just take the decalogue seriously – take the statutes and ordinances seriously too.

From Horeb to Moab

The fourth and final retrospective focus within Moses' portrayal of Israel's story is the journey from Horeb to the plains of Moab. The opening three chapters cover this period; other significant places include chapters 8 and 29:1–9. Broadly speaking, Moses focuses on two themes: the wandering in the wilderness and entry into the land, both failed and partially achieved. Moses articulates both themes with the rhetorical purpose that has characterized the rest of his history: a retelling of the past for the sake of the present; a retelling that expounds the character and actions of Yahweh and of Israel, so that Israel in Moab (and into the future) understands and acts rightly.

The message of the wilderness wanderings recounted in chapter 8 derives chiefly from verses 2–6. The general call to obey the commandment (v. 1)[15] is followed by three commands in verses 2–6, 'remember' (v. 2), 'know' (v. 5) and 'observe' (v. 6). Despite many English versions, verse 6 should be taken as closing these verses because of echoes with verse 1 ('keep, observe', šmr; 'command', miṣwâ), verse 2 ('way', derek; 'walk, lead', hlk) and the continuity of verb form between 'know' (v. 5) and 'keep' (v. 6; cf.

---

15. 'The whole commandment' (so ESV, NRSV) is preferable to 'every commandment' (NIV). Deuteronomy uses the singular 'commandment' sometimes of 'the basic demand for loyalty' in contrast to the more detailed regulations of chs. 12–26 (e.g. 6:25), and at other times (e.g. 17:18–20) as almost interchangeable with 'the whole Deuteronomic law'. For the former, see Weinfeld, Deuteronomy 1–11, p. 327; for the latter, see Richard D. Nelson, Deuteronomy, OTL (Louisville: Westminster John Knox, 2002), p. 85.

7:9–11). Their remembering of past events is to form the basis
of what they are to 'know' (v. 5); that knowledge is not simply to
be head knowledge, but is to give rise to 'observing' or 'keeping'
what Yahweh has commanded (v. 6). 'Remember . . . know . . .
keep': this threefold pattern, of bringing to mind what God has
done, using it as the basis for theological reflection that gives
rise to obedience, is equally true for the Christian. But what is
it that Moses wants them to 'remember'? There is a profound
interplay here, rooted in common vocabulary and subtly shifting
images.

In essence, he wants them to remember the way (*derek*) Yahweh
made them walk (*hlk*) (v. 2). The motif of journey in the wilderness in verse 2 is to inform the ways (*derek*) they are to walk (*hlk*)
in obedience to Yahweh (v. 6). Life in the wilderness is to connect
with life in the future. This 'way' he then unpacks further by
careful juxtaposition of language of humbling and knowing. Twice
over he talks about humbling, but the purpose of the humbling
is different in verse 2 from verse 3. In verse 2 Yahweh humbled
them, testing them so that *he* might know (*yd'*) what was in their
heart – whether they would keep his commandment or not. There
was a sense in which, within space and time, the wilderness was
a journey of discovery for God, as he 'came to know' Israel's
character.[16] Sadly, though, what Yahweh discovered was not
good. Israel's history was marked by stubborn, culpable, rebellious unbelief, sometimes issuing in flagrant idolatry (e.g. 4:3; 9:24;
29:4).

That same testing was also about Yahweh's wanting *Israel* to
understand (*yd'*) that people do not live only on bread, but on
every word that comes from Yahweh's mouth (v. 3). In the midst
of testing was Yahweh's provision: miraculous preservation of
clothing and feet, manna and quail. But more significant than
these was Yahweh's word, a word of promise, a word that did

---

16. This is not, I take it, an indication that Yahweh does not know the future.
Elsewhere in the Old Testament Yahweh clearly does so. For how to
hold together such language, see e.g. Bruce A. Ware, *God's Lesser Glory: A
Critique of Open Theism* (Leicester: Apollos, 2001), pp. 73–74.

not fail, a word on which they could depend, a word that declared provision and delivered.

Just as Yahweh's humbling and testing have two purposes (journeys of discovery for Yahweh and for Israel), so the wilderness itself has two purposes. In chapter 1 the wilderness wandering is Yahweh's punishment for lack of trust and unwillingness to enter the land; here Moses presents the other side. The punishment is a learning curve for Yahweh's recalcitrant son, Israel. The lesson is straightforward. Israel must learn the lessons of the wilderness – God's provision for them in times of need – so that they will remember them in the land in times of plenty (cf. 8:17).

The second major theme, of entry into the land, is the subject of Moses' first speech (1:6 – 3:29). Even in the prologue before that, the twin themes that shape the speech, of failed entry and partial success, appear side by side (1:2–4). As Deuteronomy starts, the narrator juxtaposes two time references that highlight failure. Verse 2 shows that it is an eleven-day journey from Horeb to Kadesh Barnea. In verse 3 Moses is speaking in the fortieth year on the first day of the eleventh month. What should have taken eleven days has in fact taken forty years. Mention of Kadesh Barnea has given a clue.[17] In 1:6 – 2:1 Moses explains more fully why. It is not that Yahweh has failed to provide. He enabled the appointing of elders and judges, only necessary because the people multiplied in fulfilment of the promises made to Abraham (1:9–18). He accompanied them on their journey in the pillar of fire and cloud (1:33). He provided through Moses reassurance that he would fight for them (1:30) and a reminder that he had carried them to this point (1:31). The reason for their failure to enter was straightforward: 'in spite of this' they had 'no trust' in Yahweh their God (1:32) and rebelled against Yahweh's command (1:26). Yahweh had revealed himself in word and action; Israel had failed to trust and obey. The result was devastating: Yahweh's wrath

---

17. Cf. J. Gary Millar, 'Living at the Place of Decision: Time and Place in the Framework of Deuteronomy', in J. Gordon McConville and J. Gary Millar, *Time and Place in Deuteronomy*, JSOTSup 179 (Sheffield: Sheffield Academic Press, 1994), p. 24.

and Israel's wandering through the wilderness for forty years until that unbelieving generation had died out. The promise remained, but the recipients would be different. That same picture was true in Jesus' day, and remains true. Failure to trust and obey cannot invalidate the promise, but it can mean exclusion from its benefits. The prominence of Israel's lack of trust in the opening chapter casts a dark shadow over the future prospects for the nation. The picture of gracious provision, wilful unbelief, anger and exile (wilderness) is one that anticipates Deuteronomy as a whole. But there is another way.

In chapter 1 the initial impetus to move from Horeb came from Yahweh's 'long enough' about their time at Horeb and his call to 'turn' (*pnh*) and 'journey' (*ns'*) (1:6–7). Because of their lack of trust, they ended up 'turning' and 'journeying' (*pnh*, *ns'*) *to the wilderness* (2:1). But after forty years, fresh impetus comes. Yahweh says 'long enough' to their going round and round, and then calls them to 'turn' (*pnh*) to the north (2:3). The opening prologue gives a prelude of failure (fortieth year). It also gives a foretaste of *success* in the way it dates the time of Moses' speaking (1:4). In chapters 2:3 – 3:29 Moses spells this out, as he reminds them how they have defeated, dispossessed and destroyed Sihon and Og. If chapter 1 casts a dark shadow, these chapters marshal hope for Moses' hearers in Moab and for subsequent generations. In anticipation of the main conquest Israel succeeds in taking the land across the Jordan (cf. 2:34; 3:4, 8, 12; 29:8). Lest this should be misunderstood as an achievement of Israel, this 'taking' is only because Yahweh has 'given' it and has fought for them (e.g. 2:24–33).

These twin possibilities carry forward into chapter 4. Alongside those who succumbed to idolatry and judgment (v. 3) are those who 'held fast' to Yahweh who are 'alive today'; the life held out in verse 1 has been a nascent reality in verse 4. Failure and success, unbelief and trust, death and life are found already in the retelling of recent history.

'Today' in Moab

'Today' is the day of Moses' speaking in the plains of Moab. The word is, as von Rad puts it, 'the common denominator of the Deuteronomic homiletic as a whole' and 'a quite fundamental

feature of Deuteronomy'.[18] In the rhetoric of the book it marks the
day of *decision* for the people confronted by Moses' teaching 'today'
(e.g. 4:39; 8:19; 11:26; 30:15–20). This chapter is focusing less on
the rhetoric of persuasion than on the storyline of Deuteronomy,
so we shall restrict our attention to the events associated with this
day, though these also have rhetorical force. Within the storyline
'today' is a day of *transition* for Moses and for Israel.

At one level 'today' is simply the first day of the eleventh month
in the fortieth year (1:3), the day of Moses' speaking. But Israel and
Deuteronomy's readers know Yahweh had declared forty years'
wandering in the wilderness as the penalty for being unwilling to
go in and take possession of the land (Num. 14:33–34). That we
are in the eleventh month of the fortieth year here says the crossing will be very soon. Given that Yahweh has also declared Moses
will not enter (Num. 20:12), Moses' death is also imminent.[19] Israel
and the readers should be on tenterhooks.[20]

The fortieth year has already marked the death of the wilderness
generation, symbolized by the death of Miriam in the first month
(Num. 20:1) and Aaron on the first day of the fifth month (Num.
20:22–29; 33:38). Moses is the last to die (Deut. 34). Throughout
Deuteronomy 'today' is the day of Moses' commanding (e.g.
4:8; 5:1). He has been asked to mediate, and now he is relaying
Yahweh's words. There is nothing else for him to do. This is
particularly evident as he writes what he has spoken (31:9–13) and
the song (31:22), mindful of his age and future (31:2). Both *tôrâ*
and song will serve as witnesses after Moses has died. Alongside
the move from Moses' spoken word to a written word that functions without him are other transfers of authority from Moses
that highlight this day of transition. Yahweh has sanctioned a
leadership structure where the different roles Moses has played

---

18. Gerhard von Rad, 'The Form-Critical Problem of the Hexateuch', in
    E. W. Trueman Dicken (tr.), *The Problem of the Hexateuch and Other Essays*
    (London: Oliver & Boyd, 1966), p. 26.
19. See Olson, *Deuteronomy*, for a sustained reading of Deuteronomy from
    this perspective.
20. Cf. Nelson, *Deuteronomy*, p. 17.

to a greater or lesser extent are divided up (16:18 – 18:22), and he commissions Joshua (31:7–8; cf. v. 23).[21] The book ends with Moses' death. Strikingly, many scholars see 'that very day' of 32:48 on which Moses dies to be the 'today' of his speaking (cf. 27:9, 11).[22]

Alongside the transition for Moses, 'today' is also a day of transition for Israel. The stepping aside of Moses obviously is a transition of *authority*. It is also a day of transition of *identity*, as they 'become' the people of God in the plains of Moab (26:16–19; 27:9; 29:9–15). They have heard Moses' words and declared their allegiance (26:17); as a result, Yahweh is their God and they are his people. In one sense, of course, they already were his people before their declaration (e.g. 7:6). Yet in the plains of Moab they reactualize that reality. As McConville notes, although the covenants at

21. The role of prophet is most explicitly tied to Moses ('prophet like me'; Deut. 18:15). But Moses has a bearing on the other roles. The king will, like Moses, be Yahweh's servant and shepherd his people. But Moses is never called a king and the king's task is not to follow Moses' role but to lead the people in obedience to Moses' word written (John Goldingay, *Old Testament Theology*, vol. 1: *Israel's Gospel* [Downers Grove: InterVarsity Press, 2003], pp. 545–556); J. Gordon McConville, 'Law and Monarchy in the Old Testament', in Craig Bartholomew, Jonathan Chaplin, Robert Song and Al Wolters (eds.), *A Royal Priesthood? The Use of the Bible Ethically and Politically*, SHS 3 [Carlisle: Paternoster, 2002], p. 76). The institution of judges has already been established to continue Moses' judging (Deut. 1:9–18; cf. 16:18–20), with provision for a central Mosaic figure to arbitrate in difficult cases (Deut. 1:17; cf. 17:9). Finally, although Moses' priestly role is stronger in Leviticus, he 'stands' (*'md*) in mediatorial role in Yahweh's presence (Deut. 5:5, 31; 10:10; cf. the Levites in 10:8 and 18:5) and he blesses the people (Deut. 33; cf. 10:8).

22. Jan van Goudoever, 'The Liturgical Significance of the Date in Dt 1, 3', in Norbert Lohfink (ed.), *Das Deuteronomium: Entstehung, Gestalt und Botschaft*, BETL 68 (Leuven: Leuven University Press, 1985), p. 451; McConville, *Deuteronomy*, p. 62; Nelson, *Deuteronomy*, p. 17. The Jewish historian Josephus, however, regards Moses' death as having taken place on the first day of the twelfth month (*Ant.* 4.8.49).

Horeb and Moab are clearly different, they are in continuity.[23] The
covenant in Moab is 'in addition' or 'besides' (29:1) that made at
Horeb, and the two codes are different ('tablets' at Horeb; 'book
of the law in Moab'). Yet they are in direct continuity. Moses
insists that the covenant at Horeb was with those standing before
him in Moab (5:2–3); yet they 'become' God's people in Moab
though they already were such at Horeb. There is a sense in which
the people of God are constituted by the preached word of God,
which comes to every generation in the continual 'today'. And the
people respond to that with covenantal renewal and commitment,
and so 'become' God's people afresh.

A further way in which 'today' is a day of transition for Israel
is that of *location*. Amid all of Moses' speaking there has been
no change in location throughout Deuteronomy. Indeed, they
have been in the plains of Moab since Numbers 22. Yet 'today'
is the day on which they are to cross the Jordan (Deut. 9:1).
Their present must give way to the future. The same is true of
Deuteronomy's storyline.

As Moses moves from past and present to the future, he speaks
both of possibilities and certainties, of a desired or imagined future
and a definite one. There are commands to be carried out, warnings to heed, judgments that will happen. From these it is possible
to trace Deuteronomy's storyline into the future – not as other
books in the Old Testament relate it, but as Deuteronomy anticipates it.

Entry to the land: conquest and covenant ceremony

The transition of authority from spoken word to written book and
from Moses to Joshua has already taken place. What lies immediately ahead for the people encamped in Moab is conquest and
covenant ceremony.

Chapters 1–3 have already highlighted the two routes open to
Israel for taking the land: lack of trust leading to Yahweh's anger
and failure (ch. 1), or doing as Yahweh has instructed, resulting in
success (chs. 2–3). As Moses looks ahead to taking possession of

---

23. McConville, 'Torah for the Church', p. 38.

the land, chapter 7 in particular spells out the approach they are
to take. Just as Yahweh gives, so they are to take and to 'devote to
destruction' (*ḥrm*) the inhabitants and destroy traces of their religion; the fundamental danger for Israel is idolatry and the snare of
the inhabitants' religion (7:3–6; 12:2–4, 29–32).[24] This taking of the
land is certain ('when', 7:1), but it will not be immediate (7:22–23).
There stands a certain tension between the land as a gift Yahweh
is giving and the land as the fruit of Israel's obedience. In 4:1
obedience is 'so that you may live and enter' the land; yet it is also
the land Yahweh is giving (cf. 1:8). How does the apparent uncon-
ditionality of the gift relate to the conditionality of appropriation?
Both are so woven through the fabric of the book that an explanation in terms of different redactional layers is unpersuasive.[25]
Further, this very tension runs right through Christian theology.
How does promise relate to task, gift to obligation? Much could
be said. Three points are important. First, Deuteronomy insists
on *both* together. One does not preclude or exclude the other.
Secondly, possession of the land is not meritorious. Israel must
never think that they somehow deserved it because of their own
righteousness (9:4–6). Thirdly, the picture of Israel as Yahweh's
son preserves the relational dimension.[26] Trusting obedience is
the means of appropriating and inheriting what Yahweh has
promised; life, of which the land is but one part, is not an arbitrary
reward for rule-keeping. Rather, it is the organic outworking of
keeping Yahweh's life-giving words. Obedience is not simply the
way *to* life; it is the way *of* life.

Alongside the imminent conquest is the covenant ceremony at
Mounts Ebal and Gerizim at Shechem (ch. 27; cf. 11:26–32). The
conquest's imminence is seen from Moses' command to them to
set up large stones 'on the day which you cross the Jordan' (27:2).
Tigay notes that Jewish interpreters took it as that very day, especially given 'that you may enter' (v. 3). Thus a manuscript found at

---

24. For more on this most demanding of commands, see chapter 6 below.

25. See esp. McConville, *Grace in the End*.

26. Christopher J. H. Wright, *God's People in God's Land: Family, Land and
    Property in the Old Testament* (Grand Rapids: Eerdmans, 1990), pp. 15–22.

Qumran shifts the carrying out of the covenant ceremony forward
in Joshua (from 8:30–35), and rabbinic commentators proposed
miracles or smaller mountains of the same name near Gilgal,
where the conquerors were circumcised and ate the Passover
(Josh. 5:1–12).[27] It is more likely that the time frame is less specific
(cf. 27:4). The phrase 'on the day' does not have to designate a
24-hour period (e.g. Gen. 2:4).[28] Moses is making an immediate
temporal and logical connection between the two days of 27:1–2:
'the "day of decision" in Moab becomes the "day of response" in
Canaan'.[29] This connection is further reinforced by writing 'all the
words of this law (tôrâ)' clearly on the whitewashed stones (27:8).
This probably is the whole body of laws that Moses has been
proclaiming: at this point this seems to be the referent of tôrâ (cf.
31:24), and the recurrence of the rare verb 'expound' (bē'ēr), last
seen in 1:5, suggests that what is 'expounded' is the same as what
was expounded in chapter 1. What was spoken in Moab will be
written in Canaan. The tôrâ placed beside the ark (31:24) will also
be in the public sphere, as a permanent reminder. They are not
merely a religious community, but a political one, with their whole
life shaped by tôrâ. Other parts to this covenant ceremony include
the building of an altar, offering sacrifices, and the declaiming of
covenant curses.

Life in the land: prosperity
Once the immediate conquest is out of view, Deuteronomy's
storyline becomes less detailed but no less certain. There is an
expectation that Israel will have a period of prospering in the land,
enjoying the blessings Yahweh provides. This is apparent from
incidental comments, from Israel's worship and, in particular, from
chapter 8.[30] Incidental comments include 4:25, 'After you have had

27. Jeffrey H. Tigay, Deuteronomy, JPS Torah Commentary (New York: Jewish
    Publication Society, 1996), p. 486.
28. Paul A. Barker, 'The Theology of Deuteronomy 27', TynB 49 (1998),
    p. 298.
29. Millar, Now Choose Life, p. 89.
30. Note also some examples of faithfulness: individual (e.g. Caleb in 1:36),

children and grandchildren and have lived in the land a long time';
12:10, 'when he gives you rest from your enemies all around so
that you live in safety'; and 30:1, 'When all these blessings . . . I
have set before you come upon you.' Passages prescribing Israel's
worship often speak of the joy that results from the experience
of blessings (e.g. Deut. 14:24; 16:10, 15; 26:11). They are thus 'in
some sense prophetic', indicating what Yahweh will do (and how
Israel should respond).[31] Most significant though is chapter 8. The
chapter as a whole urges the Israelites to remember the wilderness
lessons when they enter the land. The assumption throughout is
that there will be a time of significant prospering. Verse 10 speaks
of 'when you have eaten and are satisfied', and verses 12–13
expand on this: 'when you build fine houses and settle [in them],
and when your herds and flocks multiply and your silver and gold
multiply and all you have multiplies . . .'. Moses urges them to
be careful not to forget that it is the Lord who has provided for
them; indeed, it is Yahweh 'who gives you the power to produce
wealth' (8:18). The images speak of the land's bountiful abundance
(8:7–10; cf. 6:10–11; 11:8–15). This prospering and plenty is a sign
of Yahweh's faithfulness to his covenant (8:18) and a mark of his
generosity, goodness and blessing.

Yahweh's desire for his people is abundant blessing or 'life'; *tôrâ*
and obedience to *tôrâ* are not obstacles to this, but the means to it:
Moses declares in 4:1, 'Hear . . . do . . . so that you may live. . .' (cf.
32:47). Jesus agrees (cf. Luke 10:28). The aim is for long life in the
land (e.g. 4:40; 5:33; 32:47). And Deuteronomy declares that (for
a time) they will prosper in the land. *Tôrâ* was not an unwelcome
imposition but a gracious gift to a people Yahweh had redeemed
(cf. 5:6). How this relates to the New Testament we shall return
to later, but this understanding of Israel's *tôrâ* or law needs to be
heard in an antinomian church and culture.

---

group (e.g. those who 'held fast' to Yahweh in 4:4) and even national
(Israel's interaction with Sihon and Og in 2:26 – 3:11).

31. Cf. Timothy M. Willis, '"Eat and Rejoice Before the Lord": The Optimism
of Worship in the Deuteronomic Code', in Rick R. Marrs (ed.), *Worship and
the Hebrew Bible*, JSOTSup 284 (Sheffield: JSOT Press, 1999), pp. 284–286.

Exile from the land: turning away to idols, judgment and the curse of exile
Alongside this picture of prospering in the land is an altogether darker picture. Some aspects of Moses' rhetoric do not necessarily suggest in themselves a dark outlook, but warn of it. Ten times in Deuteronomy Moses urges the gathered people to 'be careful' or 'take care'.[32] Like a parent to a child he warns them of dangers to avoid. In 4:9 he warns them to be careful not to forget or let slip from their mind (heart) what they saw and heard at Horeb. In Deuteronomy 1 – 11 the dangers revolve around forgetting Yahweh and the covenant, and, the counterpart of that, making idols. In the central legal section Moses warns against similar dangers (12:13, 30) and more specific infringements (12:19; 15:9; 24:8). Another warning is the stark threat at the end of chapter 7. This is the chapter that outlines Israel's obligation to devote the inhabitants of the land to destruction (*ḥrm*) and to destroy their idolatrous objects. At the end Moses warns Israel not to covet their gods' silver or gold, or to bring it into their houses. If they do, they themselves will be subject to the same *ḥērem* (7:25–26). The plainest and bleakest warning of all is found in chapter 28, where Moses spells out in dreadful detail the curses that will come upon Israel if they fail to keep the covenant. Throughout Deuteronomy the picture is not of a cold and clinical punishment, but of a God who loves his people and (so) is provoked to anger by idolatry and rebellion. In 29:22–29, for example, are six different words for anger. In every case it is 'fundamental breach of the covenant' that is the problem.[33]

It is not the warnings themselves that give a darker picture. That comes from the presence of the warnings *alongside* the book's depiction of the inveterate rebelliousness of Israel. The opening chapter of the book illustrates in microcosm Israel's unbelief and the dire consequences: Yahweh fought against them, not with them (they end up at Hormah [1:44]; cf. *ḥrm*), and cast them into the wilderness, heading back to Egypt

32. Deut. 4:9, 23; 6:12; 8:11; 11:16; 12:13, 19, 30; 15:9; 24:8.
33. McConville, *Deuteronomy*, p. 418.

(1:40; 2:1).[34] This is not an isolated aberration, but captures a pattern that has been present throughout their history (9:7, 22–24). At Horeb they turned to idolatry even as Moses was receiving the tablets (9:7 – 10:11); it has continued from that day until this one (29:4). Some scholars think that until this moment they have not had the heart to obey, but *now they do* (cf. 29:9).[35] However, 'to this day' elsewhere includes 'this day',[36] and this generation has demonstrated its rebellious credentials.

Given the character of Israel, it is no surprise that the stark warnings in places yield to a certainty of judgment and exile. Three times in Deuteronomy Moses warns the Israelites of the danger, once they have eaten and are full, 'lest' (*pen*) they forget Yahweh and turn to other gods (6:11–12; 8:10–14; 11:15–16). In 31:20 Moses is convinced not merely of this danger, but of the certainty of apostasy after they have eaten their fill (same terms). The 'if' has become a 'when'. That same certainty is apparent in 28:45. The 'if' at the start of previous sections becomes a factual 'these *will* happen . . . *because* . . .'.[37] Verse 47 reinforces this certain fate: 'Precisely because you did not serve . . .'. It is now a 'foregone conclusion'.[38] While 29:22–28 graphically pictures that day almost as though a reality, chapter 31 expresses most explicitly the certainty that idolatry and judgment will be a reality (31:16–21, 29).[39]

In terms of the nature of the judgment it is a reversal of the Abrahamic promises. Instead of blessing, there will be curse (ch. 28). These build up, climaxing in exile. They will be 'few in number' (4:27; 28:62; cf. 26:5) and will be ejected from the land (e.g. 4:27; 28:63–64). It is a reversal of the redemption from Egypt. Amidst many aspects of 'de-redemption' in 28:58–68, such as

---

34. Cf. William L. Moran, 'The End of the Unholy War and the Anti-Exodus', *Bib* 44 (1963), pp. 333–342.

35. Tigay, *Deuteronomy*, p. 275; Nelson, *Deuteronomy*, p. 340.

36. Barker, *Triumph of Grace*, p. 118.

37. Olson, *Deuteronomy*, p. 122.

38. Nelson, *Deuteronomy*, p. 332.

39. Barker ('Theology of Deuteronomy 27') argues that ch. 27 anticipates a certain exile, being biased towards curse.

being afflicted again with the diseases of Egypt (28:59–60), the return towards Egypt of chapter 1 gets a sharper twist in verse 68: they will volunteer themselves for the slavery out of which they have previously been delivered. Whereas 'serving' Yahweh was the goal of the exodus from Egypt (e.g. Exod. 7:16), in the lands they are scattered to they will 'serve' gods of wood and stone (e.g. 4:28; 28:36; 29:17). The juxtaposition of the language of death and destruction, on the one hand, and exile, on the other, reveals two things: that 'death' may be an experienced reality of one still alive but cut off from Yahweh and the land; that 'life' is rooted in possession of the land (cf. Gen. 2:17; Ezek. 37:11).[40]

Restoration to the land: circumcision of the heart and return

Remarkably, Yahweh's anger and Israel's exile are not the last word. Chapter 4:23–31 begins with the call to 'be very careful' (cf. vv. 9, 15) and depicts the future. It imagines an exile, but, in a passage full of contrasts, there is hope:

Yahweh's jealousy (24)	Yahweh's mercy (31)
There (where Israel was scattered) (28)	From *there* (where Israel was scattered) (29)
Israel forgetting covenant with Yahweh (23)	Israel listening again to Yahweh's voice (30)
These things shall *find* (*ms'*) you (30)	You will *find* (*ms'*) him (29)
Israel *forgetting* (*škḥ*) *covenant* (*běrît*) with Yahweh (23)	Yahweh not *forgetting* (*škḥ*) *covenant* (*běrît*) with Abraham (31)
Israel idolatrous, acting corruptly (*šḥt*) (25)	Yahweh not destroying (*šḥt*) (31)
Exile	Return?

There is a 'return' (*šûb*) in chapter 4, but it is Israel returning to Yahweh (4:30). The passage is reticent about return from exile to the land, though mention of the covenant with their ancestors in verse 31 points to return (cf. 1:8); it also leaves unexplored the

---

40. Cf. Kenneth J. Turner, *Death of Deaths in the Death of Israel: Deuteronomy's Theology of Exile* (Eugene, Or.: Wipf & Stock, 2010), p. 75.

relationship between Israel's return to Yahweh and Yahweh's to Israel.

Both of these, and more, get a fuller airing in 30:1–10. This passage starts off with a compressed summary of the future: 'When all these things come upon you, the blessings and the curses that I have set before you . . .', before turning to 'returning (*šûb*)'. Seven times in this passage *šûb* ('turn, return, repent') is used.[41] It expresses the returning of Israel to Yahweh: verse 1 ('bring to mind'), verse 2 ('return to Yahweh'), verse 8 ('again obey') and verse 10 ('return to Yahweh'). It also expresses the returning of Yahweh (in blessing) to Israel: verse 3 ('will restore your fortunes'; 'will gather you again/back') and verse 8 ('will again delight . . .').

At first glance Yahweh's actions seem contingent on Israel's. 'When you repent . . . (vv. 1–2), *then* Yahweh your God will restore your fortunes . . . and Yahweh your God will bring you into the land . . . and Yahweh your God will circumcise your heart . . . and Yahweh your God will bring all these curses on your enemies.' Although Yahweh will do many other things in these verses, these four actions have Yahweh expressed as the subject (as opposed to a pronoun) and so are most significant. This seems to make Yahweh's action clearly consequential on Israel's repentance.

However, there are good reasons why Yahweh's enabling, expressed in his circumcising their heart, should be seen as prior. First, the very repentance spoken of in verses 2 and 10, on which Yahweh's actions seem to hang, is said to be 'with all your heart and with all your soul'; yet it is this ability to obey Yahweh with all their heart and soul that is *itself* a *result* of Yahweh's circumcision of their heart. Secondly, the catalyst for Israel's return is 'when all these *dĕbārîm* have come upon you'; *dĕbārîm* can speak of 'things' *or* 'words'. As Barker notes:

> Since these *words* which come upon Israel will lead to repentance, these words constitute gospel or grace. The point is that law and grace are not in any way opposed. It is not merely that law is a response to grace. Nor

---

41. From the NIV: v. 1 ('take'); v. 2 ('return'); v. 3 ('restore' and 'again'); v. 8 ('again'); v. 9 ('again'); v. 10 ('turn').

is it even that law depends on grace. Rather, the character of law is itself grace or gospel.[42]

This delicate dialectic between Israel's and Yahweh's actions serves a rhetorical purpose: the call is for the exiles to act; it is in and through their acting that they realize God is at work, enabling it.[43] In striking fashion, what Yahweh commanded Israel to do, to 'circumcise' their 'heart' (10:16), Yahweh will now do for them (30:6).

The reversal is complete. The curses that fell on Israel will fall on their enemies (30:7) and Yahweh's delight in Israel will be restored. In 28:63 Yahweh's delight (*śûś*) in doing good (*yṭb*) and multiplying shockingly turns to delight (*śûś*) in causing *them* to perish. Now Yahweh will 'turn back and/again (*śûb*)' delight (*śûś*) in them 'for good (*ṭôb*)' just as he had delighted in (*śûś*) their fathers.

Story in song

Standing alongside Deuteronomy's story in *tôrâ* is its story in song (32:1–43). Although this 'Song of Moses' has its own distinctive characteristics, it stands side by side with *tôrâ*, carefully embedded in its narrative context. Its structure largely follows a narrative thread. Verses 1–3 are a prologue, introducing the song; verses 4–6 introduce the twin themes of Yahweh's faithfulness and Israel's unfaithfulness; verses 7–14 then spell out further Yahweh's faithful provision and care (cf. v. 4); verses 15–18 expand on verses 5–6, exhibiting Israel's unfaithfulness; verses 19–25 spell out Yahweh's punishment, aptly fitting the crime; verses 26–35 give insights on the situation, including Yahweh's own reflection; verses 36–43 speak of Yahweh's deliverance of his people, the other side of judgment.

There are many verbal connections between the song and chapter 31 that serve to embed it: Yahweh's 'hiding' his 'face' (31:17–18; 32:20); 'heaven and earth' (31:28; 32:1); 'act corruptly'

---

42. Barker, *Triumph of Grace*, p. 150 (my emphasis; cf. 4:30, 'all these *dĕbārîm*').

43. See James E. Robson, *Word and Spirit in Ezekiel*, LHBOTS 447 (New York: T. & T. Clark, 2006), for a similar analysis in Ezekiel.

(31:29: 32:5); 'ears/hearing' (31:11, 28, 30; 32:1, 44); 'disasters' (31:17, 21; 32:23); 'end, outcome' (31:29; 32:20, 29); 'foreign' (31:16; 32:12 – only instances in Deuteronomy); 'milk' (31:20; 32:14); 'honey' (31:20; 32:13); 'provoke to jealousy' (31:29; 32:16, 19, 21, 27); 'growing fat' (31:20; 32:15[44]). Alongside these verbal connections is a close association between *tôrâ* and song. The table below gives some of the links.

Table 1: Actions predicated of both the song of Moses and the *tôrâ*

Link	Song	Tôrâ
'written'	31:19, 22	27:3, 8; 28:58, 61
'taught'	31:19, 22	4:1, 5, 10, 14; 5:31
'placed in the mouth'	31:19, 21	30;14; Josh. 1:8
'established as a witness against Israel'	31:19 (cf. v. 21)	31:26[45]
given to 'elders'	31:28	31:9
'not (to be) forgotten'	31:21	e.g. 4:9, 23; 6:12
uttered/written 'to completion'	31:30	31:24

Further links include (1) the exploited ambiguity of referent of 'these words' in 31:28, where the expected referent is the words already said, but the actual referent is the song they are about to hear (cf. the same effect in 32:46);[46] (2) the structure of chapter 31, embedding the giving of the song (31:16–22) in an ABCB′A′ pattern

---

44. NRSV and many scholars follow the Samaritan Pentateuch in emending the MT here, adding 'Jacob ate and was full . . .'; this increases the correspondence, but is unnecessary either metrically or for sense, because feeding has already happened. See J. P. Fokkelman, *Major Poems of the Hebrew Bible at the Interface of Hermeneutics and Structural Analysis*, vol. 1: *Exodus 15, Deuteronomy 32 and Job 3*, SSN (Assen, The Netherlands: Van Gorcum, 1998), p. 91.

45. For these four, see Ian Cairns, *Word and Presence: A Commentary on the Book of Deuteronomy*, ITC (Grand Rapids: Eerdmans, 1992), p. 274; Mark E. Biddle, *Deuteronomy*, Smyth & Helwys Bible Commentary 4 (Macon, Ga.: Smyth & Helwys, 2003), p. 461.

46. Tigay, *Deuteronomy*, p. 297; Nelson, *Deuteronomy*, p. 356.

within commands to Joshua (31:14–15, 23) and words about the law (31:9–13; 24–27);[47] (3) both being valedictory speeches.[48]

Such links demand that we read *tôrâ* and song in mutually interpretative fashion. The juxtaposition of *tôrâ* with song means that *tôrâ* is both a revelation to be obeyed and a witness against Israel; correspondingly, the song is not simply a witness against Israel, but is also instruction for the people. While it *is* a witness (31:31), it has a pedagogical purpose.[49] The story it tells indicts the Israel of its past, delivers the Israel of its future and so instructs the Israel of its present.

Yahweh's faithfulness

The opening three verses lead us to expect a panegyric in praise of Yahweh; the 'I' ('will proclaim') and the imperative ('ascribe') of verse 3 match those of verse 1a ('give ear', '*I* will speak'), framing the introduction. The subject is clear: 'the name of Yahweh ...' the 'greatness' of 'our God'. Verse 4 reinforces this. It begins with the stark, resplendent 'the rock', *haṣṣûr*. It is the last time that the definite article 'the' is written;[50] there is nothing to modify it, nothing to describe it; it towers at the entrance to the song.[51] 'Rock' is the dominant metaphor in the song, occurring seven times as a metaphor for 'refuge and protection'.[52] In the rest of verse 4 there is not a single finite verb or participle. There is no action, no movement; only realities.[53] Rocks do not change – they

---

47. Nelson, *Deuteronomy*, p. 357.

48. Moshe Weinfeld, *Deuteronomy and the Deuteronomic School* (Oxford: Oxford University Press, 1972), p. 10.

49. Note in this regard some of the wisdom *motifs* in the song, such as 'my teaching', 'my word' (v. 2); consulting the elders (v. 7). Cf. James R. Boston, 'Wisdom Influence upon the Song of Moses', *JBL* 87 (1968), pp. 198–202.

50. See Fokkelman, *Major Poems*, vol. 1, p. 70; in the only subsequent occurrence in v. 17 it is embedded within a word form.

51. There is no 'He is' in Hebrew. ESV and NASB capture it with 'The Rock!'

52. Nelson, *Deuteronomy*, p. 370.

53. 'God's perfections are timeless' (Fokkelman, *Major Poems*, vol. 1, p. 70).

are permanent. The significance of the metaphor becomes apparent from the structural parallel:

> *The Rock*, perfect is his work, for all his ways are justice;
> *A God of faithfulness and without injustice*, righteous and upright is he.

Positively, the Rock is 'a God of faithfulness'; negatively, he is 'without injustice' (emphasizing his justice by litotes). If verse 4 speaks of Yahweh's attributes, they are rooted in Yahweh's actions towards his people in the past.

In verse 6b Yahweh is 'your *father*' who 'created you' (*qnh*).[54] Israel existed only because of the creative will of their father. Although Israel's sonship and the exodus are closely linked (e.g. Exod. 4:22; Hos. 11:1; cf. *qnh* in Exod. 15:16), sonship seems prior, without a definite moment being identified. Further, Yahweh's creative activity did not leave them in the lurch, for he also 'established you'. The same verb is used in Psalm 40:3 of setting the psalmist's feet firmly upon the rock. Israel's father is 'a God of faithfulness'.

In verses 7–14 the call is to 'remember' Yahweh's faithful action. In verses 7–9 Yahweh moves from being father to (*executor* and) *heir*. The journey is back to the very beginning, to 'days of old' (v. 7). At that time the 'Most High' divided up the nations and allocated Israel to himself. Yahweh is spoken of as 'Most High' here because the name did not have exclusive Israelite connotations; Most High fits his executive sovereign role over the whole world, allocating nations. As far back in time as it is possible to go, Israel has been Yahweh's 'share' and 'inheritance'. Both words elsewhere are used together of the land given to Israel (e.g. 10:9). However, here 'inheritance' is not the land Yahweh gives, but the people Yahweh has received by his own allotting. As the land is to the people, a precious possession, so Jacob is to Yahweh. They have a 'high calling and noble position'.[55]

In verses 10–14 Yahweh has moved from *father* and *heir* to

---

54. This is preferable to 'bought' (NASB), given the following verb, 'made'.
55. Peter C. Craigie, *The Book of Deuteronomy*, NICOT (Grand Rapids: Eerdmans, 1976), p. 380.

redeemer. The people are again passive recipients; but here the previous economy of description changes to extravagant detail: 'he found . . . he surrounded . . . he cared for . . . he guarded' (v. 10). The plight was desperate: they were in a 'desert land', 'a howling waste'. His care was exemplary; they were 'like the apple of his eye'. And he did not leave them there, but carried them on his wings (v. 11), leading them without any help (v. 12), nourishing them (in anticipation) with the best of the best in the land (vv. 13–14). Although many elements are missing, the imagery is exodus imagery (e.g. eagles' wings: 32:11; Exod. 19:4) depicting the move from Israel's helplessness to their enjoying lavish abundance in the land. From time immemorial and through the historical particularity of a journey to the land, Yahweh has done everything as *father*, *heir* and *redeemer*.[56]

Israel's unfaithfulness

It is thus all the more heinous that Israel should respond so ungratefully. That Israel's unfaithfulness should be in view at all is something of a surprise, given the announced theme. 'After all this praise Moses' audience must feel hit by a sledge-hammer.'[57] But verses 5–6 contrast with verse 4 and distil what verses 15–18 spell out: Israel's unfaithfulness. Where Yahweh is 'upright/straight', they are 'crooked'; his work is 'perfect', but they are a 'blemish';[58] he is 'righteous', but they are 'perverse';[59] he is a God of 'faithfulness', but they have 'acted corruptly'. In short, where Yahweh is their 'father' (v. 6) they are 'not his sons'. What a foolish way to repay their father (v. 6)![60]

---

56. Note also the maternal imagery. In v. 13 Yahweh suckled him with honey from the rock; in v. 18 Israel has forgotten the 'rock' that 'bore' them (in more than 85% of cases, the verb *yld* is used of the mother, according to BDB) and 'the God who gave you birth' (the verb is used of giving birth through the pains of labour).

57. Fokkelman, *Major Poems*, vol. 1, p. 71.

58. In sacrificial contexts an animal is 'perfect', *tāmîm*, or it has a 'blemish', *mûm* (Lev. 22:21; Num. 19:2).

59. These are opposites in Prov. 8:8.

60. A fool (*nbl*) is 'someone who, within a particular sphere of influence,

When the song returns to the theme of Israel's unfaithfulness in verses 15–18, the ingratitude and folly take the breath away. Though the song is uttered on the edge of the Promised Land, it looks back to feeding on the land's abundance (vv. 13–15) and on Israel's rebellion (vv. 15–18). In their folly (*nbl*, v. 5) they treated Yahweh with contempt (*nbl*). This is how Jeshurun (meaning, ironically, 'upright/straight one'), the inveterately crooked, treated Yahweh, 'the rock of his salvation'. Contempt in times of plenty for the one who had provided for them; idolatry with gods who had done nothing for them at all (cf. v. 12), and indeed were no gods at all; forgetfulness of the God to whom they owed their very existence, who had made them, borne them and given birth to them (vv. 15, 18) – the catalogue of unfaithfulness is shocking. We await Yahweh's reaction with some trepidation.

Yahweh's judgment
The next chapter of the story paints Yahweh's devastating but fitting judgment. It begins with the summary of verse 19, which spells out Yahweh's rejection of his sons and daughters because of their provocation. There follows an astonishing window first into Yahweh's plans (vv. 20–25), then into his internal deliberations (v. 26) and reflections (vv. 27–30). Yahweh's plans for judgment initially seem to consist in abandonment, hiding his face and then seeing what their end will be, rather than involvement (v. 20). Gradually, his involvement becomes more direct, from his actions to make jealous and provoke (v. 21) to kindling a fire without an end necessarily envisaged (v. 22), to firing his arrows at a definite target – them (v. 23). The judgment is related to the infraction. Verse 21 makes this particularly clear: Yahweh repeats the two verbs 'make jealous' and 'provoke to anger' (*qn'*, *k's*) from verse 16, anchoring the punishment in 21b to the crime. Having made Yahweh 'jealous' with 'strange (gods)' (v. 16) who are 'no god' (v. 17), Yahweh will make them 'jealous' with a 'no people'; having 'provoked' Yahweh 'to anger' as a 'senseless' (*nbl*, v. 6) people who

counts for nothing, has nothing to offer, gives no help, commands no respect, is nothing' (*HALOT* 663).

'scoffed' (*nbl*) at the rock of their salvation (v. 15), Yahweh will
'provoke' them 'to anger' with a 'senseless' (*nbl*) nation. Assonance
further reinforces the link between sin (*hblym*, 'idols') and punishment (*nbl*, 'senseless' nation).[61] The identity of the 'no people' is
'deliberately obscured',[62] but their actions in verse 25 complement
the arrows Yahweh sends in verse 24.[63] The personified sword
bereaves. Merisms, pairs of opposites indicating totality, show
that death is total and nowhere is safe: inside and outside; man
and woman; suckling child and grey-haired man. The imagery is
terrifying. Perhaps, then, Yahweh wonders, he will make an end of
his people (v. 26). Yahweh 'is quoting himself!',[64] giving an unprecedented window into his consciousness. He relents, not because
of the people's repentance, but because of fear of 'provocation
to anger' (*k's*) from the rampaging 'no people', that they will take
the kudos (27).[65] Judgment is devastating; destruction is almost
complete.

Yahweh's restoration

Even in the midst of judgment 'a hint of hope may remain, for the
divine plan is to make Israel "jealous"',[66] and Yahweh relents from
total destruction for his own sake (cf. Ezek. 36:22–23). But we
have to wait until verse 34 before there is something definitively
positive. Prior to that, in verses 28–33 there is a 'subtle interplay between the accusation of the enemy and that of Israel'.[67]
Language describing the vicious 'no people' suits Israel: 'void of
counsel', 'no understanding in them' (v. 28); 'if they were wise'
(v. 29; cf. v. 6); 'vine' (v. 32). On the surface it is this vicious nation
that is supposed to draw conclusions about the terrible devastation

61. Tigay, *Deuteronomy*, p. 308.

62. Nelson, *Deuteronomy*, p. 373.

63. Cf. Fokkelman, *Major Poems*, vol. 1, p. 103.

64. Ibid., p. 59.

65. The versions struggle with the notion of Yahweh 'fearing'; see *BHQ*,
    Deuteronomy, p. 148*.

66. Nelson, *Deuteronomy*, p. 374.

67. McConville, *Deuteronomy*, p. 457.

on Israel; yet the underspecified 'them' of verse 30 invites every hearer and singer of the song to come to the same conclusion: defeat was not because Yahweh was powerless. No, it was because 'their rock had sold them', because Yahweh, the faithful covenant God, had 'given them up' (v. 30). Only in Yahweh then could a future be found. Perhaps Israel first needed to have a right perspective on their plight. The beginnings of that future are in verses 34–35 but continue through to the end of the Song.

First, there is *destruction of the nations*. Vengeance belongs to Yahweh (v. 35); calamity and doom are near at hand for the 'no people' who treated Israel so brutally (vv. 35, 40–43). Even at the moment of reasserting vengeance on his adversaries and declaring that he will 'repay those that hate me' (v. 42), there are echoes of his covenant with Israel ('repay' 'those that hate me'; 7:10). Future judgment of Yahweh's enemies is of a piece with the judgment he has carried out on his people. There is no partiality.

Alongside this judgment of the nations, indeed a counterpart to it, is the *vindication of his people* (v. 36). The first verb is 'judge', meaning 'judge in favour of' (cf. Ps. 135:14). With vindication is compassion. There is no suggestion of Israel's repentance or turning back to Yahweh. Instead, Yahweh will look on their pitiable, powerless condition and have compassion (cf. Amos 7:1–6; Judg. 10:16). This vindication of and compassion for his people largely consist in the destruction of enemies, both Yahweh's (v. 41) and his servants' (v. 43). Yahweh does not spare Israel's blushes about the past even as he 'rises up' and 'helps', as he 'makes alive' and 'heals' (vv. 37–39). Israel has sacrificed to 'no gods', scorning the God of their salvation and throwing their lot in with johnny-come-lately pseudo-deities (vv. 15–18). The taunt comes, 'Let them rise up and help you' (v. 38). Through judgment and restoration comes the revelation that only Yahweh is God (v. 39).

Yahweh will also '*cleanse* (or *atone for*) *his people's land*' (v. 43). The cleansing may be from the defiling activity either of the marauding nations and their bloodshed (cf. Num. 35:33) or of idolatrous Israel (cf. Lev. 18:27). Either way the land will no longer be unclean.

A contested final part of the future restoration is the *nations rejoicing* (v. 43). The text of the verse has been discussed extensively.

The Greek Old Testament (the Septuagint [LXX]) and manuscript 4QDeutᑫ from Qumran have longer versions (and are different from each other). The Hebrew MT may be translated, 'Rejoice, nations, [with] his people' (cf. NIV), or 'Make his people rejoice, nations' (NIV footnote). Few scholars regard the MT as reflecting the original.[68] Most scholars and some English translations largely follow 4QDeutᑫ (e.g. ESV, NRSV), while the NIV reflects a version closer to the MT. Retaining the MT can still yield a more nationalistic sentiment (cf. NIV footnote). Strikingly, in the Greek Old Testament the nations are called to rejoice along with Yahweh's people (cf. Rom. 15:10). Although at first glance puzzling given the nations' destruction, other parts of the Old Testament also insist that the judgment of the earth is a cause for wide celebration (Pss 22:27–28; 96; 98); the reason seems to be that blessing to the nations is tied up with the restoration of Israel (Ps. 47).[69] Further, 'the language of vengeance is applied to "adversaries," "those who hate me," and "the enemy," but never to Gentiles *per se*'.[70]

Reflecting on the song's story

The song, as with the rest of Deuteronomy, tells a story of Yahweh and Israel. As poetry, 'the speaking of God (to, from, and about God) in the Bible is *figural* and *non-literal*; it is *indirect* and *open*'.[71] Not only is it memorable (cf. 31:21), but it is self-involving; its ambiguities and imagery invite, even demand, engagement. It

---

68. See Nelson, *Deuteronomy*, pp. 379–380; Tigay, *Deuteronomy*, pp. 314–315, 516–518; *BHQ, Deuteronomy*, pp. 152*–153*; note, however, McConville, *Deuteronomy*, p. 450; Fokkelman, *Major Poems*, vol. 1, p. 130.

69. Christopher J. H. Wright, *Deuteronomy*, NIBC (Peabody, Mass.: Hendrickson, 1996), p. 304.

70. Lincicum, *Paul*, p. 161.

71. Patrick D. Miller, 'The Theological Significance of Biblical Poetry', in Samuel E. Balentine and John Barton (eds.), *Language, Theology and the Bible: Essays in Honour of James Barr* (Oxford: Clarendon, 1994), p. 225 (emphasis original).

captures a reality and opens new vistas. Its aesthetic fittingness leads singer and reader to embrace its condensed articulation of Yahweh and Israel's relationship.

The form is different from the rest of Deuteronomy; so too is the standpoint. Whereas in the rest of Deuteronomy the perspective is that of Moses addressing the people in the plains of Moab and anticipating entry, the song looks back on entry into the land, to prospering in the land, to wilful rebellion and to devastating judgment. It inhabits the moment of greatest disaster and loss, anticipating vindication and restoration. As such, 'narrative chronology and historical specificity are both subjugated to rhetorical and didactic concerns'.[72] Yet it does so in a remarkably stylized fashion. The Song is deliberately devoid of definitive historical referent. Although Israel are clearly Yahweh's people (vv. 9, 36, 43), there is no mention of the promises to Abraham, the giving of *tôrâ* at Horeb or the delivering of statutes and judgments at Moab. Although sonship and wilderness wandering cohere with the rest of Deuteronomy, the particularities of Egypt, exodus and life in the wilderness are missing. Although Yahweh's leading brought them into the land of plenty (vv. 13–14), there is no hint of conquest or even of actual entry. Although the song looks back on destruction, the identity of the human agent is hidden from view. Although it anticipates future vindication, it is both distinctive and general. It is radically theocentric, with no hint of any action on Israel's behalf. In articulating cleansing of the land and destruction of the enemy, it goes beyond the rest of Deuteronomy, but in full rhetorical imagery empty of detail.

Alongside these significant differences there is nonetheless a fundamental continuity of storyline: (1) Israel has a special relationship with Yahweh by virtue of Yahweh's distinctive action; (2) Yahweh shows lavish generosity and faithfulness throughout his dealings with Israel; (3) Israel is guilty of wilful and heinous idolatry, spurning Yahweh; (4) in anger Yahweh enacts catastrophic judgment almost to the point of annihilation; (5) the other side of

72. David M. Allen, *Deuteronomy and Exhortation*, p. 32.

judgment, Yahweh punishes the nations and restores his people, without ultimate dependence on Israel's actions.

Concluding reflections

Deuteronomy is a word with a story. Although the central section of Deuteronomy, chapters 12–26, is closely akin to a law code, the book as a whole is more than 'law': it is a book that tells a story of the relationship between Yahweh and Israel. One of the problems of translating the Hebrew *tôrâ* by the Greek *nomos* and then translating that Greek word into English, 'law', is that the dimension of story can be lost. This can have the effect of hindering interpretation of some significant New Testament passages, such as Matthew 11:13, 'For . . . the law prophesied until John came,' or Matthew 5:17, where Jesus declares that he has come to 'fulfil' the 'law', or Romans 10:4, where Christ is the 'end/goal/fulfilment' of the law.

What is more, as story it has a constitutive function. The people of God are such by virtue of owning this story. As they tell and retell, as they teach and learn, they are constituted by this story of their past, present and future. They are a people united by a shared story. The events of the story and the narrative of these events both serve to form this people.

Further, as with all stories, there is a prescriptive function too. Not only does the story form a people, but it shapes a people. It articulates beliefs, attitudes and behaviours that are life-giving and those that are not. It frames them within a context that helps interpret them and assists the process of memorization (cf. 31:21). To put it a different way, theology and ethics are profoundly connected to history. They are not abstract. Abstracting a theology from the text, a systematic theology, is an important enterprise, given that the Scriptures all speak with God's voice. Yet the rootedness of Israel's theology and ethics in a narrative needs to be privileged.

God's faithfulness is articulated in statements both figuratively, as 'the rock', and literally, 'a god of faithfulness' in 32:4. Such statements are not detached from history, but are rooted in Israel's experience of this God, Yahweh, in history. Not only has he created them, but he has provided for them (32:6); he is one who inherited Israel as his people (32:8–9) and lavished all good things upon them in the journey from the wilderness to the land (32:10–14). In similar fashion, declarations about Yahweh's uniqueness do not stand detached from history, but are founded upon that history. In Deuteronomy 4:32–40 some of the strongest statements of Yahweh's uniqueness are found: 'So acknowledge today and take to heart that Yahweh is God in heaven above and on the earth beneath; there is no other' (v. 39; cf. v. 35). They are to draw this conclusion from what they have *experienced* of Yahweh. No other deity has spoken to his/her people as Yahweh has; no other deity has delivered his/her people from slavery as Yahweh has. That is true even if the question is asked at any moment since creation itself (vv. 32–34). They are to draw the same conclusions in 32:39, again on the basis of what Yahweh has *done in history*, in judgment and restoration.

Israel's election, identity and character again become clear through this story. They know they were not chosen on their merits, *because* they were chosen when they were few in number (7:6–8). Because it is a story of a people, there is a particularity about it. There is a 'when' and a 'where'. There are, of course, universal implications, which Deuteronomy's story barely touches upon, but its particularity, and the particularity of Israel's election, is not an awkward embarrassment, but a necessary entailment. Israel's character, or, more specifically, Israel's heart with its failings, is something that comes to light through narrative, through event. Indeed, Yahweh himself speaks about testing them 'so that *he* might know what was in their heart, whether they would keep his commandments or not' (8:2).

Israel's obligations too come within this narratival framework. 'Law' (or, more neutrally, their obligations) is not an abstract entity, but something for a time and a place. There *is* something enduring about it, as we shall see. But it is also rooted to a historical situation. It does not give ethical ideals for any and every situation, but works with the realities of a people with uncircumcised hearts at a point in time. It was, as Jesus reminded the Pharisees, because of their hardness of heart that Moses wrote the law on divorce (Mark

10:5; Deut. 24:1–4). Further, the story makes it clear that the law was given to a people whom Yahweh had *already* redeemed (5:6). The Decalogue and the statutes and commandments were never meant to be a means of earning favour, still less a way of being redeemed. No, they were given to a people whom Yahweh had brought *out of* slavery.

This story also helps illuminate the theological relationship between the covenant made with Abraham and that at Horeb. They form part of the *same* story. The covenant Yahweh made at Horeb was not an aberration or a cruel imposition, but was in direct continuity with the promises made to Abraham. The blessings Yahweh promised Abraham were in principle no different from those that Deuteronomy held out. Yahweh's laws at Horeb were the means of Israel, his son, appropriating the land that Yahweh had promised as an inheritance. They were also the means of Israel becoming numerous, receiving blessing and, ultimately bringing blessing to the nations (Deut. 28; 4:6–8). Israelite unfaithfulness to the Horeb covenant brought a reversal of the *Abrahamic* promises: curse, exile from the land, reduction in number (Deut. 28, esp. vv. 62–64). Thus the apparent conditionality of the Horeb covenant was never absolute. Behind the covenant made at Horeb was the oath sworn to Abraham (Deut. 4:31; 30:1–20). While a generation that turned to other gods would cease to benefit from that inheritance, the promise remained as a reality.

Appreciating Deuteronomy's story also helps makes sense of the strands of optimism and pessimism present in Deuteronomy. It is in the outworking of history, in the interaction between the life-giving commands of a gracious king (33:5) and the uncircumcised heart of a rebellious people that resolution can be seen. It was a 'command' that was 'for life' but it turned out 'for death' (Rom. 7:10).

But of course the book of Deuteronomy, with its story, exists within the canon of Scripture with its own story. It is to that story, and Deuteronomy's relation to it, that we now turn.

3. A WORD IN A STORY

The book of Deuteronomy tells its own story. It also comprises events in the plains of Moab and, in the final chapter, on Mount Nebo. The task of this chapter is to consider how the story Deuteronomy tells relates to the wider story from Genesis to Revelation. There is also the subsidiary question of how the events in the book of Deuteronomy relate to the wider Old Testament story. This is, of course, an almost impossible task![1]

---

1. C. Marvin Pate, J. Scott Duvall, J. Daniel Hays, E. Randolph Richards, W. Dennis Tucker, Jr., and Preben Vang, *The Story of Israel: A Biblical Theology* (Leicester: Apollos, 2004), is a book-length attempt to do so, based on the 'pattern of sin–exile–restoration' (p. 22). Behind this articulation lies the sixfold pattern of Odil H. Steck, *Israel und das gewaltsame Geschick der Propheten: Untersuchungen zur Uberlieferung des deuteronomistischen Geschichtsbildes im Alten Testament, Spätjudentum und Urchristentum*, WMANT 23 (Neukirchen-Vluyn: Neukirchener, 1967), pp. 184–189. Steck's six stages are (1) Israel's entire history is characterized by 'stiff-necked' disobedience; (2) Yahweh sent prophet after prophet exhorting

It will inevitably entail selectivity and (over)simplification. Some important preliminary comments, observations and questions of method precede the chapter's main focus: to highlight the main points of connection and difference between Deuteronomy's story and the Bible's story. At the risk of jumping ahead, the main argument will be that later writers in the Old and New Testaments see themselves as living in Deuteronomy's story, bringing to fulfilment what Deuteronomy anticipates.

The preliminary comments all revolve around the dangers, real and potential, of talking about 'a story'. A first danger is that language of 'story' could be understood as downplaying history or suggesting that events did not happen. But to talk about 'story' is not necessarily to cast doubts on historicity. Rather, it may be, and is here, simply a recognition that much of the Bible has many of the characteristics of literary artistry. Attention to plot and characterization are an important part of interpretation, but questions of history are not thereby excluded.[2]

A second danger is that, by focusing exclusively on the Bible's storyline, biblical theology is narrowed to redemptive history. This, then, excludes the so-called wisdom literature (Proverbs, Job, Ecclesiastes), the Psalms and the Song of Songs. In response, the focus here on the Bible's story should be seen for what it is, a self-consciously limited perspective rather than an attempt to be exhaustive that marginalizes these books.

A third danger lies in the word 'a'. Might it not justly be said

---

Footnote 1 (*cont.*)

repentance; (3) Israel consistently rejected the prophets, sometimes with violence; (4) in Yahweh's anger, he exiled them; (5) even in exile, there is the chance for repentance; (6) if there is repentance, Yahweh will restore them to the land and bestow covenant blessings on them.

2. See esp. V. Philips Long, *The Art of Biblical History*, Foundations of Contemporary Interpretation 5 (Grand Rapids: Zondervan, 1994). For literary readings of biblical books, see Robert Alter and Frank Kermode (eds.), *The Literary Guide to the Bible* (London: Fontana, 1987); Leland Ryken and Tremper Longman III (eds.), *The Complete Literary Guide to the Bible* (Grand Rapids: Zondervan, 1993).

that there are *many* stories, rather than *a* story? After all, there are two main accounts of Israel's history, the Primary History (Genesis–Kings) and the Secondary (or Chronistic) History (Chronicles–Nehemiah), which largely cover the same period and do so with distinctive perspectives. According to David Clines, the existence of two histories serves to 'problematize the past for all their readers'. He continues:

> This is because the Old Testament itself simply juxtaposes the two
> Histories, without offering any hermeneutical key to their dual
> existence, nor even any historical key to their comparative value
> for the reconstruction of the history of the Jewish people.[3]

Rather than being a problem, the existence of different perspectives on the same events, even perspectives hard to blend, is one of the beautiful characteristics of divinely inspired Scripture. Human voices are not drowned out, nor are distinctive viewpoints always amalgamated: there are, after all, four Gospels. Unity is found alongside the diversity, a unity rooted in the ultimate author, God, and his plans to bring everything together under Christ (Eph. 1:10). This unity means it is right to speak of 'a' story, though readers should not decide in advance what the characteristics of God's story-telling should be!

A fourth danger arises out of the third. It is the assumption that because there is 'a' story, there is *one* way of articulating it. But there are many possible different ways, as evidenced by a variety of attempts, popular and scholarly, to speak of this story. Graeme Goldsworthy has spoken of the unifying pattern of God's kingdom, of God's people in God's place under God's rule;[4] Elmer Martens frames his Old Testament theology around

---

3. David J. A. Clines, 'The Old Testament Histories: A Reader's Guide', in *What Does Eve Do to Help? And Other Readerly Questions to the Old Testament*, JSOTSup 94 (Sheffield: JSOT Press, 1990), p. 92.

4. Graeme Goldsworthy, *Gospel & Kingdom: A Christian Interpretation of the Old Testament* (Homebush West, NSW: Lancer, 1981), p. 47. Cf. also his *According to Plan: The Unfolding Revelation of God in the Bible* (Leicester:

God's fourfold plan as revealed in Exodus 5:22 – 6:8 (salvation, covenant community, knowledge of God and land), and briefly traces this design in Matthew and Romans;[5] Marvin Pate and others have used the story of Israel, seen through the characteristically Deuteronomic lenses of election, sin, exile and restoration, as a unifying theme for the Bible storyline;[6] Christopher Ash has characterized the Bible storyline in terms of the scattering and gathering of God's people;[7] finally, Scott Hahn sees divine covenanting (of different types) as a way of finding unity in diverse traditions within the canon.[8]

A final danger, one already alluded to, is that the volume and diversity of biblical material make any retelling or analysis simplistic. What follows makes no attempt to be exhaustive. But selectivity can be illuminating.

In terms of preliminary observations, two need making at this point.

First, and strikingly, the *events* of Deuteronomy hardly feature elsewhere. Although language characteristic of Deuteronomy is found in many other parts of the Old Testament, the main events of Deuteronomy resound only within the book of Deuteronomy itself. The covenant in the plains of Moab, 'in addition' (29:1) to the one at Horeb, is never mentioned elsewhere. The reason for this may well be the way in which the events in Moab combine

---

Footnote 4 (*cont.*)

    Inter-Varsity Press, 1991); *Preaching the Whole Bible as Christian Scripture* (Leicester: Inter-Varsity Press, 2000); and the lucid framing by Vaughan Roberts: *God's Big Picture: Tracing the Story-Line of the Bible* (Leicester: Inter-Varsity Press, 2003).

5. Elmer A. Martens, *God's Design: A Focus on Old Testament Theology*, 2nd ed. (Grand Rapids: Baker; Leicester: Apollos, 1994).

6. Pate et al., *Story of Israel*.

7. Christopher Ash, *Remaking a Broken World: A Fresh Look at the Bible Storyline* (Milton Keynes: Authentic Media, 2010).

8. Scott W. Hahn, *Kinship by Covenant: A Canonical Approach to the Fulfillment of God's Saving Promises*, Anchor Yale Bible Reference Library (New Haven: Yale University Press, 2009).

with those at Horeb: 'The relationship of the Moab covenant to the Horeb covenant is not one of clean distinction, but rather a new realization.'⁹ Further, the actual transition of leadership from Moses to Joshua (ch. 31) as an event is not picked up elsewhere. That Joshua would be Moses' successor had been anticipated a while before Moses' death (Num. 27:12–22; cf. Deut. 3:28; 31:1–8). Within the storyline the transition is a necessary event to explain Joshua's significance in the book bearing his name. Yahweh's words in Joshua 1:5 pick up on this: 'Just as I was with Moses, [so] I will be with you', and open the way for a certain typological relationship between them (of which more below). But outside Deuteronomy nothing is made of the transition event itself. Finally, Moses' death outside the land has very little prominence. Judgment on Moses is pronounced in Numbers 20:11–12; his death is referred to in passing in Joshua 1:1. But beyond this, the death of the foundational leader and lawgiver has none of the significance it has in Deuteronomy.

Secondly, Deuteronomy's own retelling of the past is typically selective. Alongside some omissions (e.g. Gen. 1 – 11, of which more below) and additions (e.g. the allocating of the nations by the Most High in 32:8–9) there is often a distinctive rhetorical purpose when Deuteronomy covers the same events. It is not merely repeating events and narratives (is there such a thing as *mere repetition*?). One example is the appointing of judges in Deuteronomy 1:9–18. The appearance of the passage is somewhat abrupt, since this appointment has not been mandated by Yahweh in 1:6–8, nor do the judges appear subsequently. Further, it breaks the flow from the command to set out (1:7) and the recounting of that setting out (1:19). Given the repetition of Moses' not being 'able' (*ykl*) to bear 'alone' (*lĕbad*) the burden of the Israelites, he is recalling the appointing outlined in Exodus 18:13–27 and Numbers 11:10–25. In Exodus it is Moses' father-in-law, Jethro, who takes the initiative and identifies the problem. In Deuteronomy it is Moses. In Exodus there is no mention of the consultation with the people that is a critical component of the

9. McConville, *Deuteronomy*, p. 409.

account in Deuteronomy. A further example of distinctive retelling is the sending out of the spies, which is at the initiative of the people in Deuteronomy, while mandated by Yahweh in Numbers 13:1–3. In both these passages Moses identifies the significant role played by the people, a characteristic theme in the democratizing Deuteronomy. Selectivity and rhetorical purpose characterize Deuteronomy's retelling.

As far as questions of method and approach are concerned, the main point is that characterizing indebtedness is complex, not least because every narrative operates with certain constraints and freedoms.[10] Constraints in telling obviously arise from the events themselves. They also arise from earlier retellings of these events. Alongside these constraints are freedoms, freedoms that arise from the newness of the situation in which the retelling takes place. In other words future accounts owe a debt to the past (events and retelling) and yet are free to reframe it in the light of the present. As such, the relationship between Deuteronomy and the wider story is not straightforward to characterize. Claims of indebtedness to a previous tradition may be genuine, but there may be substantial departures from that tradition: by including, by excluding, by rewriting, by condensing, by surpassing. It may even be possible that claims of indebtedness are, in fact, a way of subverting even at the moment of apparent endorsement.[11] Just as Deuteronomy stands in a line of tradition and interpretation, so do subsequent works. As we look beyond Deuteronomy to the wider story of the Old and New Testaments, the relationship between

---

10. Cf. Michael Fishbane, *Biblical Interpretation in Ancient Israel* (Oxford: Clarendon, 1985), p. 428, who speaks of 'an ongoing interchange between a hermeneutics of continuity and a hermeneutics of challenge and innovation'.

11. So Bernard M. Levinson, *Deuteronomy and the Hermeneutics of Legal Innovation* (Oxford: Oxford University Press, 1998), argues that the authors of Deuteronomy have produced an 'impious fraud' (p. 150). There are better ways of construing the relationship, though. See e.g. Hindy Najman, *Seconding Sinai: The Development of Mosaic Discourse in Second Temple Judaism*, JSJSup 77 (Leiden: Brill, 2003).

these works and Deuteronomy will not be straightforward to characterize. What I shall do is look at the most significant points of contact and departure, using as a basis the story Deuteronomy tells. Given that Deuteronomy occurs early in Israel's history and is the gateway from the Pentateuch to the rest of the biblical story, the bulk of the time will be spent looking forward. But there is one significant backward glance we must first make.

Deuteronomy and Genesis

At critical moments in Deuteronomy Moses refers back to the promises Yahweh made to Abraham. These form the bedrock of the claims to the land, whether in Moab or after the exile (1:8; 4:31; 30:20). When articulated to a multitude standing before Moses, they give ample demonstration of Yahweh's faithfulness (1:10–11). The language of relationship between Yahweh and Israel, typified in the phrase 'your/our God', has these promises as its ultimate source.

There are glimmers of a history behind these promises in Deuteronomy, with talk of creation (4:32) and of Yahweh referred to as Most High, allocating nations and receiving Israel as his inheritance (32:8–9). For the most part, though, these promises to Abraham constitute the initial landmark event in Deuteronomy's story. In Genesis there is history behind these promises (Gen. 1 – 11). This (hi)story consists in large measure of a cycle of Yahweh's creative activity, humanity defying that order, Yahweh's judgment and, finally, Yahweh's fresh (re-)creative act.[12] Together, humanity's defiance and Yahweh's judgment constitute a kind of 'decreation', with death, exclusion and fragmentation of relationships in stark contrast with the very goodness of creation.

In their context in Genesis the promises Yahweh makes with Abraham are intimately connected to the context (cf. Gen. 11:27–32) and declare that Yahweh's purposes for *creation* are now being

---

12. Cf. Joseph Blenkinsopp, *Creation, Un-Creation, Re-Creation: A Discursive Commentary on Genesis 1–11* (London: T. & T. Clark, 2011).

carried forward through Abraham and his offspring. One way in which this is evident is when the promises to Abraham in Genesis 12:1–3 are compared with the creation purposes in Genesis 1:28.[13]

In Genesis 1:28 God commands humanity, 'be fruitful and multiply (*rbh*)'; numerical growth is part of Yahweh's creation purpose. In 12:2 Yahweh promises to make Abraham into a great nation. Throughout the rest of Genesis the issue of 'offspring/seed (*zera‘*)' dominates the plotline. That concern for multiplication (*rbh*) is explicitly picked up as a fulfilment of the promises made to Abraham in Deuteronomy 1:10–11.

Alongside the concern for numerical growth is God's 'blessing'. After making humanity in his image, male and female, 'God blessed them . . .' (Gen. 1:28). Blessing spoke of prosperity and fertility (cf. 1:22). That God went on to speak with them points to more than this in the case of God and humanity: it speaks of a harmonious relationship between God and his people.[14] The 'blessing' God gave to man and woman in chapter 1 he also promises to Abraham (12:1–3). Five times in these three verses Yahweh speaks of blessing. Explicitly, in verse 2, he declares that he will 'bless' Abraham.

A third component found in both places is that of 'land' (or, more neutrally, 'place', 'space' or 'territory'). In Genesis 1:28 God commands humanity, 'Fill the earth (*'ereṣ*) . . .'. In the context of the chapter *'ereṣ* is the dry ground that has appeared after God has gathered the waters into one place (1:9–10). Humanity is to populate this land and 'subdue' it. It belongs to them as the place they are to live.[15] In Genesis 12 Yahweh commands Abraham to

---

13. I follow Gordon J. Wenham, *Pentateuch*, p. 40, in seeing four elements to the promises.

14. Cf. Gordon J. Wenham, *Genesis 1–15*, WBC 1 (Dallas: Word, 1987), p. 33.

15. This is not a mandate for mistreatment of creation. See Richard J. Bauckham, *Bible and Ecology: Rediscovering the Community of Creation*, Sarum Theological Lectures (Waco: Baylor University Press, 2010). The forcefulness of the depiction here needs to be read alongside language of Adam's 'serving' and 'keeping' the garden of Eden in 2:15. These two words (*'bd, šmr*) occur together like this elsewhere only in connection with the priests looking after the tabernacle (Num. 3:7–8).

'go from your land (*'eres*) . . . to the land (*'eres*) that I will show you'. In the subsequent narrative that 'land' receives greater definition: 'this' land (12:7); 'all the land you can see' and 'for ever' (13:15); 'from the river of Egypt to the great river, the river Euphrates' (15:18); 'all the land of Canaan' (17:8).[16] The scope of the territory differs between Genesis 1 and 12 – 25, but the common term *'eres* and the reality of a promise of 'land' held out as a place to live point to a common concern. Later interpretation came to see the promise of territory to Abraham to be rather larger, perhaps carrying through the expansive logic of the promises;[17] in line with this, Paul speaks in Romans 4:13 of the promise that Abraham would inherit the *kosmos*. On this reading, the promise to Abraham of 'land' has not a smaller but a greater orbit than the initial creation mandate.

The final part of the promise is the blessing of 'humanity' more generally. In Genesis 1:28 God's blessing is for humanity in its entirety. By Genesis 12 there might seem something parochial about the calling of a wandering nomad. But the promises to Abraham do have wider humanity in view. There is God's curse for those who curse Abraham, God's blessing for those who bless Abraham, and the final promise that 'in you all the families of the earth shall be blessed'. The blessing pronounced in Genesis 1 is an ultimate purpose of the call to Abraham. 'God's choice of Abraham constitutes an initially exclusive move for the sake of a maximally inclusive end. Election serves mission.'[18]

Genesis 12 then carries forward God's creation purposes expressed in Genesis 1. Deuteronomy's appeal to the promises to Abraham means that Deuteronomy is intimately connected with

---

16. Gordon J. Wenham, *Story as Torah: Reading the Old Testament Ethically*, OTS (Edinburgh: T. & T. Clark, 2000), p. 22.

17. C. E. B. Cranfield, *Romans*, 2 vols., ICC (Edinburgh: T. & T. Clark, 1975–9), vol. 1, pp. 239–240; Douglas J. Moo, *The Epistle to the Romans*, NICNT (Grand Rapids: Eerdmans, 1996), p. 274.

18. Terence E. Fretheim, 'The Book of Genesis: Introduction, Commentary, and Reflections', in Leander E. Keck (ed.), *New Interpreter's Bible*, vol. 1 (Nashville: Abingdon, 1994), p. 417.

God's plans for creation. Before looking at some implications, there are some striking parallels that corroborate the link between Deuteronomy and the start of Genesis.

The analogy of Yahweh's 'hovering' like an eagle matches the Wind of God 'hovering' over the water (*rḥp*; Gen. 1:2; Deut. 32:11);[19] the 'formlessness' of creation matches the 'formlessness' of the wilderness (*tōhû*; Gen. 1:1; Deut. 32:10); so at the end of Deuteronomy God's act of redemption is associated with his act of creation.[20]

Deuteronomy describes the land in creation terms, as 'good' (Deut. 1:25–35; cf. Gen. 1), with Edenic abundance. There are many parallels between Adam and Eden, on the one hand, and Israel and the land, on the other. Dumbrell notes:

> Like Adam (Gen 2:8), Israel was formed outside of the land. Placed in the land by God, she was given a code which was to regulate life there. In the land she was promised particular access to the divine presence, but the threat existed that if the regulations were not kept, she would be expelled from the land.[21]

Further, Israel as the son of God inheriting the land (Deut. 8:5; 14:1; 32:5–6) matches Adam as the son of God receiving the gift of Eden.[22] The sanctuary nature of the garden, where Yahweh walks about is matched by the sanctuary nature of the camp where Yahweh walks about (hithpael of *hlk*; Gen. 3:8; Deut. 23:14), and ultimately by the sanctuary nature of the land where Yahweh will

---

19. These are the only two occurrences of the piel of *rḥp* in the Old Testament.

20. Deuteronomy's connection of redemption with creation is also apparent in its grounding of the sabbath command in deliverance from Egypt, mirroring Exodus's grounding of it in creation.

21. William J. Dumbrell, *The Faith of Israel: Its Expression in the Books of the Old Testament* (Leicester: Apollos, 1988), p. 56.

22. The notion of Adam as God's son, articulated in Luke 3:38, is clear from the parallel between language of 'image' and 'likeness' used of Adam's son Seth (Gen. 5:3), and of God's creating of Adam (Gen. 5:1).

make his name dwell (Deut. 12) and where he will be near his people (Deut. 4:7). The choice of life or death, prosperity (lit. 'good', *ṭôb*) or destruction (lit. 'evil', *rāʿ*), confronting the people on the edge of the Promised Land is precisely the same choice that confronted Adam and Eve in the garden (Deut. 30:15; Gen. 2:17). Finally, 'the verbs "multiply" and "bless" [in Deut. 1:10–11] recall the creation account (Gen. 1:28); God's initial words of blessing are enacted in Israel, who is the carrier of YHWH's will for all creation'.[23]

The first implication of the connections between Genesis 1 – 3 and Deuteronomy is that Deuteronomy's concern for land, for an embodiment of life lived before God in space and time, is neither an aberration nor a temporary concern restricted to a particular point in salvation history. Rather, it is part of God's single redemptive plan, a plan not to scrap creation, but to redeem it. There is always a 'where', a place where humanity's relationship with God is lived out. Further, this 'where' is profoundly physical and material. In the beginning God's forming and fashioning work in creation was 'good'. The rest of the Bible does not consist in a flight *from* this creation, but a redeeming and renewing of it. Redemption is not about disembodied souls floating in the ether, playing harps. This fails on at least two counts: it downplays human physicality and it ignores the rest of God's good creation.

That redemption of humanity is profoundly physical is apparent from the language of 'save' and 'salvation' in the Gospels:

> It is fascinating to see how passages like this [about 'saving' as physical healing] – and there are many of them – are often juxtaposed with others which speak of 'salvation' in larger terms, which seem to go beyond present physical healing or rescue. . . . The future rescue which God had planned and promised was starting to come true in the present. We are saved, not as souls, but as wholes.[24]

The most obvious signs of God's ongoing commitment to human physicality are Jesus' incarnation and his resurrection as the

---

23. Brueggemann, *Deuteronomy*, p. 27.
24. Tom Wright, *Surprised by Hope* (London: SPCK, 2007), p. 211.

first fruits of the general resurrection (1 Cor. 15). The Christian hope is of resurrection *of the body*.

Further, redemption of humanity fits within God's larger redemptive plans for creation. Humanity had the task of being God's vicegerents in creation. They failed in that task, but the intimate relationship between humanity and creation remains in the Old Testament and in the New (Deut. 8; Col. 1:20; Rom. 8:18–27). The goal of redemption is a redeemed humanity in a new heavens and a new earth (Rev. 21 – 22). In that new heavens and new earth 'God's people are promised a new type of bodily existence, the fulfilment and redemption of our present bodily life' (cf. Rom. 8:23).[25] There is a danger in assuming there is an inherent contrast between 'spiritual' and 'physical', especially if there is a tacit implication that 'physical' is bad. In the New Testament 'spiritual' is to do with the heavenly realms, and may be profoundly physical. The food Israel ate was 'spiritual' (1 Cor. 10:3); the resurrection *body* will be 'spiritual' (1 Cor. 15:44).[26] 'The adjective describes, not what something is *composed of*, but what it is *animated by*.'[27] Thus the 'spiritual blessings in Christ' in Ephesians 1:3 do not describe their non-physicality, but their location and what animates them. Recreation is the goal, not an escape from creation. Dietrich Bonhoeffer in his *Life Together* brilliantly illustrates one way in which this shapes our thinking about church life. It is no shame to long for the 'physical' presence of other Christians. He notes shrewdly that familiarity can breed contempt, but 'the prisoner, the sick person, the Christian in exile sees in the companionship of a fellow Christian a physical sign of the gracious presence of the triune God'.[28]

A second implication is that Deuteronomy's nationalism is rela-

––––––––––––––––––

25. Ibid., p. 159.

26. It would be a grotesque oxymoron for the 'spiritual body' (*sōma pneumatikon*) to be non-physical. See the discussion in N. T. Wright, *Christian Origins and the Question of God*, vol. 3: *The Resurrection of the Son of God* (London: SPCK, 2003), pp. 348–352.

27. Ibid., p. 352 (emphasis original).

28. Bonhoeffer, *Life Together*, p. 9.

tivized. Read in isolation, Deuteronomy appears one of the most narrowly nationalistic books in the Old Testament. Blessing for Israel involves their being 'high' above the other nations (26:19; 28:1), lending to them and ruling over them without borrowing from them (15:6; 28:12). The 'election' of Israel also may be seen to fit here. Out of all the nations on earth Yahweh had chosen Israel, and Israel alone, to be his 'treasured possession' (7:6; cf. 26:18–19). Most striking, though, are chapters 7 and 20. Few who have read the stark accounts of the 'ban' (*ḥērem*) in these chapters would dispute Deuteronomy's nationalism. Without wanting to minimize the shocking nature of these chapters, in particular, and the more general nationalistic stamp, it is important to read Deuteronomy within the wider Bible storyline. Within that story-line God's choice of Israel is integral to his redemptive purposes for the *whole of creation*. God's ultimate purpose is for the good of creation and of the nations within it. It is perhaps because of this that even judgment could be seen as a grounds of rejoicing for the nations.[29]

Related to this, hostility to Israel, the vehicle of God's creation purposes, is not simply an illustration of one nation's antipathy to another in the ancient world. It is a demonstration of opposition to God's purposes in creation. Yahweh's declaration that he will bless those who bless Abraham and curse those who curse him (Gen. 12:3), and his ongoing commitment to Israel within this rubric fits within this framework. It is not about myopic, parti-san support for a morally dubious clan or nation, but about the carrying through of a redemptive plan to renew the cosmos and to bless humanity as a whole.[30] A striking illustration of this point is to be found in the plague narratives in Exodus. Yahweh's cre-ation purposes are being fulfilled in Israel (e.g. Exod. 1:7; cf. Gen. 1:21, 28; 9:1). Pharaoh opposes Israel, and in so doing opposes Yahweh's creation purposes. Picking up creation language of Israel's being numerous (Exod. 1:9; cf. 1:7), three times over

---

29. See chapter 2, n. 69.

30. Neither the patriarchs, Jacob in particular, nor Israel as a nation, could claim the moral high ground.

Pharaoh attempts to thwart the multiplication. First he imposes
stiffer burdens, and then instructs the midwives to kill Hebrew
boys; finally, he instructs his people to hurl every Hebrew boy
into the Nile. As Pharaoh resists Yahweh's purposes, Yahweh in
turn gives to Pharaoh the de-creation for which he has fought.
There are ecological disasters with the Creator unleashing creation's power. In some, creation boundaries are crossed (e.g. the
frogs leaving their prescribed habitat, or darkness taking over from
light). The final creation day, the sixth day, saw the creation of
animals, climaxing in humanity; the final plague is the destruction
of Egypt's firstborn, both animal and human.

A third implication arising from the connection between
Deuteronomy and the early chapters of Genesis is that commands
framing God's pre-existing relationship with his people are not an
innovation at Horeb, still less an anomaly. Keeping the commands
in Genesis was not a means of earning entry into the garden or a
means of establishing a relationship with Yahweh. Rather, it was
the way of maintaining the relationship and enjoying the blessings
of life. The same is true of the commands at Horeb and Moab.
They were not a means of earning entry into the land or establishing a relationship with God. Rather, they were the means of
already-redeemed Israel appropriating and enjoying the blessings
held out to them. Death was a possibility, but 'life' was God's good
intention for his people; hence Moses' call to 'Choose life!' (Deut.
30:19; cf. v. 15; Gen. 2:17). That same dynamic is to be found in
the New Testament. With Deuteronomic overtones, Jesus declares
that those who love him will obey his commands (John 14:15; cf.
Deut. 7:9; 11:1) and that those who obey his commands will remain
in his love (John 15:9). This is not the way of becoming linked to
Jesus, the true vine, or of earning his love, but the way of remaining
in that love. And Jesus precludes erroneous understandings that
see this dynamic as transactional, demeaning or coldly conditional
by declaring that this is nothing other than how he responds to
his Father, 'Now remain in my love. . . . just as I have obeyed my
Father's commands and remain in his love' (John 15:9b).

A final implication is that Deuteronomy, as the counterpart and
end of something started in Genesis, permanently leaves every
subsequent generation *outside the land*, with a sense of anticipation,

expectation and demand. As the Pentateuch ends, Israel are ready
to enter the land, to inherit what they have been promised but do
not yet possess. They no longer have their charismatic prophetic
leader, Moses, but they do have *tôrâ* in his stead.

Determining the beginning and end of a work is critical for any
reading strategy. Scholars have often located Deuteronomy within
a different corpus than a Pentateuch. Some scholars have seen
Deuteronomy not as the end of the Pentateuch but as part of a
'Hexateuch' climaxing with Joshua.[31] Certainly, similar language
and thought forms in Joshua and Deuteronomy bind both books
together.[32] There is a sense of narrative closure on a grand canvas
with the possession of the land, promised since Genesis 12 but
taken only in Joshua. That closure is matched by the destiny of
Joseph's bones, which ties Genesis to Joshua. Joseph urged his
sons to take his bones with them when they left Egypt (Gen. 50:25);
the bones make a brief appearance in Exodus 13:19 as the Israelites
leave; they finally come to rest at the end of Joshua (24:32).

A different viewpoint, articulated most eloquently by Martin
Noth, is that Deuteronomy takes its place not in a Pentateuch
or Hexateuch, but as the start of a work that extends to the
end of Kings.[33] This importantly recognizes the links between
Deuteronomy and the subsequent history books that tell the story
of conquest to exile (Joshua, Judges, Samuel, Kings). Without
further development, though, the 'Deuteronomistic History'
leaves behind a 'Tetrateuch', from Genesis to Numbers, 'a torso-
like composition which has never been fully justified'.[34]

----

31. Alexander Geddes, a Scottish Roman Catholic priest, first proposed this
    in 1792 (T. Desmond Alexander, *From Paradise to the Promised Land*, 2nd ed.
    [Carlisle: Paternoster, 2002], p. 10). Perhaps Gerhard von Rad is the name
    most naturally associated with this view. See e.g. Gerhard von Rad, *The
    Problem of the Hexateuch and Other Essays*, tr. E. W. Trueman Dicken (New
    York: McGraw-Hill, 1966).
32. See esp. Gordon J. Wenham, 'The Deuteronomic Theology of the Book
    of Joshua', *JBL* 90 (1971), pp. 140–148.
33. Noth, *Deuteronomistic History*.
34. Childs, *Introduction*, p. 232.

A more satisfying account of Deuteronomy's connections both backward and forward is to think of a Primary History from Genesis to Kings.[35] Certainly, there is a unified unbroken narrative that moves from creation to exile.

But within this there is a clear demarcation of a Pentateuch, marked by the connections we have seen between Genesis and Deuteronomy. The final shape of the Hebrew canon is 'unambiguous in maintaining the literary integrity of the Pentateuch'.[36] This Pentateuch permanently enshrines God's people in the Old Testament outside the land, on the edge of the land, looking in, confronted by the choice of life and death, with the call to choose life and to embody *tôrâ*. The Pentateuch permanently enshrines *tôrâ* as the definitive revelation. With Deuteronomy there is a line drawn underneath, an end to revelation (cf. Deut. 4:2; 12:32). For all the internal variety and updating of laws within the *tôrâ*, *tôrâ* now is complete.

'Israel's existence is characterized by an election, but this only can anticipate in faith the possession of her heritage.'[37] Along with this anticipation is an expectation that Deuteronomy's future will become a reality, and a demand that they should act in such a way that this reality is brought closer.

Deuteronomy and the Old Testament story

With much of Deuteronomy's story of the future there is a blend of what Israel *should* do and what *will* happen. How the story unfolds will relate to both of these: Did Israel do what they were supposed

---

35. The methodological issues here are not straightforward. For a recent discussion of these issues and criteria for identifying literary works, see Thomas B. Dozeman, Konrad Schmid and Thomas Römer (eds.), *Pentateuch, Hexateuch, or Enneateuch? Identifying Literary Works in Genesis Through Kings*, Ancient Israel and Its Literature 8 (Atlanta, Ga.: Society of Biblical Literature, 2011).

36. Childs, *Introduction*, p. 233.

37. Ibid., p. 224.

to do, and did what Deuteronomy said would happen, happen? In examining the relationships there is potential for paralysis over terminology (intertextuality, influence, allusion, quotation) and over the direction of borrowing.[38] The relationship between Old Testament texts is much more complex and contested than that between Old and New Testament texts, partly because secure dating of Old Testament material is so hard to come by and partly because there was a dynamic of mutual interpretation and updating. For our purposes it is the narratival priority that is significant, not the temporal. We are concerned to see how the portrayal of Israel's history as found in Deuteronomy relates to what follows.

Given both the constraints (of past events and prior text) and the freedoms (of new situations), we would expect to see points of connection and points of departure. There is no doubt that the account of Israel's history from Joshua to Kings bears a significant debt to Deuteronomy. Scholars discuss whether material is Deuteronomic (connected to the core of Deuteronomy) or Deuteronomistic (connected to the subsequent reworking of Deuteronomy and associated with the exile). A fair amount of our attention will be taken with these works, but we shall also at points move beyond the so-called Deuteronomistic History to other parts of the Old Testament in our examination.

Entry to the land

The book of Joshua picks up the story that Deuteronomy left off. The events happen 'after the death of Moses' (1:1); Joshua, Moses' successor, addresses the people with a speech that echoes his own commissioning in Deuteronomy (Josh. 1:1–9; Deut. 31:6–8, 23; cf. 11:24–25) and is filled with motifs characteristic of Deuteronomy (such as those of 'all' Israel, 'all the land').[39] Joshua is a figure like Moses in a number of ways, such as his exaltation (4:14), his intercession for the people (7:6–9; cf. Deut. 9:25) and his identity

---

38. For a helpful recent discussion on all this, see Michael A. Lyons, *From Law to Prophecy: Ezekiel's Use of the Holiness Code*, LHBOTS 507 (New York: T. & T. Clark, 2009), pp. 47–75.

39. See esp. Gordon J. Wenham, 'Deuteronomic Theology', pp. 140–141.

as the 'servant of Yahweh' (Deut. 34:5; Josh. 1:1; etc.; cf. Josh. 24:29). But he remains subordinate to Moses. He is not a revelation receiver or *tôrâ*-giver, but a *tôrâ*-keeper, calling on others to submit to the book of *tôrâ* (1:8) and be obedient to the commands of Moses himself (e.g. 1:7; 8:31; 11:12, 15; 14:2, 5; 20:2).

Given the narrative continuity, it is not surprising that the conquest and the covenant ceremony are prominent. Chapters 1–12 spell out the crossing of the Jordan (1:1 – 5:12) and the taking of the land Yahweh has given (cf. 11:16, 19, 23). Alongside foundational issues of community identity and belonging (note the contrast between the included outsider, Rahab, and the excluded insider, Achan) the narrative raises the question of whether Israel did as instructed and devoted to *ḥērem* the inhabitants (cf. Deut. 7:1–4). Nonetheless, the taking of the whole land is clearly emphasized, for conquest gives way to dividing up the land (chs. 13–21). Everything has happened as Yahweh had promised (21:43–45). Amid the accounts of conquest Joshua carries out the covenant ceremony mandated by Moses in the plains of Moab (Josh. 8:30–35; cf. Deut. 27:1–8). The carrying out of this ceremony 'just as Moses, the servant of Yahweh, had commanded at the first' (8:33b) shows continuity with what they should have done.

Alongside the continuity, though, there are some significant elements of discontinuity. There was a certain discontinuity between what was commanded in Deuteronomy and what was carried out. There had been no instruction to send out the spies (Josh. 2), though to do so may not necessarily have been disobedient. Achan's plundering and hiding of what should have been given to Yahweh as *ḥērem* and the covenant with the Gibeonites were clearly wrong (cf. 9:14). Alongside the largely triumphant account of chapters 1–12 is a clear sense in chapters 13–19 that there is more to be done. Yahweh declares to Joshua, 'You are old and advanced in years, and very much of the land still remains to be possessed' (13:1; cf. 23:1–2). Further, the sense of unity that characterizes the opening chapters gives way to a certain resentment (17:14–18) and division (22:10–34). The opening chapter of Judges gives an even more fragmented picture, with growing problems as the chapter progresses. Deuteronomy had acknowledged there would not be immediate total conquest (7:22–23), but the grounds there do not overlap with those in Judges.[40]

Alongside the somewhat idealized account of Joshua, which highlights Yahweh's faithfulness and continuity in conquest and covenant ceremony, there is an awareness of a more negative reality when Israel is under the spotlight.

Life in the land

The story Deuteronomy tells of life in the land is condensed. It forms the backdrop for warnings or anticipations of disaster, but there *is* a positive aspect to it, best characterized as prosperity. In the subsequent history this picture is not contradicted, but the retelling expands the picture in ways barely hinted at or unmentioned.

The anticipation of a land Yahweh had 'prepared' for the incoming people is indeed a reality (Josh. 24:13; cf. Deut. 6:10–11; 8:7–10). Somewhat surprisingly, in view of Israel's 'heart' through history up to that point (cf. Deut. 29:4), there was even a time of due worship and service of Yahweh (Josh. 24:31; Judg. 2:7).[41] These high points of Israel's obedience function to highlight the imminent departure from such reverence, though elsewhere individuals did seem to have Yahweh's word on their hearts in obedience as Deuteronomy 6 enjoined (e.g. 2 Kgs 23:25; Pss 40:8; 119:11).

In the years that followed, there were periods of rest. With the era of the judges Yahweh granted rest while the judges were alive, but such rest did not endure. Quickly the cyclical pattern of

---

40. Judges gives five reasons for the delay (which may well overlap): (1) superior weapons of the Canaanites (1:19); (2) God's judgment for disobedience in making treaties (2:1–3); (3) violation of the covenant made with their forefathers (2:20–21); (4) God's testing of Israel's faithfulness (2:22–23; 3:4); (5) opportunity for skills in warfare (3:1–2).

41. The centre of human will and thinking in Deuteronomy is *lēbāb* or, much less frequently, *lēb*. It is usually rendered as 'heart' but sometimes as 'mind' or left untranslated in what are regarded as idioms (e.g. 8:17, 'say in your heart' = 'say to yourself' in NRSV, NIV).

idolatrous rebellion, swift retribution from Yahweh, some kind of request from Israel, a rescuer from Yahweh and renewed rest would resume (cf. Judg. 2:11–19), although departures from the pattern show something of a downward spiral rather than a recurring cycle. Later, in David's day, Yahweh finally granted the kind of rest from enemies that echoed Deuteronomy (2 Sam. 7:1; Deut. 12:10). But even this rest was not a settled reality, for conflict within David's family soon arose within Israel.

There was also a certain institutional continuity in subsequent history that Deuteronomy anticipated. Moses had spoken of Yahweh's raising up prophets like himself (Deut. 18:15–22); Yahweh did indeed raise up prophets, but none was quite like Moses (Deut. 34:10). Deuteronomy, uniquely of the Pentateuchal law codes, makes provision for a king, and the subsequent historical books never have monarchy far from the centre of the stage. Judges sees the first exploration into monarchy with Abimelech (Judg. 9) and finishes with a refrain connecting lack of kingship with everyone doing what they thought right (Judg. 21:25); the books of Samuel and Kings in turn are dominated by the institution of the monarchy and the history of Israel in relation to that monarchy. But that continuity should not obscure a profound discontinuity. The kind of king Deuteronomy spoke of was essentially the 'model Israelite';[42] in many ways Solomon is the very kind of king Deuteronomy warned against, who was not to keep many horses (17:16b; cf. 1 Kgs 4:26); not to go to Egypt to get more horses (17:16b; cf. 1 Kgs 10:28); not to have many wives lest his heart strayed (17:17a; cf. 1 Kgs 11:1–8); not to amass silver and gold (17:17b; cf. 1 Kgs 10:14–29). And Solomon was not the exception.

Deuteronomy's depiction 'is directed exactly against the style of kingship adopted by every king after David'.[43]

There are a number of other ways in which there is a certain discontinuity or complicating developments. Continuing with the

---

42. Hans W. Wolff, *Anthropology of the Old Testament*, tr. M. Kohl (London: SCM, 1974), pp. 196–197.

43. McConville, 'Law and Monarchy', p. 76.

theme of kingship, in subsequent history the promise of long life for obedience is now directed towards the king (1 Kgs 3:14; cf. Deut. 5:33). Perhaps this is an indication that the destiny of the people is now bound in with the destiny of the king. The splitting of the kingdom under Rehoboam (1 Kgs 12) is an ugly breach of the Deuteronomic emphasis on 'all' Israel and Israelite unity. Language of blessing that dominates Deuteronomy is remarkably absent from the books that follow. People bless Yahweh or proclaim Yahweh's blessing on others, 'May Yahweh bless you . . .', but the reality of Yahweh's stated blessing of people is almost absent (Judg. 13:24; 2 Sam. 6:11). Finally, the apparent nexus of obedience leading to prosperity and disobedience to cursing in Deuteronomy acquires a more nuanced hue in subsequent history. Length of reign did not always relate to whether the king did what was evil or right in Yahweh's eyes. Manasseh, one of the longest reigning kings in Judah, was also one of the wickedest (2 Kgs 21). As we shall see later, Deuteronomy does not have a mechanistic framework of retribution, but its stark polarities speak of an order that simplifies lived history.

One place where continuity seems most evident at first glance is the reign of Josiah. The continuity is so great that most scholars see Deuteronomy (or at least part of it) as the impetus for Josiah's reforms. Certainly, there are many close connections, not least the fact that Josiah uniquely is said to have turned to Yahweh 'with all his heart, soul and might' (2 Kgs 23:25; cf. Deut. 6:5). Nonetheless, there are also some points of discontinuity. One of the key terms in the verses that describe the reforms (2 Kgs 23:4–20), 'high places' (*bāmôt*), does not occur in Deuteronomy; there is no mention of 'the book of the law' in these verses and some of the reforms carried out cannot be derived from Deuteronomy alone (e.g. the desecration in vv. 6b, 14).[44]

Exile

Deuteronomy blends warnings, depictions of Israel's chronic rebellion and declarations of certain judgment. While Moses'

---

44. See further, Robson, 'Literary Composition'.

constant refrain in Moab is to 'keep' or 'do' the commandments, statutes or judgments, the negative counterpart to this is not so much 'disobedience' as idolatry (e.g. 6:10–19; 28:14, 20; 29:24–26). This is rooted in the start of the Decalogue (5:6–10): Yahweh is the one who has redeemed them, so they should have no other deities but him. Deuteronomy is less concerned with 'rule-keeping' per se and more with loyal allegiance to Yahweh, expressed in observing his statutes and commandments. Yahweh's anger is not that of a fastidious deity trawling though an itemized checklist, but of a consuming fire, a *jealous* God who demands love and loyalty from the people he has redeemed in his love. The judgment that comes, the covenant curse, is the 'death' of exile, a reversal of patriarchal promises and redemption from Egypt; after the trauma of siege and expulsion, there lies an idolatrous life scattered among the nations.

Elsewhere in the Old Testament are a number of places where there is sustained reflection on the crisis of Judah's exile in the sixth century BC. Alongside the narrative from Joshua to Kings, which many scholars see as a history governed by (the core of) Deuteronomy and that ends in exile, are the prophetic books of Jeremiah and Ezekiel and the haunting Lamentations. Chapters 40–55 of Isaiah also engage with the rhetorical situation of the exile, as, probably, do a number of psalms (e.g. Pss 74, 79, 89). Finally, there are other parts of the Pentateuch (notably Lev. 26) that deal explicitly with expulsion.[45] Comparing such extensive, diverse material with Deuteronomy allows only the sketching of some contours.

First, there are some kinds of continuity. Alongside calls to obey, a certain pessimism is to be found. Joshua declares his own allegiance to Yahweh, but shockingly declares amid his exhorta-

---

45. Ackroyd is representative of many critical scholars who believe that a Priestly writer (P) working in the exile is responsible for much of Leviticus and Numbers and that earlier traditions were taken and 'subordinated to the uncertainty of the exilic age'; this is evident, for example, in the focus on purification and atonement. See Peter R. Ackroyd, *Exile and Restoration*, OTL (London: SCM, 1968), pp. 101–102.

tion, 'you cannot serve Yahweh' (Josh. 24:19). The downward spiral in Judges highlights Israel's incapacity to be faithful. The book of Jeremiah seems to show initial calls to repent subsequently contextualized within a book where repentance has not been forthcoming (Jer. 2:1 – 4:4).[46]

There is a continuity in the nature of expulsion. Lamentations 4 speaks of the brutal realities of being besieged, including parents eating their children (Lam. 4:10; cf. Deut. 28:53–55; also Ezek. 5:10). Ezekiel and Jeremiah speak of being 'scattered among the nations' (Jer. 9:16; 18:17; Ezek. 12:15–16; cf. Deut. 4:27; 28:64). In exile idols entice. Isaiah 40 – 55 lampoons Babylonian idols (e.g. 44:9–20; 46:1–2), presumably because there is a temptation to give up on Yahweh (cf. 40:27). Ezekiel 20:32 imputes to the exiles a conscious *desire* to worship gods of wood and stone (cf. Deut. 4:28; 28:36, 64).

There is also a continuity in the grounds of that expulsion. Idolatry features large in Israel's actions. The narrative from Joshua to Kings, while not giving much attention to exile,[47] still highlights idolatry as the catalyst. The benchmark for the assessment of kings in the northern kingdom of Israel is the paradigmatic sin of Jeroboam (1 Kgs 12:25–33). Persistence in this sin resulted in exile for the north at the hands of the Assyrians (2 Kgs 17:18–23). Judah foolishly followed that example (2 Kgs 17:19), culminating in the idolatrous actions of Manasseh that precipitated exile (2 Kgs 21:1–15). Ezekiel spotlights idolatry as he declares an end for Jerusalem. He speaks of 'abominations' and 'idols' (literally 'dung pellets' or 'droppings') and 'detestable things'; his vision in chapters 8–11 focuses on idolatry in the temple; his extended metaphors depict Israel as a loose woman consorting, even cavorting,

---

46. See J. Gordon McConville, *Judgment and Promise: An Interpretation of the Book of Jeremiah* (Leicester: Apollos, 1993), pp. 27–41. Another example is the two stories of the potter in Jer. 18 and 19. For a sustained analysis of the preaching of Jeremiah and Ezekiel from this perspective, see Thomas M. Raitt, *A Theology of Exile: Judgment / Deliverance in Jeremiah and Ezekiel* (Philadelphia: Fortress, 1977).

47. The main places are 1 Kgs 8:15–53; 2 Kgs 24 – 25.

with other nations and their gods (Ezek. 16; 23). These actions are
said to be rebelling against or not walking in accord with Yahweh's
statutes and judgments (e.g. Ezek. 5:6–7). With Israel's idolatry
comes Yahweh's anger and his just punishment. Isaiah 40 – 55
declares that Israel has now received sufficient punishment (Isa.
40:2), that Yahweh has not forgotten about Israel (Isa. 40:27–31),
and that Yahweh had given up Israel in his anger because they
would not walk in his ways (Isa. 42:24–25). By connecting the
destruction of Jerusalem with Israel's idolatry, Kings, Jeremiah
and Ezekiel look to vindicate Yahweh. For Ezekiel those escaping
the destruction of Jerusalem who join those already in Babylon
after the first deportation will illustrate the rightness of Yahweh's
actions (Ezek. 12:16). Yahweh's anger is a thread that runs through
the different texts (e.g. 2 Kgs 24:20; Isa. 42:25; Jer. 7:20; Lam. 1:12;
Ezek. 5:13). Sometimes the specific language of 'curse' occurs to
describe Yahweh's judgment for their rebellion, a curse under the
terms of the covenant/law (e.g. Jer. 11:3; Dan. 9:11).

Alongside these various continuities are some discontinuities. In
contrast to the anticipation of 'swift' destruction in Deuteronomy
once idolatry has taken root (e.g. 4:26), the history from Joshua
to Kings has a rather longer time frame. Further, while in Judges
there is a cycle of judgment for abandoning Yahweh, in Kings
there seems to be a cumulative effect.

Secondly, while Deuteronomy focuses chiefly on idolatry, other
texts highlight different dimensions of Israel's sinfulness that precipitated exile. Kings speaks of Manasseh's shedding of innocent
blood as another ground for judgment (2 Kgs 21:16; 24:4). For
Ezekiel moral sins precipitating exile included failure to help the
poor and needy in a way far worse even than in Sodom (16:47–50;
cf. 18:7–9). Jeremiah categorizes Judah's sin as 'falseness', where
lies and deceptions abound (9:2–9).[48]

Thirdly, the picture of reversal of either the patriarchal promises
or of redemption is not at all prominent. Ezekiel, for example,
has very little reference to history prior to the exodus. Abraham

---

48. J. Gordon McConville, *Exploring the Old Testament*, vol. 4: *Prophets*
(London: SPCK, 2002), p. 63.

is mentioned only in 33:24, on the lips of those spared exile who wrongly lay claim to the land!

Finally, there is what might be called a voice from the margins that gives a different perspective. Psalm 137 indicates a distressed piety in exile. Lamentations, while not disputing the rightness of Yahweh's judgment, resolutely focuses on Jerusalem's response and gives a perspective that laments the downfall.[49]

Restoration/return to the land

As we move from judgment to restoration, tracing the Old Testament story acquires a new complexity. The breadth and variety of material remains great. New complexity arises because alongside exilic voices that look *forward* to a future after the exile there are now voices that speak *after* the return, sometimes long after. Rooted in how that future turned out, in hopes realized and disappointed, these voices rose in new situations that proved a fertile ground for further theological reflection. Unsurprisingly, the other voices do not speak in identical fashion. Solomon's prayer at the dedication of the temple acknowledges the possibility of exile and the need of prayer and repentance in exile, but makes no mention of a return (1 Kgs 8:46–51). Distinctive perspectives may also be found in works spawned in the same era. Jeremiah, for example, never mentions the 'Spirit', while his contemporary Ezekiel owes much to the Spirit both in his ministry and in his message. There is also, of course, a methodological complexity about dating works. As before, we shall be working synchronically, following the rhetorical perspective of the works.

There are (at least) seven main points of continuity between Deuteronomy's story of restoration and that found elsewhere.

First, there is a *renewed covenant relationship* (cf. Deut. 30:1–10; especially the 'again'/'return' of vv. 8–9). The pattern of Israel's returning to Yahweh and Yahweh's turning away from his anger, love and healing of their disloyalty finds profound expression in Hosea 14:1–4 against the backdrop of the northern kingdom's

---

49. Cf. Lena-Sofia Tiemeyer, 'To Read – Or Not to Read – Ezekiel as Christian Scripture', *ExpTim* 121 (2010), pp. 481–488.

dalliance with Assyria. The command to comfort that rings out
at the start of Isaiah 40 juxtaposes 'my people' and 'your God'
(cf. Ezek. 36:28) before the comforting message is heard.[50] The
most formal articulation of this is found in Jeremiah's Book of
Consolation, where Yahweh declares that he will make a 'new covenant' with them, putting his *tôrâ* on their hearts (31:31–34); this
will be 'an everlasting covenant with them' (32:40).

Secondly, as part of this renewed covenant relationship there
will be a *sustained obedience* to *tôrâ* and this will be *brought about by
Yahweh* (cf. Deut. 30:6–8). Yahweh promises through Ezekiel a
heart of flesh rather than a heart of stone, a new spirit, and that
(by these gifts) he will '*make* [them] *follow* [his] statutes and be
careful to observe [his] ordinances' (Ezek. 36:26–27). In Jeremiah
the gift of the law on the heart (Jer. 31:31) is matched by the gift
of 'one heart and one way' '*so that*' they will 'fear' Yahweh 'for all
time' (Jer. 32:39). Isaiah 54:13 declares that 'all your children shall
be taught by Yahweh'.[51] Strikingly, Yahweh will do for Israel what
earlier he has commanded them to do. In Deuteronomy Moses
called on Israel to 'circumcise the foreskin of your heart' (Deut.
10:16); Yahweh will himself do this for them (Deut. 30:6). In
Ezekiel the call is to 'get for yourself a new heart and a new spirit'
(Ezek. 18:31); but Yahweh will himself give them a new heart and
a new spirit (Ezek. 36:26; cf. 11:19). In Jeremiah the heart change
they need to do (Jer. 4:4) is something Yahweh will effect (Jer.
31:31–33; 32:39–40).

Thirdly, there will be a *return to the land*. Although 1 Kings

---

50. Contrary to many English versions, v. 2 does not contain the message of
    comfort, but the grounds for being able to offer it. The message comes in
    v. 9, 'Behold your God!' See John Goldingay, *The Message of Isaiah 40–55:
    A Literary-Theological Commentary* (London: T. & T. Clark, 2005), p. 15.

51. This emphasis on renewed commitment to *tôrâ* carries through into
    Ezra-Nehemiah, where Ezra's preaching of *tôrâ* along with Nehemiah's
    wall-building serve together to mark out the firm boundaries of the
    community back in the land. Cf. Douglas J. Green, 'Ezra-Nehemiah', in
    Leland Ryken and Tremper Longman III (eds.), *The Complete Literary Guide
    to the Bible* (Grand Rapids: Zondervan, 1993), pp. 206–215.

8:46–51, like Deuteronomy 4, does not talk explicitly about return, elsewhere return to the land features strongly (cf. Deut. 30:1–10). The climax of Ezekiel's vision in the valley of dry bones is bringing the people back to the land and putting them on their own soil (Ezek. 37:12–14). Isaiah 40 portrays Yahweh's return to the land with his people. In verse 10 we see the strong arm of the warrior, coming with the plunder of battle. In verse 11 there is the compassionate arm of the shepherd, leading the nursing ewes and carrying the lambs close to him. The juxtaposition of the images and the parallels with 49:9–10 show Yahweh is bringing his people back with him. Jeremiah 29 echoes Deuteronomy 30's restoration of Israel's fortunes, gathering of the scattered and bringing the people back to the land, while adding the figure of seventy years (Jer. 29:10–14). When Nehemiah hears of the pitiable state of Jerusalem, he prays before Yahweh and recalls the Deuteronomic promise of Yahweh's gathering what had been scattered (Neh. 1:9; cf. Deut. 30:4). Throughout the opening chapters of Ezra-Nehemiah[52] the return to the land that Cyrus mandated is characterized in terms of a new exodus, giving great significance both to those returning and to the destination.

Fourthly, the restoration of Israel is in some sense '*life after death*'. In Deuteronomy this is apparent from the depiction of exile as death that we saw above (cf. 32:39). Most famous elsewhere is Ezekiel's vision when Yahweh's *rûaḥ* (spirit, wind) picks him up and deposits him in a valley of dry bones (Ezek. 37:1–14). The exiles conceive of their experience in terms of death: 'Our bones are dried up, and our hope is lost; we are cut off completely' (Ezek.

---

52. Originally these were one book. Internal evidence includes the otherwise under-specified 'twentieth year' (Neh. 1:1), the lack of introduction to Ezra (Neh. 8:2) and the fact that Neh. 8 – 12 is the climax not just of Neh. 1 – 7, but also of Ezra's ministry recorded in Ezra 7 – 10. See further Michael W. Duggan, *The Covenant Renewal in Ezra-Nehemiah (Neh. 7:72b–10:40): An Exegetical, Literary, and Theological Study*, SBLDS 164 (Atlanta, Ga.: Society of Biblical Literature, 2001), p. 36. For external evidence, see H. G. M. Williamson, *Ezra, Nehemiah*, WBC 16 (Waco: Word, 1985), pp. xxi–xxiii.

37:11). For Ezekiel return to the land and restoration is resurrec-tion. Donald Gowan characterizes the message of the prophets more generally as *The Death and Resurrection of Israel* because of the certain end to exile that they declared and the hope for Israel beyond that end ('death').[53]

Fifthly, as a counterpart of the restoration of Israel comes *Yahweh's judgment on the oppressing nations* (cf. Deut. 30:8; 32:35–43). In Ezekiel the oracles against the nations (25 – 32) function as a bridge between judgment on Israel, climaxing in the fall of Jerusalem (24), and oracles of salvation (33 – 48), but strikingly Babylon is missing. Instead, particular focus is given to the nations who capitalized on Judah's defeat. The conqueror of Judah and Jerusalem, Babylon, *is* the subject of oracles of devastating destruc-tion, though, in Isaiah 47 and Jeremiah 50.

Sixthly, in a number of places the people's *repentance (šûb) is seen to play a significant role in restoration* (cf. Deut. 4:29–30; 30:1–3, 9–10). In Solomon's prayer of dedication, repenting *(šûb)* 'with all their heart and soul' is a prerequisite for Yahweh to hear their prayers (1 Kgs 8:46–51). The same picture is found in Leviticus 26:40–46. Ultimately, the significant penitential prayers of Daniel, Ezra and Nehemiah and the reappropriating of Solomon's prayer from 1 Kings 8 in Chronicles indicate the ongoing importance of repent-ance even as the physical reality of exile from the land has receded (Dan. 9; Ezra 9; Neh. 9; 2 Chr. 7:14–15).

Finally, in Deuteronomy and in some other places there is some sense of *restoration's surpassing what had been there before the exile*. In Deuteronomy it is the circumcision of the heart, something unprecedented, and the greater prosperity and mul-tiplication (30:5–6).[54] Similarly, in Jeremiah future obedience is assured because of Yahweh's action on the heart. In Ezekiel it is the guaranteeing of obedience through the new heart and the new spirit and the outpouring of the Spirit (Ezek. 36:26–27; 39:21–29).

---

53. Donald E. Gowan, *Theology of the Prophetic Books: The Death and Resurrection of Israel* (Louisville: Westminster John Knox, 1998).

54. Thus 'restore your fortunes' in Deut. 30:3 is more than simply 'restore to an earlier state of well-being' (as Nelson, *Deuteronomy*, p. 345, claims).

In Isaiah 40 – 55 there will be multiplication akin to the promises to Abraham, but surpassing what had preceded (Isa. 51:2; cf. 54:1–3).

Other instances of the future hope surpassing what has preceded, such as a magnificently adorned and secure Jerusalem (Isa. 54:11–17), move away from the Deuteronomic hope and illustrate the fact that alongside the lines of continuity there are significant discontinuities. These occur partly because of prophetic or hymnic characterization and partly because of the realities of life after the return from exile.

The first discontinuity is the place of *repentance*. Some see in Deuteronomy the temporal priority of repentance, of Israel's return to Yahweh, before restoration comes (Deut. 4:29–30; 30:1–10).[55] Restoration in the prophets, on the other hand, is often said to be grounded not in anything Israel does but in divine initiative.[56] The discontinuity is less sharply defined than this. Deuteronomy 32 makes no mention of repentance and Deuteronomy 30 preserves a delicate dialectic between Israel's and Yahweh's actions. Further, while it is true that the prophets do not ground oracles of salvation in the explicit action of the people, and Ezekiel, for example, declares that salvation will not be for Israel's sake but for Yahweh's (Ezek. 36:22, 32), there may still be a place for repentance. In Ezekiel the calls to repent cannot easily be relegated. Their ongoing presence alongside oracles of salvation indicates that the response itself will be divinely enabled.[57] While rejecting a sharp disjunction, though, it must be said that repentance plays a less significant role in prophetic salvation oracles than it does in Deuteronomy.

A second discontinuity is the place of a *renewed Davidic monarchy*. Deuteronomy as a whole downplays the role of the monarchy: Yahweh is the king who gives laws (Deut. 33:5; cf. the treaty

---

55. E.g. Nelson, *Deuteronomy*, p. 347: 'Both Yahweh and Israel "turn", but Israel makes the first move.'

56. So e.g. Raitt, *Theology of Exile*; Paul M. Joyce, *Divine Initiative and Human Response in Ezekiel*, JSOTSup 51 (Sheffield: JSOT Press, 1989).

57. See Robson, *Word and Spirit*.

structure of much of the book); the king is the *tôrâ*-keeping model
Israelite (Deut. 17.14-20). Some works addressing the exilic situation have a distinct hope for a renewed Davidic monarchy (cf.
2 Sam. 7:12–16). Ezekiel envisages a new David (Ezek. 34:23–24;
37:24–25), although there seems a certain diminishing of his significance by designating him a 'prince' (*nāśî'*) and circumscribing his
role in the temple vision.[58] Jeremiah anticipates a righteous branch
raised up for David and reaffirms that covenant as unbreakable
(Jer. 23:5; 33:15–22). The book of Kings ends with the release
of the captive Judahite king, Jehoiachin, but the picture remains
somewhat forlorn (2 Kgs 25:27–30). Isaiah 55:3 picks up on the
promise to David, though reapplies it to the people more generally. Although not explicitly said to be Davidic, the one speaking
in Isaiah 61:1–3 has the Spirit on him, like the servant (42:1),
and is anointed, like a king. Cyrus, though, was the last anointed
figure (Isa. 45:1) and this figure is a preacher. There seems to be
a deliberate coalescing of various offices in a 'messianic' figure.[59]
Soon after the return Haggai speaks favourably of Yahweh's signet
ring (Hag. 2:20–23). Although renewed hopes for the monarchy
fade from view in Ezra-Nehemiah, Chronicles reaffirms Nathan's
promise to David of a king on the throne 'for ever' (1 Chr.
17:12), echoes it in 2 Chronicles 13:5 and 21:7, and gives David's
genealogy right down to his own day (1 Chr. 3), despite the exile
and lack of a king after the return.[60] Finally, after the apparent failure of the covenant with David and the spurning of the

---

58. Cf. Daniel I. Block, 'Bringing Back David: Ezekiel's Messianic Hope',
   in P. E. Satterthwaite, R. S. Hess and G. J. Wenham (eds.), *The Lord's
   Anointed: Interpretation of Old Testament Messianic Texts* (Grand Rapids: Baker,
   1995), pp. 175–176; Paul M. Joyce, 'King and Messiah in Ezekiel', in John
   Day (ed.), *King and Messiah in Israel and the Ancient Near East: Proceedings of the
   Oxford Old Testament Seminar*, JSOTSup 270 (Sheffield: Sheffield Academic
   Press, 1998), pp. 331–332.

59. H. G. M. Williamson, *Variations on a Theme: King, Messiah and Servant in the
   Book of Isaiah* (Carlisle: Paternoster, 1998), pp. 187–188.

60. Leslie C. Allen, *1, 2 Chronicles*, Mastering the Old Testament 10 (Dallas:
   Word, 1987), pp. 18–19.

Davidic king in Psalm 89, there is still a Davidic royal hope (e.g. Ps. 132).

A third point of discontinuity is the prominence of *Yahweh's reign*. In Deuteronomy Yahweh's kingship is seen principally in its structure and language, which closely resemble ancient Near Eastern vassal treaties. Yahweh has the role of suzerain, or overlord, while Israel is like a vassal state. Yahweh's kingship is also evident as a lawgiver upholding justice and righteousness and, on one occasion, he is specifically referred to as a king (Deut. 33:5).[61] After the exile and the end of the monarchy in Book 3 of the psalter, many of the psalms in Book 4 celebrate Yahweh's kingship, declaring *yhwh mālak* (best translated 'Yahweh has become king'). It is not that Yahweh was not king before, but that a new action, a new victory, speaks of the start of a new reign. In similar fashion Isaiah 40 – 55 celebrates the kingship of Yahweh because of his redeeming of his people and the salvation he has brought (Isa. 52:7–10; cf. Mark 1:14–15).

Fourthly, the *temple* has great significance. In Deuteronomy there is no explicit reference to the temple and only one to the 'tent of meeting' (Deut. 31:14). Yahweh dwells in heaven (26:15), while his name is to be found in the place he will choose to make it dwell (e.g. 12:5). Although this does not indicate Yahweh's absence,[62] yet there is a distinctive articulation of divine presence. While in Isaiah 40 – 55 the temple is not especially prominent within a restored Zion (only 44:28), in Ezekiel the entire vision of chapters 40–48 consists of a new temple. The journey of Yahweh's glory connects judgment and restoration. In the first half of Ezekiel Yahweh's glory leaves the temple (chs. 8–11) and encounters Ezekiel in exile (1:28; 3:12, 23). In chapter 43:1–7 Ezekiel has a vision of the glory returning to the rebuilt temple. For the early post-exilic prophets Haggai and Zechariah, rebuilding the temple was instrumental in the process of restoration (cf. also Ezra 1 – 6). Strikingly, no

---

61. For God as the referent, see Tigay, *Deuteronomy*, p. 322; cf. McConville, *Deuteronomy*, p. 466.

62. See Ian Wilson, *Out of the Midst of the Fire: Divine Presence in Deuteronomy*, SBLDS 151 (Atlanta, Ga.: Scholars Press, 1995).

post-exilic work speaks of Yahweh's return to the temple, although Malachi looks forward to that day (Mal. 3:1).[63]

Fifthly, there is a new *sense of hope for the nations*. We noticed above how the LXX (and possibly the Hebrew MT) of Deuteronomy 32:43 highlights the nations' rejoicing. Elsewhere in Deuteronomy the nations are enemies, observers and, sometimes, beneficiaries.[64] As enemies they are either the inhabitants of Canaan to be destroyed or the nations that come against rebellious Israel and will be judged. As observers they see Israel's obedience to *tôrâ* (ideally) and Yahweh's actions of judgment on his people, and may draw wrong (9:28; 32:27) or right (4:6–8; 29:24–28) conclusions. As beneficiaries Yahweh loves the resident aliens (10:18), so the people should also (10:19; cf. 1:16; 24:20); they may participate in the religious life (e.g. Deut. 5:14; 16:11); there is an acknowledgment of 'brotherhood' towards the Edomites (2:3–8) and the possibility of incorporation into the assembly (23:7–8). However, there are hard barriers to Moabites and Ammonites (23:3–6) and the hopes held out more generally are not strong.

Elsewhere there is a certain sense of 'universalism', not just that Yahweh is God of the whole world, but that the nations willingly acknowledge him as God.[65] Isaiah is the prophetic book most commonly associated with this (e.g. Isa. 2:2–4; 19:19–25; 56:3, 6–7; 60 – 62), with the Servant instrumental in this task (42:1–9; 49:1–6). In Zechariah the nations will join with God's people (Zech. 2:11; cf. 8:20–23; 14:16–19); the same picture is found in Psalm 87. This is not to deny an ongoing particularism. Zion remains very much central in the future hope for the nations. Nor is it to deny the reality within Israel's history of the outsider's being incorporated,

---

63. Jesus talks of the one who 'lives' in the temple (Matt. 23:21), but this is hardly expansive, and v. 38 subverts it immediately. See N. T. Wright, *Christian Origins and the Question of God*, vol. 2: *Jesus and the Victory of God* (London: SPCK, 1996), p. 571, n. 120, p. 623, n. 40.

64. See Millar, *Now Choose Life*, pp. 147–160.

65. Precisely how to define 'universalism' and its relation to 'particularism' is not straightforward. Cf. Joel S. Kaminsky, 'Election Theology and the Problem of Universalism', *HBT* 33.1 (2011), pp. 34–44.

with Rahab being the obvious example. But it is to say that there is an expanded hope for the nations as part of restoration.

Sixthly, a number of prophets, in particular, highlight the significant role in restoration to be played by the *Spirit, rûaḥ*. In Deuteronomy Joshua has the '*rûaḥ* of wisdom' because Moses placed his hands on him (Deut. 34:9). Elsewhere the Spirit's role is much more expansive. For Ezekiel *rûaḥ* is intimately linked by marvellous interplay between a renewed moral will and the dead becoming alive, figurative of the restoration of the exiles (36:26–27; 37:1–14; cf. 39:29).[66] In Joel 2:28 the outpouring of Yahweh's Spirit is associated with a democratized knowledge of Yahweh, with the day of Yahweh being imminent. In Isaiah 44:3 the outpouring of *rûaḥ* is associated with Yahweh's blessing.

Seventhly, as part of the restoration of Israel there is a *creational and cosmic dimension*. Deuteronomy envisages something of this, for a restoration of blessing entails right relations with the land (Deut. 30:9). Ezekiel's characterization of a renewed land is very much in line with this (Ezek. 36:29–30, 35). Sometimes, though, the creational dimension surpasses what has been found before: there is extravagant language of a new harmony (e.g. Isa. 65:17–25); the inanimate creation joins in the celebratory throng (Isa. 55:12–13), particularly as 'Yahweh has become king' (Pss 96:10–13; cf. 98). It may well be that language speaking of cosmic effects sometimes refers in reality to real-world geopolitical events (e.g. Joel 2:30–31), but nonetheless there is a picture of cosmic implications of Israel's restoration.

The final point of discontinuity to highlight is perhaps in some sense the starkest. It is that *life after the actual return from exile was not as had been hoped for*. In the immediate aftermath of the exile the building of the temple started, only to stop quickly. It needed the preaching of Haggai and Zechariah to set the building process in motion again. The book of Ezra-Nehemiah articulates clearly the 'now' of a genuine work of Yahweh in salvation history. As a book it takes disparate historical events over a long time frame (e.g. Ezra 7:1 covers a gap of more than sixty years) and connects

---

66. Cf. Robson, *Word and Spirit*, chs. 5–6.

them into a continuous narrative of Yahweh's working: many have
returned from exile, rebuilt the temple and celebrated the Passover
in Judah again (Ezra 3; 6:13–22); under Nehemiah the walls of
Jerusalem have been rebuilt in the face of opposition (Neh. 3 – 4,
6); Jerusalem has been reinhabited (Neh. 11) and the walls have
been dedicated with great joy (Neh. 12:27–43); they have become
a new community in continuity with the old (cf. Ezra 2 and Neh.
7);[67] they have gathered around God's Word (Neh. 8); they have
'new life' (to some extent) (Ezra 9:9).

But alongside this is the 'not yet'; things are not ideal – they
are not as they should be. There is disappointment in the temple,
with elders who saw the original weeping (Ezra 3:12), and with the
prophets Haggai and Zechariah trying to temper this (Hag. 2:3;
Zech. 4:10). Although there is a certain quietist deference to the
Persian rulers, with a recognition that God's hand is behind some
of their actions (e.g. Ezra 1:1), and no hint of longing for Davidic
monarchy, yet there is an undercurrent of dissatisfaction.[68] Ezra
6:22 refers to the Persian king Darius as 'king of Assyria', a creative
anachronism to connect Persian rule with the days of Assyrian
oppression. More conspicuous still is the sentiment enshrined
in prayer that they are 'slaves' under foreign oppression (Ezra
9:7–9; Neh. 9:32, 36–37). Another dimension of dissonance is the
shadow of sin that rests across the community. There is the issue
of intermarriage in Ezra 9 – 10 (cf. Ezra 9:1–2 and Deut. 7:1–4),
and Nehemiah ends on an anticlimax as the joyful celebrations
fade into a narrative of sustained failure (Neh. 13).

Against such a backdrop there were broadly three (potentially
overlapping) responses: Chronicles illustrates the response of
'keep living'; it does not try to answer the questions of the exile

---

67. 'Membership of the community depended principally on establishing
    one's physical descent from pre-exilic Israel (Ezra 2:2–63 = Neh. 7:6–65;
    13:3)' (Brian E. Kelly, 'Ezra-Nehemiah', in T. Desmond Alexander and
    Brian S. Rosner [eds.], *New Dictionary of Biblical Theology* [Leicester: Inter-
    Varsity Press, 2000], p. 197).
68. See further Daniel L. Smith-Christopher, *A Biblical Theology of Exile*
    (Minneapolis: Fortress, 2002), p. 37.

and why it happened, but tries to make sense of the present by connecting present-day institutions, temple worship in particular, to the life of an otherwise distant past.[69] The future perspective, while not absent, is muted. A second response, 'keep praying', is found in some of the psalms of lament,[70] and, especially, in the penitential prayers of Ezra 9, Nehemiah 9 and Daniel 9. They rehearse the sins of the past, the faithfulness of Yahweh in the past, and the plight and sins of the present, echoing the language of Deuteronomy (e.g. Ezra 9:12; cf. 9:1; Neh. 9:25; Dan. 9:4). The emphasis on Yahweh's righteousness in keeping his promises and in punishing provides one major ground for hope set against Israel's own lack of righteousness (Ezra 9:15; Neh. 9:8, 33; Dan. 9:7, 16; cf. Deut. 32:4). The other major ground is Yahweh's 'love' (ḥesed, Ezra 9:9; Neh. 9:17, 32; Dan. 9:4) or mercy (raḥĕmîm, Neh. 9:19, 27–28, 31; Dan. 9:9, 18). A third response is to 'keep hoping', looking for Yahweh's dramatic intervention and expressing it in cosmic language. In Isaiah 24 – 27, for example, cosmic imagery such as slaying Leviathan (27:1) is found with the destruction of death (25:8) and a magnificent 'banquet' (25:6).

Deuteronomy and the New Testament story

The story Deuteronomy tells and is a part of unsurprisingly continues in the intertestamental literature and on into the New Testament. As N. T. Wright puts it, 'the great story of the Hebrew Scriptures was . . . inevitably read in the second-temple period as a story in search of a conclusion'.[71] This is hardly surprising:

---

69. Sara Japhet, *The Ideology of the Book of Chronicles and Its Place in Biblical Thought*, BEATAJ 9 (Frankfurt am Main: Peter Lang, 1989), pp. 403–404.

70. Cf. Donald E. Gowan, 'The Exile in Jewish Apocalyptic', in Arthur L. Merrill and Thomas W. Overholt (eds.), *Scripture in History and Theology: Essays in Honor of J. Coert Rylaarsdam*, PTMS 17 (Pittsburgh, Pa.: Pickwick, 1977), pp. 219–220.

71. N. T. Wright, *Christian Origins and the Question of God*, vol. 1: *The New Testament and the People of God* (London: SPCK, 1992), p. 217.

When we survey the entire Old Testament, we find ourselves involved in a great history of movement from promise toward fulfilment. It flows like a large brook – here rushing swiftly, there apparently coming to rest in a quiet backwater, and yet moving forward as a whole toward a distant goal which lies beyond itself.[72]

As we turn to Deuteronomy and the New Testament story, the aim is to explore the main contours of Deuteronomy's place in that New Testament story. There are a number of preliminary comments that should be made.

First, Deuteronomy was a key work within second-temple Judaism.[73] As such, it was not so much an abstract authority to be quoted from as a book to be recited, to be heard, to be prayed, to be discussed, to be taught, to be learnt, to be lived. There is a sense in which it provided part of the air that a first-century Jew would have breathed. Within that, certain texts had particular prominence: the Shema (Deut. 6:4–5) and its surrounding context, including the Decalogue (5:1 – 6:9); 10:12 – 11:21; and the Song of Moses (Deut. 32:1–43).[74]

Secondly, how to conceive of Deuteronomy's place within the New Testament story depends in part on discerning Deuteronomy's influence. This may be nuanced in three ways.

1. It is possible to discern the New Testament's connections with Deuteronomy through a descending hierarchy from quotation marked by explicit acknowledgment to unmarked quotation to paraphrase to allusion/echo to more generic conceptual indebtedness.[75]

---

72. Walther Zimmerli, 'Promise and Fulfillment', in Claus Westermann (ed.), James Luther Mays (tr.), *Essays on Old Testament Hermeneutics* (Richmond: John Knox Press, 1963), p. 111.

73. Cf. Timothy H. Lim, 'Deuteronomy in the Judaism of the Second Temple Period', in Steve Moyise and Maarten J. J. Menken (eds.), *Deuteronomy in the New Testament: The New Testament and the Scriptures of Israel*, LNTS 358 (London: T. & T. Clark International, 2007), pp. 6–26; Lincicum, *Paul.*

74. Lincicum, *Paul*, p. 57.

75. Cf. ibid., pp. 13–14. This in turn is closely related to Stanley E. Porter,

2. As the connection moves 'down' the hierarchy, the significance of the connection may be less obvious. Richard Hays famously gives seven criteria for identifying an intertextual allusion:[76] (a) Availability – was the proposed source of the echo available to the author and/or original readers? (b) Volume – how 'loud' is it? This may be in terms of repetition of vocabulary or syntax or rhetorical stress in the quoting work; it may be, how loud is the original in other scriptures? (c) Recurrence – how much does this word or theme recur elsewhere in the corpus of the particular author? (d) Thematic coherence – how well does this fit with the logic, flow and other points of the quoting writer? (e) Historical plausibility – would it be anachronistic to give the meaning that might be suggested? (f) History of interpretation – have other readers, critical or pre-critical, noticed this before or drawn similar conclusions? (g) Satisfaction – does it make sense? Does it help illuminate the passage and give a new coherence to the particular understanding? These criteria are helpful for identification, but discerning the *purpose* of the allusion or echo may not be straightforward.

3. The third way of nuancing our thinking about Deuteronomy's influence is to recognize that Deuteronomy may be influential in three 'interlocking' ways: as 'ethical authority', governing the life of the church; as theological authority, governing the beliefs of the church; and as providing the lens of history, shaping the story the Bible writers tell.[77]

Thirdly, just as Deuteronomy was operating with its own constraints and freedom when retelling the past or framing the present, so too do New Testament texts working with Deuteronomy. The New Testament is written from the conviction that in the life, death and resurrection of Jesus God's promises to Israel, *including those in*

'Allusions and Echoes', in Stanley E. Porter and Christopher D. Stanley (eds.), *As It Is Written: Studying Paul's Use of Scripture*, SBLSS 50 (Atlanta, Ga.: Society of Biblical Literature, 2008), p. 29.

76. Richard B. Hays, *Echoes of Scripture in the Letters of Paul* (New Haven, Conn.: Yale University Press, 1989), pp. 29–32.

77. Lincicum, *Paul*, p. 122.

Deuteronomy, have been fulfilled. There is, then, a profound sense of continuity. At the same time there is a certain sense of discontinuity. God had acted, God's king was present, but not in the way that was expected or imagined. Jesus' parables both endorsed and subverted expectations: 'every scribe who has been trained for the kingdom of heaven is like the master of a household who brings out of his treasure what is new and what is old' (Matt. 13:52 NRSV). The disciples constantly failed to understand, and they were the ones following Jesus. To narrow it down, Deuteronomy influences, because it is authoritative; but at the same time there is a certain reappropriation that bursts the banks of Deuteronomy's own articulation. One good example of this is the incorporation of Jesus *within* the Shema (Deut. 6:4) in 1 Corinthians 8:6 'yet for us there is one God, the Father, from whom are all things and for whom we exist, and one Lord, Jesus Christ, through whom are all things and through whom we exist' (NRSV). Deuteronomy remains authoritative; the Shema is authoritative; yet 'Paul has redefined it christologically, producing what we can only call a sort of christological monotheism.'[78]

Exile

The title of this section may raise a few eyebrows, for had not the return from exile happened hundreds of years earlier, following Cyrus' edict (Ezra 1)? The suggestion that the New Testament story begins with a sense of Israel's expulsion from the land is hotly contested: to what extent was the exile believed to be an ongoing reality in second-temple Judaism? The conviction that 'the great majority of Jesus' contemporaries believed that they were still in exile, in all the senses that really mattered' is one that N. T. Wright has argued for strongly.[79] Although Wright was neither the first, nor the only recent, voice to advocate this, his articulation of it has been highly significant and controversial.[80] Questions have

---

78. N. T. Wright, *The Climax of the Covenant: Christ and the Law in Pauline Theology* (Edinburgh: T. & T. Clark, 1991), p. 129.

79. N. T. Wright, *New Testament*, pp. 268–272; N. T. Wright, *Jesus*, pp. xvii–xviii and *passim*.

80. See James M. Scott (ed.), *Exile: Old Testament, Jewish, and Christian*

revolved around how an enduring 'exile' could relate to the physical reality of a return to the land and a certain degree of restoration, notably of the worshipping life of the temple.

It should be said that there is significant agreement that for first-century Judaism(s) things were not as they should be; they were waiting for God to act. For Snodgrass, for example, the exile may have been over, but the effects were not.[81] There is also agreement that many second-temple texts do use the language of exile. Wright explains by way of qualification that 'exile' refers to *a period of history with certain characteristics*, not to a geographical situation'.[82] This is at one level helpful, given the reality of many people back in the land. But the historical does not marginalize the geographical. The land remains contested space. 'Spatial matters would be unavoidable for anyone presenting a hope for "Israel".'[83] There is a rich symbolism to the language of 'exile' that speaks of enduring realities as the era of the New Testament dawns. Debate about the appropriate term should not detract from these realities.

Within second-temple Judaism there are many places outside the New Testament that speak of the ongoing plight in exilic

Conceptions, JSJSup 56 (Leiden: Brill, 1997), for a number of essays supporting the view. For stimulating discussion and some agreement and disagreement, see Carey C. Newman (ed.), _Jesus & the Restoration of Israel: A Critical Assessment of N. T. Wright's_ Jesus and the Victory of God (Downers Grove: InterVarsity Press, 1999).

81. Klyne R. Snodgrass, 'Reading & Overreading the Parables in _Jesus and the Victory of God_', in Carey C. Newman (ed.), _Jesus & the Restoration of Israel: A Critical Assessment of N. T. Wright's_ Jesus and the Victory of God (Downers Grove: InterVarsity Press, 1999), p. 62.

82. N. T. Wright, 'In Grateful Dialogue: A Response', in Carey C. Newman (ed.), _Jesus & the Restoration of Israel: A Critical Assessment of N. T. Wright's_ Jesus and the Victory of God (Downers Grove: InterVarsity Press, 1999), p. 259. The decision to use 'exile' is governed by the texts themselves.

83. Matthew Sleeman, _Geography and the Ascension Narrative in Acts_, SNTSMS 146 (Cambridge: Cambridge University Press, 2009), p. 68, commenting on Acts 1:6 and the disciples' question to Jesus about the restoring of the kingdom to Israel (cf. p. 87, n. 126).

language.[84] According to Jesus ben Sira (c. 180 BC) in Ecclesiasticus 36,[85] Israel awaits God's mercy (v. 1) and new signs and wonders (v. 6). He pleads, 'Gather all the tribes of Jacob, and give them their inheritance, as at the beginning' (13, 16). What is needed is a new exodus and new entry into the land. In 2 Maccabees 2 (first century BC) Jeremiah has told those hunting for the cave where he had hidden and sealed the 'tent and the ark and the altar of incense' (v. 5), 'The place shall remain unknown until God gathers his people together again and shows his mercy' (v. 7 NRSV). The location of the sacred artefacts awaits Yahweh's gathering of his people, for many are still in exile. The Greek translation of 2 Chronicles 29:9 ends not with 'are in captivity for this' (NRSV, following the MT), but 'are in captivity in a land not their own, as it is even now'. Captivity and exile are enduring realities.

When we come to the New Testament, a very similar picture is to be found. In Matthew's Gospel the genealogies that dominate chapter 1 have three pivotal moments before Christ, separated by fourteen generations: Abraham, David and deportation/exile (Matt. 1:17). Jesus is so named because he will save 'his' people from their sins. Jesus himself becomes an exile, carried off to Egypt (Matt. 2:13), awaiting a redemption (cf. Hos. 11:1). Later Jesus appoints twelve apostles who will judge, reconstituting and restoring Israel (Matt. 10:2; 19:28).[86] In Mark, John the Baptist's initial ministry is summarized as a voice crying in the wilderness, 'Prepare the way of the Lord, make his paths straight' (Mark 1:3). He quotes from Isaiah 40:3, part of a chapter that promises comfort because the *exile* is over. One of the caveats I raised earlier is how to discern significance, in this case of a quotation. Jesus'

---

84. See further Craig A. Evans, 'Jesus & the Continuing Exile of Israel',
    in Carey C. Newman (ed.), *Jesus & the Restoration of Israel: A Critical
    Assessment of N. T. Wright's* Jesus and the Victory of God (Downers Grove:
    InterVarsity Press, 1999), pp. 77–100; Thomas R. Hatina, 'Exile', in
    Craig A. Evans and Stanley E. Porter (eds.), *Dictionary of New Testament
    Background* (Leicester: Inter-Varsity Press, 2000), pp. 348–351.
85. The verse numbering and translation follows the NRSV here.
86. Evans, 'Jesus & the Continuing Exile', pp. 91–93.

message in Mark 1:15 is that 'the time has come, the kingdom of God has come near'; this connects with the words of comfort in Isaiah 40, 'Behold your God' (Isa. 40:9), and the message coming later, where Yahweh is returning to Zion (52:8), beginning his reign (52:7) and ushering in salvation (52:10). In the ministry of Jesus there is a sense in which the Lord is returning to Zion.[87]

Within Luke-Acts are a number of further pointers. For Zechariah they are still in the hands of their enemies (Luke 1:74); the message of the angels was of 'good news of great joy for all *the* people', because they were, like Simeon, waiting for the consolation of Israel (Luke 2:25), or, like Anna, waiting for the redemption of Jerusalem (Luke 2:38). Because Jesus' birth was good news for Israel ('*the* people'), it was good news for the world. At the transfiguration Moses and Elijah talk with Jesus about Jesus' departure ('exodus') that he is going to 'accomplish' in Jerusalem (Luke 9:31). Through his death there will be a new redemption like the exodus from Egypt. Jesus reads out from the Isaiah scroll in the temple, declaring that Isaiah 61:1–3 is fulfilled in their hearing. This figure embodied a ministry of rescue and redemption, liberating captives. In similar fashion Jesus answers John the Baptist's questions about Jesus' identity by referring back to Isaiah 35 (Luke 7:22). There a revelation of Yahweh accompanies the healing of the blind and deaf and the *returning (šûb) to* Zion of those redeemed by Yahweh. The pictures of restoration indicate a desperate plight. In Acts Stephen explicitly works within Steck's Deuteronomistic pattern as he indicts the leaders for their uncircumcised hearts, opposing of the prophets and failure to keep God's law (Acts 7:51–53), 'living words' declared by one who spoke of raising up a prophet like him (Acts 7:37–38; cf. Deut. 18:15; 30:15–20; 32:47).[88]

John's Gospel, without explicitly using the language of exile, indicates by what Jesus brings the plight they are in: darkness, ignorance and death.

For the apostle Paul, as he surveyed the landscape from his new

---

87. Cf. N. T. Wright, *Jesus*, pp. 612–653. Note esp. the Lucan parable of the talents and the cleansing of the temple (cf. Mal. 3).

88. See n. 1 above (ref. to Steck).

vantage point as a servant of Christ and an apostle, Jerusalem was in slavery (Gal. 4:25; cf. Ezra 9:8 9; Neh. 9:36), enmeshed within the 'present evil age' (Gal. 1:3–4), under the curse of the law (Gal. 3:13; cf. Dan. 9:11). Jew, like Gentile, was a child of wrath (Eph. 2:3), under the power of darkness (Col. 1:13). The real problem was the lack of circumcision of the heart (Rom. 2) and the hardening of Israel's heart in unbelief (Rom. 11:7–8; cf. Deut. 29:4; Isa. 29:10).

For Hebrews the dominant paradigm is 'then' and 'now', of 'typological promise and models' and 'fulfilment' rather than the pattern of sin–exile–restoration. Yet the exilic motif endures in the sense of the addressees being confronted by the choice 'today' (Heb. 3), the danger of an unbelieving heart, and the opportunity of entering the rest that Joshua did not (Heb. 4:8). They, like their forefathers, are in one sense 'strangers and exiles' (Heb. 11:13–16, 39–40).[89]

As Jesus arrives on the scene, Israel is waiting for God to act. There is a sense in which the exile endures to that day. This should not be pushed too far, not least because some of the New Testament writers can also conceive of believers in Jesus after Jesus' life, death and resurrection being a 'diaspora' in exile (Jas 1:1; 1 Pet. 1:1; cf. Deut. 30:4 LXX). However, exile does convey with it a certain point in time and space within the story of Israel. Within the framing of questions about world views that stories articulate, 'in exile' answers both 'Where are we?' and 'What time is it?'[90] Restoration, redemption, return are awaited. Having a Pentateuch enshrines God's people outside the land, waiting to inherit. As the New Testament dawns, Israel are in a sense in the same place and time as that of the final provenance of Deuteronomy: outside the land, ready to inherit, with the *tôrâ*'s demand and story shaping them.

Restoration/return to the land

Fundamental to any analysis of the New Testament's depiction of restoration, redemption and return is the sense of 'now' and 'not

---

89. For these points on Hebrews, see David M. Allen, *Deuteronomy and Exhortation*, pp. 221–222.

90. Cf. N. T. Wright, *Jesus*, p. 138.

yet', or 'here' and 'not here'. Something new, radical and decisive is happening in and through Jesus' life, death, resurrection, ascension and the pouring out of the Spirit. God is acting (at last). But it awaits final consummation. Jesus' parables spell this out clearly. The kingdom is present, but it is not as people expected. There is wastage and failure as well as fruitfulness (Mark 4:1–20). There is gradual growth (Mark 4:26–32). The sifting of the wicked from the righteous comes only at the end, as the parable of the wheat and the weeds illustrates (Matt. 13:24–30, 36–43). Jesus' quoting of Isaiah 61:1–3 in Luke 4:18–19 gives the same picture, as it notably stops before the declaration of vengeance (Isa. 61:2). As the rest of the New Testament expresses, he came the first time to deliver; the second time he comes to deliver his people finally and to judge (Acts 17:31; Heb. 9:25–28).

But the time has changed. Jesus declares, 'The time is fulfilled, and the kingdom of God has come near; repent, and believe in the good news' (Mark 1:14). In Luke the storyline opens with two remarkable pregnancies and Zechariah's song, celebrating that God has acted to redeem his people (Luke 1:68) and has fulfilled his promises to Abraham (Luke 1:73). This is the salvation for which John the Baptist prepared the way, calling for repentance as the voice proclaiming the end of the exile (Luke 2:11, 30; 3:3–6; cf. Deut. 30:2; Isa. 40:3–5). The story of Luke finishes with the possibility of 'repentance' and 'forgiveness of sins' being proclaimed to all nations in accordance with the Scriptures (Luke 24:47). In between, Jesus has embodied 'salvation' in his life and ministry, he has accomplished a new 'exodus' by his death, resurrection and ascension in Jerusalem (Luke 9:31),[91] inaugurating a new covenant through his blood (Luke 22:20; cf. Jer. 31:31). Acts continues that story, with the outpouring of the Spirit and the spreading of the gospel even to Rome. But this is precisely connected with 'the hope of Israel' (Acts 28:20); the Jewish people's failure to listen is in accord with the hardness of their hearts (Isa. 6:9–10; cf. Deut. 29:4).

---

91. Cf. Darrell L. Bock, *Luke*, 2 vols., BECNT (Grand Rapids: Baker, 1994–6), vol. 1, p. 870.

It is perhaps with Paul, though, that the Deuteronomic story-line of restoration and return the other side of 'exile' is most evident.[92] For Paul the period of the law acting as a *paidagōgos*, a 'tutor' (NASB), 'guardian' (ESV) or 'disciplinarian' (NRSV) to Israel, the child and heir, is over (Gal. 3:23–24); during that time, being a child was little different from being a slave (Gal. 4:1–2). But now the time has changed: 'when the fullness of time had come, God sent his Son, born of a woman, born under the law, in order to redeem those who were under the law, so that we might receive adoption as children' (Gal. 4:4–5). Through Jesus' death the curse of the law has been taken away (Gal. 3:13). Given how Paul continues, this is not a reference to an individual's relationship to God, but to a salvation-historical event: just as the curse was for Israel, so too was its removal.[93] There were two purposes of this, as Paul goes on to say: 'in order that in Christ Jesus the blessing of Abraham might come to the Gentiles, so that we might receive the promise of the Spirit through faith' (Gal. 3:14 NRSV). Behind this promise of the Spirit lies Jesus' resurrection that declared him Lord and Christ (Rom. 1:3–4), hence with authority to judge (Acts 17:31), the outpouring of the Spirit at Pentecost and the Spirit's ongoing availability to all who believe in the Messiah. It is a new-covenant blessing. This sense of the time moving on explains why Paul sees Peter's and the other Jewish Christians' ceasing to have table fellowship with the Gentiles as 'not in step with the truth of the gospel' (Gal. 2:14). God has done something decisive in and through Christ, such that the Gentiles are now welcome (cf. Eph. 1). To insist on circumcision and to deny Gentile table fellowship

---

92. For more on Paul and Deuteronomy's story, see James M. Scott, 'Restoration of Israel', in Gerald F. Hawthorne and Ralph P. Martin (eds.), *Dictionary of Paul and His Letters* (Leicester: Inter-Varsity Press, 1993), pp. 796–805; and esp. Lincicum, *Paul*, pp. 142–167.

93. N. T. Wright, *Climax*, pp. 144–156. This is not to deny relevance to individuals, but to see that relevance in its proper place. Although Deut. 27:26 in its immediate context refers to individuals, Paul is reading it within its wider context and through the lenses of passages such as Dan. 9:11. See Lincicum, *Paul*, pp. 144–145.

are both to wind the clock back, denying what God has done in Jesus in opening the door for Gentile inclusion. It is a different gospel from the gospel God declared to Abraham, which includes Gentiles (Gal. 3:8). To allow oneself as a Gentile Christian to be circumcised is a disastrous return to enslaving 'weak and worthless elementary principles' (Gal. 4:9; cf. v. 3), albeit this time through *tôrâ* rather than through their prior paganism, because the way of the 'works of *tôrâ*' has, in reality, led only to Israel's slavery (Gal. 4:25b).

In tandem with the inclusion of the Gentiles is the circumcision of the heart (Rom. 2:25–29). Remarkably for Paul, this was an 'alternative' to physical circumcision, not something in addition.[94] Now 'the uncircumcised can be the true Jew'.[95] To do this they need to believe in the word that is near them, the word that is Christ himself (Rom. 10:5–13; cf. Deut. 30:11–14); after all, *anyone* who calls on the name of the Lord (Jesus; see Rom. 10:9) will be saved (Rom. 10:13).[96] Alongside this Gentile inclusion Paul is in anguish over the unbelief of his own people (Rom. 9:1–5). But this is not somehow a denial of God's righteousness or a thwarting of his purposes. For this was part of God's purposes, with God's giving Israel a 'spirit of stupor' (Rom. 11:8; cf. Deut. 29:4; Isa. 29:10). It was in and through this inclusion of a Gentile 'no-people' that God was making Israel 'jealous' (Rom. 10:19; 11:11–14; cf. Deut. 32:21).[97] The next stage in the song of Moses is the vindication of God's people (Deut. 32:36–43) and, according to the LXX, Israel *and* the nations rejoicing (Deut. 32:43). As Romans 11 ends, Paul looks forward to that day of the vindication

----

94. Lincicum, *Paul*, p. 150.

95. Ibid., p. 152.

96. The momentum for connecting the law with Christ already begins in Deuteronomy, with characteristics of Yahweh also predicated of Yahweh's word: 'near' (*qārôb*, 4:7 + 30:14); 'righteous' (*ṣaddîq*, 32:4 + 4:8); 'your life' (30:20 + 32:47); note also 'perfect' (*tāmîm*, 32:4 + Ps. 19:8); 'consuming fire' (4:24 + Jer. 23:29).

97. For Paul's approach of reading the epithets beginning with 'no'/'not' (e.g. Rom. 9:25–26) as speaking of the Gentiles, see Lincicum, *Paul*, p. 163.

of God's people, and sees the Gentiles joining in praise of God's mercy in fulfilment of Deuteronomy (Rom. 15:9–10; cf. Deut. 32:43). It is no wonder that Richard Hays wrote of the Song of Moses that 'it contains Romans *in nuce*'.[98]

Conclusion

There are, then, fundamental streams running through the rest of the Old Testament and into the New Testament that have Deuteronomy either as their source or as a major tributary. That is not to deny certain discontinuities in both Old and New. In the Old Testament the monarchy as conceived in Deuteronomy (17:14–20), for example, stands in some tension with Israel's kings, whether in Samuel–Kings or in the Psalms. Within the New Testament Jesus as the Davidic Messiah, inaugurating God's kingdom, is something at which Deuteronomy does not begin to hint. The agency of God's Spirit is not explicitly envisaged in Deuteronomy's vision of restoration. Further, even where Old and New Testament narrative conforms to the Deuteronomic story there is a sense of newness rather than simply ploughing Deuteronomy's furrow. For example, although in many senses the exile is over, the 'return' to the land is something that remains a vision for the future. Often on Jesus' lips 'entering the kingdom' is something future; it remains a future reality that 'the meek will inherit the land/earth' (Matt. 5:5) and that the descendants of Abraham will inherit the 'cosmos' in accordance with the promise (Rom. 4:13). This should not be surprising. Deuteronomy stands in a tradition; it shapes subsequent tradition, but is always read in dialogue with the events and circumstances in which readers find themselves.

Deuteronomy provides a definitive telling of events: a history where God's faithfulness is met by Israel's unfaithfulness, where Israel's unfaithfulness is met by God's judgment seen supremely in the curse of the death of exile, where God acts so their hearts are circumcised and his people turn to him in repentance. This telling of events is appropriated and followed through the Old Testament

---

98. Hays, *Echoes*, p. 164.

and into the New. It provides the foundation for other connections that are made. Jesus unlike Israel is the faithful son of God in the wilderness (Matt. 3:17; 4:1–11; cf. Deut. 8:1–6; Exod. 4:22). He is the one who supremely cares for the poor and marginalized. He is Lord of the sabbath, embodying sabbath rest (Mark 3:27–28; Matt. 11:29–30; cf. Deut. 5:12–15; 12:9). The mountain on which they will worship is neither Zion nor Ebal, but in spirit and truth on Christ himself (John 4:20–24). The 'one' God they worship has Jesus firmly within rather than subordinate (1 Cor. 8:6). The 'word of faith' that is near is now the gospel of Jesus Christ (Rom. 10:6–15). Love issuing in obedience is no longer love for God resulting in obedience to Moses' commands, but love for Christ and obedience to his words (John 14:15). Deuteronomy constrains the New Testament portrayal, which in turn creatively appropriates Deuteronomy's testimony.

There are a number of implications as we read Deuteronomy.

First, Deuteronomy forms part of the story in which I find myself as a Christian living in the twenty-first century. As a Gentile I am grafted into the olive tree (cf. Rom. 11), so there is a certain otherness about it. Yet as I read Deuteronomy, it is my story. I am there in the plains of Moab. I am confronted by the choice of 'life' and 'death'.[99] This, and not our own lives, is where salvation history takes place. By analogy the church is like Israel. But it is more than an analogy. It is a personal, organic connection.

Secondly, though in a sense I am there (as is the church), yet the story has moved on. Though I, and the church, may exhibit many of Israel's characteristics of hard-heartedness, stubbornness and rebellion, yet in Christ God has done something definitive. There is for the believer a circumcised heart, the presence of the Spirit, a real desire to follow Christ and the enabling of God to do so. That is not to say that sinless perfection is possible. But it is to caution against an unreflective flattening of salvation history that considers the Christian as *no* different from the Israelite. Ironically, to do that is not so very far from insisting on circumcision for the Gentile. It

---

99. Cf. Bonhoeffer, *Life Together*, p. 38, quoted above on pp. 23–24.

is to wind back the clock and forget that the 'fullness of time' has come (Gal. 4:4).

Thirdly, to preach, teach or read Deuteronomy is to relate its story to the wider story. It needs to be read in its widest canonical context and not to be abstracted from it. The hope the New Testament holds out needs to be understand and interpreted within the framework and storyline of Genesis through Deuteronomy and on. That is to say, God's commitment is to a renewed creation and a renewed humanity within it, not to some other-worldly ethereal salvation.

Fourthly, the Christian can and should rejoice in the faithfulness of God to his word and promises. The Christian looks back with gratitude and celebration to what Deuteronomy anticipated. Naturally there is still more to come; there is a 'not here' as well as a 'here', a 'not yet' as well as a 'now'. But the 'now' and 'here' of what God has already done in Christ, the climax of Deuteronomy and the rest of the Old Testament promises, is grounds for joy.

PART 2

A WORD TO SHAPE THE LIFE
OF GOD'S PEOPLE

Deuteronomy's storyline is critical for its interpretation. For many
Christians reading Deuteronomy that comes as something of a
relief, because the central section of laws can on such a reading be
downplayed or even bypassed. It seems rather easier to connect
Deuteronomy's narrative than its laws with the New Testament.
What Deuteronomy anticipated has now arrived. Further, the
powerful rhetoric that characterizes Deuteronomy 1 – 11 and 29 –
30 lends itself more straightforwardly to a new, Christian context,
even if the precise content of that rhetoric has changed somewhat.
For example, the call to 'Choose life!' comes originally in the
context of the choices of 'life' and 'death' set out before the people
in the plains of Moab. It transfers naturally to an urgent appeal,
whether evangelistic or for ongoing commitment.

However, an emphasis on Deuteronomy's narrative and
rhetoric must not be at the expense of attention to the more specific commands, particularly those in Deuteronomy 12 – 26.[1] This

---

1. There are also other places in Deuteronomy where Moses gives specific
injunctions to the people (e.g. 7:1–6).

is not because many scholars see these chapters, or parts of them, as the oldest part of Deuteronomy (sometimes called *Ur-Deuteronomium*, *Urdeuteronomium* or *Urdt*), though they do. Rather, it is because the rhetoric of the book as a whole establishes their central importance. In chapter 5 the people urged, and then Yahweh mandated, Moses to stay and listen to Yahweh after the revelation of the Decalogue (5:22–31). What Yahweh revealed to Moses he is *now* relaying to them in the plains of Moab: 'These are the decrees and laws you must be careful to follow in the land that Yahweh, the God of your fathers, has given you to possess' (12:1; cf. 5:31). These decrees and laws unpack what it means to love Yahweh (Deut. 6:4–5). Deuteronomy's narrative does not obviate the need for obedience, but demands it. That Israel failed to do so – indeed in a profound sense was always going to fail to do so – within Deuteronomy's narrative does not invalidate this observation. As we shall see, the detailed instructions, as with the more general demand for loyalty, are part of an enduring vision for the community life of the people of God. At the same time, there are significant issues surrounding interpretation and appropriation. In Part 2, chapter 4 outlines Deuteronomy's vision for Israel; chapter 5 discusses five dead ends in interpreting the laws; chapter 6 looks at some of the challenges for contemporary Christian appropriation; the final chapter proposes how to appropriate Deuteronomy's vision of community life more generally, and gives one example of appropriating specific injunctions.

4. DEUTERONOMY'S VISION FOR ISRAEL

Deuteronomy's vision for what Israel *should be* is rooted in its vision of what Israel *is*. There are at least five (in some ways overlapping) characteristics of Israel as a people, which Deuteronomy insists are foundationally true.

What Israel is

First, they are a *redeemed* people. Israel's identity is rooted in the fact that they were a people in slavery in Egypt, but have now been redeemed by Yahweh. Yahweh 'brought them out of Egypt, out of slavery'. Because of that, they are to live a particular kind of way. Yahweh's redemptive work is the basis of the obligations of the Decalogue (5:6) and of more general calls to loyalty and exclusive worship (e.g. 6:12; 8:14). Within chapters 12–26 the reality of Israel's slavery in Egypt is to shape their care for those on the margins of society (e.g. 15:15; 24:18). This is all far removed from some modern notions of freedom that emphasize freedom *from* but have no conception of freedom *for*. Yahweh redeemed

Israel from Egypt, from the house of 'slavery' (*'bd*) that they might 'serve' (*'bd*) him (6:12 13).

Secondly, they are a *loved* people. With Deuteronomy, the language of God's love (*'hb*) for Israel (7:8) and their ancestors (e.g. 4:37; 10:15) is first found. Most scholars trace the origin of such language to the Northern Kingdom and (indirectly) to the preaching of Hosea. Eichrodt, for example, explores the loving dimension of Yahweh's holiness (cf. Hos. 11:1–9), and comments, 'For the first time in the history of Israel, *the message of the love of God* is heard in Hosea's proclamation as the center of God's action with his people.'[1] There are, though, some striking differences in Deuteronomy's articulation of Yahweh's love, most notably the absence of the marriage metaphor so prevalent in Hosea. Vang has recently contended that the direction of indebtedness should be reversed: Hosea has taken over Deuteronomy's theme and then developed it in the light of his own 'personal tragedy about a failed marriage'.[2] There is an emotive aspect to Yahweh's love for his people in Deuteronomy, seen in language of Yahweh's 'setting his heart' on you (7:7) and expressions elsewhere of his mercy (e.g. 4:31) and jealousy (e.g. 4:24). Within that, there is a conditional dimension whereby remaining within the orbit of Yahweh's covenantal love, or *ḥesed*, is rooted in obedience (5:9–10; 7:9–10). The declaration of a conditionality within a love that does not depend on Israel's qualities may seem puzzling to the point of incoherence (7:9–10; cf. 7:7–8). The point is that love demands a response. Although Yahweh has made a binding promise and can withdraw only his favour, not his love, Israel may spurn that love and so forfeit its benefits. Further, the difference between judgment for three or four generations and steadfast love (*ḥesed*) for a thousand indicates that 'mercy finally outweighs judgment'.[3]

1. Walther Eichrodt, 'The Holy One in Your Midst: The Theology of Hosea', *Int* 15 (1961), p. 263 (emphasis original). For more on Yahweh's holiness as love, see James E. Robson, 'Forgotten Dimensions in Holiness', *HBT* 33 (2011), pp. 121–146.

2. Karsten Vang, 'God's Love According to Hosea and Deuteronomy: A Prophetic Reworking of a Deuteronomic Concept?', *TynB* 62 (2011), p. 193.

3. McConville, *Deuteronomy*, p. 127.

A third characteristic of Deuteronomy's Israel is that they are a *chosen* people. Just as with language of Yahweh's 'love' for Israel, Deuteronomy is the first book in the Pentateuch to use language of Yahweh's 'choosing' (*bḥr*) Israel: they are 'elect'. Prior to this there was, of course, a particularity about God's calling of Abraham; indeed, Israel's own election is rooted in Yahweh's love for Abraham (4:37). But here in Deuteronomy the language of choice or election appears and the picture of Israel's election flourishes. Israel's election is closely related to Yahweh's redemption and love, for it was in and through God's loving action in redeeming them that Yahweh chose them and they became his people. This is particularly evident in the structure of Deuteronomy 7:7–8:

7	Not because of your being more numerous than all the peoples	A
	did Yahweh desire you	X
	and so choose you	
	(for you [were] the least of all the peoples)	
8	But rather, because of Yahweh's loving you	B
	and because of his keeping the oath he swore to your fathers	
	did Yahweh bring you out by a strong hand	Y
	and redeem you from the house of slavery . . .	

There is a contrast set up in verse 7: 'it was *not* because of A that X happened'. This basic structure of reason and event is then repeated in verse 8, but with variation in the content: '*but rather* because of B that Y happened'. The implication of this parallel structure is that A and B formally correspond, as do X and Y. In both cases the reason for the action (A, B) precedes the action itself (X, Y), directing primary attention to these reasons. It was *not* for the reason that they might have expected, but for a different reason altogether. There is an emphatic contrast between A and B. The statements X and Y, on the other hand, are less prominent. They correspond with each other, almost as synonyms. In other words the syntax connects 'Yahweh set his heart on you and chose you' with 'Yahweh brought you out with a strong hand and redeemed you from the house of slavery.' The same thing is being said with different words. Election is effected in and through Yahweh's action in history (cf. 4:20).

Strikingly, in Deuteronomy election is focused not on a king (David) but on the people (Deut. 4:37; 14:2; cf. 2 Sam. 6:21; Pss 78:70; 89:19). It is democratized. Although the king *is* chosen (Deut. 17:15), this merely emphasizes that it is Yahweh who chooses; the king's status is in no sense exalted.[4] There are certain similarities with Isaiah 40 – 55, which also is concerned for Israel's election (e.g. Isa. 41:9; 44:1) and in some ways democratizes the promise made to David, applying it to the people more generally (Isa. 55:3). This does not mean, though, that the concept of Israel's election *arises* from a rhetorical situation that includes the demise of the Davidic king, with the purpose of assurance to a beleaguered people. It is already found in Amos, where Yahweh declares to Israel, 'you only have I known of all the families of the earth' (Amos 3:2; cf. Gen. 18:19), and in Hosea ('not my people', Hos. 1:9).[5] Questions about the origin of the concept should not detract from the dignity that election confers to the people as a whole.

A further significant point about Deuteronomy's concept of 'election' is its rhetorical deployment. Far from being the grounds for complacency and smugness, it occurs in contexts that emphasize Israel's obligations. Because Yahweh has *chosen* them, they are to keep his commands (e.g. 4:37–40; 7:6–11). 'It is the proclamation of the Decalogue over her which puts Israel's election into effect.'[6] Language of election is inseparable from Israel's responsibility and vocation.[7]

A fourth characteristic closely related to these is that Israel is a

4. A. D. H. Mayes, *Deuteronomy*, NCBC (London: Marshall, Morgan & Scott, 1979), pp. 60–61.
5. Cf. Dale Patrick, 'Election', *ABD*, vol. 2, p. 438.
6. Gerhard von Rad, *Old Testament Theology*, tr. D. M. G. Stalker, 2 vols. (Edinburgh: Oliver & Boyd, 1962–5), vol. 1, p. 192.
7. Cf. Moberly's 'preferred conceptuality' for conceiving of election: 'For everyone to whom much has been given, much will be required.' See R. W. L. Moberly, 'Is Election Bad for You?', in Jill Middlemas, David J. A. Clines and Else K. Holt (eds.), *The Centre and the Periphery: A European Tribute to Walter Brueggemann*, Hebrew Bible Monographs 27 (Sheffield: Sheffield Phoenix Press, 2010), p. 106.

holy-to-Yahweh people (e.g. Deut. 7:6; 14:2, 21; 26:19). In Leviticus in particular, holiness is a *task* for Israel. They are told, 'Be holy, for I, Yahweh your God, am holy' (Lev. 19:2; cf. Exod. 19:6). In Deuteronomy 'holy' describes what the people *are*, 'a reality that has already been established'.[8] Yet Deuteronomy never speaks of Israel as 'holy' as if it were some kind of independent status; they are 'holy-to-Yahweh'. Israel is what it is by virtue of the special relationship with Yahweh. They are fundamentally a people in *covenant* relationship with Yahweh. Yahweh is their God and they are Yahweh's people. These are summed up by describing Israel as Yahweh's *səgullâ* or 'treasured possession', 'a kind of small trove of gold and pearls which a rich man keeps in his innermost chambers, to admire and enjoy'.[9]

All of the characteristics convey the sense of particularity about Yahweh's relationship with Israel. Yahweh remains God of the whole world (cf. Deut. 4:32–40), yet in a particular relationship with Israel. This particularity is ultimately for the sake of the nations, but Deuteronomy itself does not afford many glimpses of this more universal perspective.[10]

The fifth characteristic is that Israel is a *fraternal* people, or 'broth-erhood'. The democratization seen in Deuteronomy's concept of election, from 'king' to 'people', is also seen in Yahweh's parenthood; while in Psalm 2:7 the king is the 'son' of God, in Deuteronomy the whole community are 'children of God' (Deut. 14:1).[11] Deuteronomy expresses in a remarkable fashion the resultant relationship they have with each other, using the egalitar-ian language of 'brother' (*'āḥ*). Everyone in the community is a 'brother'. King and priest, male and female slave are all 'brothers' (17:15; 18:2; 15:12); so too are judge and prophet, the debtor and

8. Nelson, *Deuteronomy*, p. 100.

9. Alexander Rofé, 'The Monotheistic Argumentation in Deut. 4:32–40: Contents, Composition and Text', *VT* 35 (1985), p. 440.

10. There are close similarities between these characteristics and those found in Exod. 19:3–6, although the language of 'election' is absent there.

11. The masculine 'sons' is used in Hebrew, but both men and women are included, as the reference to 'sons and daughters' in 32:19 indicates.

the needy (1:16; 18:15; 15:3, 7). Deuteronomy may even be commanding love for one's enemy through seeing him as a 'brother': Deuteronomy picks up the law in Exodus on an enemy's ox or donkey straying, speaks of the person not as an 'enemy' but as a 'brother' (*'āḥ*), and emphasizes and expands on the duty of care found in Exodus (22:1; cf. Exod. 23:4–5).[12] Deuteronomy 'envisages a society that is quite distinct from every other known society in its world: based on the absolute respect for all its members, all equally enjoy the protection of the law of God'.[13] This fraternal relationship grounds many of the laws, and, behind the legal framework, the attitude that members of the community are to have.

What Israel should be

What Israel *should be* is rooted in what Israel *is*: a redeemed, loved, chosen, holy-to-Yahweh fraternal people. While chapters 12–26 articulate the detailed obligations most specifically, Deuteronomy as a whole sets out to give a particular shape to Israel's life. The fundamental obligation is to 'love' Yahweh (Deut. 6:4–5), a love characterized by obedience. The many verbs that recur in Deuteronomy's parenesis reinforce this: 'do' (*'śh*, 163 times), 'hear' (*šm'*, 91 times), 'keep/observe/watch' (*šmr*, 73 times), 'fear' (*yr'*, 37 times), 'serve' (*'bd*, 35 times). Broadly speaking, Israel as a people should be marked by four characteristics.

First, they should be a people that *listen obediently*. Expressed like this, the focus is on hearing and obeying words. An objection may come that Deuteronomy puts great significance on what the people have experienced or seen. The relationship in Deuteronomy between seeing and hearing needs teasing out carefully. It is true that sight gives validity and credence to the activity

---

12. Cf. Braulik, 'Deuteronomy and Human Rights', pp. 147–148.
13. J. Gordon McConville, 'Deuteronomy, Book of', in T. Desmond Alexander and David W. Baker (eds.), *Dictionary of the Old Testament: Pentateuch* (Leicester: Inter-Varsity Press, 2003), p. 189.

of Yahweh. On many occasions they are to 'remember' or 'not forget' what Yahweh has done; the focus of memory is a historical event. This 'remembering' goes hand in hand with what they (or their 'eyes') have 'seen' (*r'h*) (e.g. Deut. 4:9; 7:18–19). They are to draw conclusions on the basis of what they have seen and experienced. This is true of Joshua, seeing what Yahweh had done to Sihon and Og (3:21). It is also true of their 'seeing' Yahweh's differentiating between the idolaters at Baal Peor and those who held fast to him (4:3). Yahweh 'showed' (*r'h*) them miraculous signs in delivering them from Egypt (4:34–35; cf. 10:21) and 'his great fire', 'his glory and his greatness' at Horeb (4:36; 5:24). With rhetorical flourish Moses claims that their own eyes, not their children's, have seen everything (11:2; cf. 4:10, 15), yet Deuteronomy has already made clear that the exodus generation has died out (1:34–40; 2:14). All this serves to demonstrate that Yahweh has acted in history in a unique, dramatic fashion that remains significant for them in the plains of Moab and into the future. Seeing and experiencing is important. What is remarkable is what Deuteronomy 4 does with that. Carasik sums it up well:

> All agree that true knowledge of the divine realm comes through the eye; at Horeb, Israel had a visual experience giving them true knowledge; the true knowledge they acquired was that true knowledge comes through the ear.[14]

Or, to put it differently, what Israel 'saw' and 'experienced' was in fact the primacy of Yahweh's revelation in *word*. Nowhere is this expressed in more striking fashion than in Deuteronomy 4:12. Most translations make this rather bland, changing the 'very dramatic'[15] participles expressing ongoing action into the aorist, 'heard'/'saw', and by rendering the final phrase 'there was only a

---

14. Michael Carasik, 'To See a Sound: A Deuteronomic Rereading of Exodus 20:15', *Proof* 19 (1999), p. 261. He is summarizing with approval the argument of Stephen A. Geller, 'Fiery Wisdom: Logos and Lexis in Deuteronomy 4', *Proof* 14 (1994), pp. 103–139.

15. Craigie, *Deuteronomy*, p. 134.

voice'.[16] But the Hebrew says, 'you were hearing the sound (*qôl*) of words but a form you were not seeing – except a voice (*qôl*)!' The final phrase is not a verbless clause in its own right ('there was only a voice'), but an exception to what they did not see. It gives the remarkable picture of 'seeing' 'a voice'. This is not suddenly to reify the voice as if it could literally be seen; that would undercut the notion of not seeing any form. Rather, it stresses rhetorically that the theophany (appearance of God) was in fact a theophony (voice of God).

Deuteronomy's insistence on 'revelation-in-word' has a number of implications.

1. Worship of Yahweh should be aniconic, unlike Canaanite worship. Because Israel saw no form, they should use no physical form for representing Yahweh in their worship (Deut. 4:15–19). They are to relate to Yahweh in word.

2. The Moab generation and every subsequent generation are not connected with Horeb only through the cultural memory of an encounter at Horeb, handed down from one generation to the next. Nor, it should be added, is connection to be sought in trying to repeat the direct encounter of Horeb, of 'seeing' again. Instead, there is an immediacy of access to Horeb, because there is access in Moab and beyond *to Yahweh's voice*. The words of the Decalogue and the words given in Moab are the divine voice, Yahweh's address, to every generation into the future. Deuteronomy answers the 'problem' of making 'the commandments that each generation was to teach the next as *immediate* a part of Israelites' experience as the mighty deeds that God had performed "before your eyes"'.[17] In Exodus the tabernacle is a 'portable Sinai'[18] that Israel could take with them as they left the mountain, enshrining Yahweh's presence and graded access. In Deuteronomy the *tôrâ* is a portable Horeb. Every time they gather and hear the words God spoke at Horeb in order to learn to fear Yahweh and to teach their children,

---

16. An exception is Craigie, ibid.

17. Carasik, 'To See a Sound', p. 261 (my emphasis).

18. Nahum M. Sarna, *Exodus*, JPS Torah Commentary (Philadelphia: Jewish Publication Society, 1991), p. 173.

they are gathering again around Horeb (Deut. 4:10). This unique 'day of the assembly' (Deut. 9:10; 10:4; 18:16), or, as the Greek translation renders it, 'day of the *ekklēsia*', is paradigmatic of every 'assembly', whether of synagogue or of church. They hear God's voice with the same immediacy as the generation that stood there. Although for the church gathered around the risen Christ the mountain is Zion, not Horeb (cf. Heb. 12:18–25), God's word is an immediate, contemporary word and the issue remains the same: whether those gathered will refuse the one who 'speaks' (present tense; Heb. 12:25).[19]

3. This explains the distinctive Deuteronomic emphasis on 'teaching' and 'learning' (different forms of *lmd*).[20] Access to Horeb is preserved by the teaching of these 'statutes and commandments' (4:1).[21] Moses 'teaches' them in Moab (4:1, 5, 14; 5:31; 6:1) and they are to 'learn' them (4:10; 5:1); in turn, they are to 'teach' them both when they gather (4:10) and to their children at every opportunity (11:19). Their uncompromising stand towards the nations in Canaan stems in part from concern that those nations will 'teach' them 'abominations' (20:18) and they will 'learn' them (18:9). This teaching ministry of Moses extends to the song (31:19, 22; 32:1–43). The 'teaching' and 'learning' is not simply a cognitive

---

19. The logic here is similar to that of John 20, where sight is very important for establishing Jesus' resurrection and for belief (20:8, 18, 20, 25); yet Jesus upbraids Thomas for not believing. This is not because seeing is unimportant, but because the testimony of others to what they had seen was sufficient. He should have believed because others have seen (20:29; cf. 3:11; 6:46; 19:35). Every subsequent generation is in the same place as Thomas. The same pattern is also present in the dramatic revelations at Jesus' baptism and transfiguration, where God enjoins to 'listen to him' not 'look at him'.

20. The same Hebrew root lies behind both. To 'teach' (*lmd*, piel) is to 'bring about learning'.

21. In the context of Deuteronomy as a whole these cannot be restricted just to chs. 12–26 (note 12:1), but is 'a generalizing term for the whole of Mosaic preaching' (Nelson, *Deuteronomy*, pp. 63–64). Cf. Millar, 'Living', pp. 36–41.

grasp, but one issuing in obedience (e.g. 4:1) and 'fear' of Yahweh (e.g. 4:10; 17:19; 31:12–13).

Secondly, they should be a people who *worship exclusively*. No other deity had done for any nation what Yahweh had done for Israel in redeeming them from slavery and in speaking out of fire (4:32–34). Yahweh showed them this 'so that [they] would acknowledge that Yahweh is God; there is no other besides him' (4:35). The particular privileges Israel had experienced through Yahweh's action in history, of being redeemed, chosen, loved and holy-to-Yahweh, come with the obligation to worship Yahweh exclusively. This is expressed positively in the emphatic declarations in Deuteronomy 6. Most famously, the Shema declares, 'Hear O Israel, Yahweh our God, Yahweh is one, *and* you shall love Yahweh your God with all your heart . . .' (6:4–5). In context Yahweh as 'one' is saying less about Yahweh's essence or even about monotheism as a concept than about Israel's relationship to Yahweh, which is to be exclusive. This is apparent from four factors.

1. Verse 5 continues with 'and' (in the Heb., not in many modern English translations), which has the force of 'so' or 'therefore' (NAB). Yahweh as 'one' entails a relational response of 'love' that is exclusive and total.

2. The best parallel for the use of 'one' in Deuteronomy 6:4 is Song of Songs 6:8–9. Here the dove, the young woman, is 'one' to her lover and her mother. She is not the only woman in the world, and almost certainly is not her mother's only daughter. It is not about absolute existence but about the relationship between them: she matters in a way that others do not.

3. The only time the Shema is explicitly picked up in the Old Testament is in Zechariah 14:9. It looks into the future and declares, 'And Yahweh will become king over all the earth; on that day Yahweh will be one and his name one.' This is clearly not about Yahweh's essence changing, so that he will be 'one' then while he is 'many' now; nor is it about Yahweh's character changing, so that he will be faithful and consistent then, while he is not now; nor is it even about how many gods there are in the world. There will not be only one God then, while there are many now. Rather, it is to do with everyone acclaiming Yahweh as the king then although they do not do so now. He 'will be one'. All will

acknowledge him as king, their king. They will not acclaim anyone else.

4. A final pointer towards exclusivity of relationship rather than absolute monotheism comes from references elsewhere in Deuteronomy to 'other gods' (e.g. Deut. 5:7).

The exclusivity is expressed further in terms of Yahweh's jealousy (6:15), and is encapsulated in the emphatic commands of 6:13. In each clause in this verse the object appears in front of the verb in Hebrew. This order draws attention to possible alternative objects of worship and excludes them. In English the force may be captured either by copying the word order in Hebrew ('The LORD your God you shall fear', NRSV) or by a 'cleft' clause ('It is the LORD your God you shall fear', ESV) or with a change of tone. The force of the verse is, 'Yahweh your God (and not others) you shall fear and him (and not others) you shall serve and in his name (alone, and not others) you shall swear.' Positively, they are to worship Yahweh exclusively.

The negative counterpart to this is evident in warnings against idolatry. Idolatry is *deadly*. It provokes Yahweh in his jealousy to anger and brings the punishment of death and exile; to flirt with idolatry is to invite for themselves the uncompromising destiny that Israel is to inflict on the inhabitants of the land (Deut. 7:25).

Idolatry is also *foolish* (32:6). The idols are nothing other than the produce of human hands (4:28) and contrast sharply with Yahweh, who is jealous (4:24) and compassionate (4:31), active to command, scatter and drive (4:23, 27), responsive to prayer and repentance (4:29) and faithful to his covenant (4:31). He alone has spoken from the fire; he alone has redeemed his people in such dramatic fashion (4:32–34). 'Under judgment they will have to do what they had freely chosen to do – serve other gods. But they will then discover precisely the impotence of those gods.'[22]

Not only is idolatry deadly and foolish, but it is also *varied*. Although many of the injunctions relate to physical objects that the Canaanites had set up (Deut. 7; 12), there are pointers that

22. Christopher J. H. Wright, *Deuteronomy*, p. 53.

idolatry is more varied than this. It is not just worshipping the wrong deity (Deut. 5:7; 32:17) or worshipping Yahweh the wrong way, using physical representations (Deut. 4:15–19). It may be seen also in an arrogant superiority over Yahweh's word spoken through Moses. In Deuteronomy 4:2–3 the commands not to add to or subtract from the 'word' are juxtaposed without a conjunction or an explanation with recollection of the punishment (for idolatry) at Baal Peor. This suggests that 'such punishment will also be meted out to those who dare to change God's word!'[23] To tamper with Yahweh's word is to tamper with Yahweh.

There is also the idolatry of ideology or false faith in Deuteronomy 7 – 10. Moses has just set out the essence of Israel's covenant obligation in terms of undivided loyalty and faithfulness to the one true God (Deut. 6:1–25). Now he highlights three dangers to faith and obedience that would arise in the new setting of the land, each introduced by the phrase 'do not say in your heart' (7:17; 8:17; 9:4–5). Their heart was to be the place where Yahweh's words were to be found (Deut. 6:6), but it also has the capacity for idolatry.[24] Olson characterizes the dangers as 'the gods of death – militarism, materialism, and moralism'.[25] An alternative formulation is self-importance, self-satisfaction and self-righteousness. Self-importance puts an undue focus on one's own strength, or lack of it, rather than on trusting Yahweh (7:17; cf. vv. 7–8).[26] Self-satisfaction claims the credit for what has in fact been achieved only through Yahweh's gracious gift (8:17). Self-righteousness makes the mistake of interpreting present blessings,

---

23. Geller, 'Fiery Wisdom', p. 117.

24. Cf. Calvin's comment about human nature being 'a perpetual factory of idols' (John Calvin, *Institutes of the Christian Religion*, 2 vols., ed. John T. McNeill, tr. Ford Lewis Battles, LCC 20–21 [Philadelphia: Westminster, 1960], 1.11.8 [p. 108]).

25. Olson, *Deuteronomy*, p. 52.

26. Olson (ibid., p. 54) perceptively comments, 'both despair and arrogance are simply other facets of the wrongful worship of the false god of militarism and numerical strength. Despair does not trust God enough; arrogance trusts too much in its own human ability and calculation.'

in Israel's case possession of the land, as a sign of moral superiority (9:4). Idolatry then and now may, but need not have, physical form.

Idolatry is also *wicked*. Part of this is the robbing of Yahweh of the worship that rightfully belongs to him, especially given all he has done for them (32:15–18). But idolatry has ethical implications. Most conspicuously, the idolatrous practices of the Canaanites involved 'every abhorrent thing that Yahweh hates', even burning their children in the fire (Deut. 12:31). What is perhaps less recognized is that many of the laws illustrating Deuteronomy's humanitarian concern (e.g. Deut. 14:28–29; 15:1–18) occur precisely in the section of laws from 12:1 to 16:17 that emphasize the need to worship at the place Yahweh will choose rather than at the varied places of the Canaanite inhabitants. Deuteronomy links inhumanity with idolatry and humanitarian laws with right worship.[27]

The danger of idolatry and apostasy lies behind many of the laws, especially in chapters 7 and 12–13. In chapter 7 the command to *ḥrm* is rooted in the danger of religious compromise. It speaks of devotion to Yahweh, usually to destruction. After the initial command to *ḥrm* (7:2bα), there are several prohibitions, beginning with 'do not make a covenant with them' and ending with 'do not take his [the Canaanite inhabitant's] daughter for your son'. The danger is that they would turn aside from following Yahweh and serve other gods, to their destruction (7:4). The counterpart to what they should *not* do comes in verse 5. Every one of the positive commands that serve to explicate the command to *ḥrm* is about religious iconoclasm. That is not to say that the inhabitants of the land are suddenly secure (see e.g. 7:16, 23; cf. 7:2, 'show them no mercy'), but it is to suggest that 'what we have is a retention of the (in all likelihood) traditional language of *ḥērem*, but a shift in the direction of its acquiring significance as a metaphor'.[28] The sparing

---

27. The church should examine itself and its own ethical conduct *before* it seizes on the link between idolatry and inhumanity to indict those outside the church.

28. R. W. L. Moberly, 'Toward an Interpretation of the Shema', in

of Rahab is thus not an act of disobedience but an appropriate response to one who has made the characteristically Israelite confession (Josh. 2:11; cf. Deut. 4:39).

In chapter 12 the Israelites are to destroy the 'places' (*māqôm*, pl.) of idolatry of the land's occupants, blot out the 'name' (*šēm*) of such idols (12:1–3) and instead go to the place (*māqôm*, sg.) where Yahweh will choose to put his 'name' (*šēm*). Deuteronomy is well known for its insistence on worshipping not in multiple locations but in the place Yahweh will choose. This restriction of worship is not predicated on the fact that Yahweh is 'one' but it does seem to be contrasted with the Canaanite idolatry that happens elsewhere. The ultimate focus is not *Kulteinheit* ('unity of worship' at a central sanctuary), but *Kultreinheit* (purity of worship), although unity of worship is Deuteronomy's way of ensuring purity of worship. Even after they have been destroyed, they are not to show any inquisitiveness about the worship of the inhabitants because of the detestable nature of their practices (Deut. 12:31). The command was not the product of xenophobia, rooted in ethnic hatred. In 7:25–26 idolatrous Israel is liable to the same *ḥrm*. Chapter 13 demands an uncompromising response to idolatry within Israel, whether prophet, family member or town. The command to *ḥrm* is now applied to an apostate town (Deut. 13:15). Even the command to execute the stubborn rebellious son may derive from the dangers of idolatry (21:18–21). The Decalogue links honouring father and mother with children's days being long (5:16). In the previous chapter their days being long results from obedience to the statutes and commands (4:40). Presumably this fits with Deuteronomy's insistence that the home was to be a place not just of order, but of passing on the faith (Deut. 6:4–9). For a son to be 'stubborn and rebellious' was not, then, simply about being naughty. Rather, it was about threatening the covenant, fabric and order of society through idolatry.

Footnote 28 (*cont.*)

Christopher R. Seitz and Kathryn Greene-McCreight (eds.), *Theological Exegesis: Essays in Honor of Brevard A. Childs* (Grand Rapids: Eerdmans, 1999), p. 136. There are significant problems with regarding the command exclusively as 'metaphorical', as we shall see below.

Thirdly, they should be a people who *trust implicitly*. Within the sections surrounding the central law code this trust relates particularly to possession of the land. It is first introduced in Deuteronomy 1:32 in the context of Israel's failure to take the land. Although Martin Noth claimed that chapters 1–3 have 'nothing in common with the Deuteronomic law but [are] directly related to the Deuteronomistic history',[29] and thus connect more closely with Joshua than the rest of Deuteronomy, this has been justifiably criticized.[30] Israel's failure to take the land was at its heart a culpable failure of 'trust' despite all that Yahweh had done for them (Deut. 1:32). The result was a return towards Egypt into the desert, an exile. In the opening three chapters Moses sets this unbelief in stark contrast with the success that comes when they take Yahweh at his word, as happened with Sihon and Og. The two choices, of wilful unbelief and obedient trust, ultimately of 'death' and 'life', are ones that endure for the people in the plains of Moab and into the future (cf. Deut. 30:19). As they prepare to cross into the land, they are to trust and not be afraid. The exhortation to the first generation that met with unbelief (1:21, 29) echoes afresh to Joshua as he prepares to lead the people across the Jordan to take possession (3:22; 31:6, 8): 'do not fear/be afraid'. Elsewhere it is Yahweh they are to 'fear', not the inhabitants of the land. There is a right and a wrong object of fear.

Within the central legal section this implicit trust is expressed in obeying laws that are profoundly costly to the one obeying them.[31] It means taking Yahweh at his word and obeying him when common sense and self-interest might suggest otherwise. Male and female slaves join in with the celebration of the sabbath and the various sacrifices in the place Yahweh will choose as the place for his name, with the feasts of weeks and booths specifically mentioned (5:14; 12:12, 18; 16:11, 14). When the slaves are resting on the sabbath or celebrating at the festivals, they are not working

---

29. Noth, *Deuteronomistic History*, p. 29.

30. See Millar, 'Living', pp. 16–32.

31. J. Gordon McConville, *Law and Theology in Deuteronomy*, JSOTSup 33 (Sheffield: JSOT Press, 1984), p. 15.

for their masters. In similar fashion, bringing sacrifices – especially the firstlings – to Yahweh, leaving parts of the field for the poor to glean, setting apart a tithe for the Levites and the marginalized, cancelling debts, all are costly acts of trust (Deut. 12:6; 24:19–22; 14:27–29; 15:1–11). McConville captures the paradox of the laws:

> [A] demand for self-denial and a renunciation of one's rights runs through them. But the result of such self-denial is the continued enjoyment of all the fruits of the land. The principle involved is in fact a paradox. Enjoyment of the land and its benefits depends upon a readiness to relinquish them . . . it is . . . a regular principle that where blessing is promised it is in the context of self-restraint.[32]

Underpinning obedience to all these laws is a trust that Yahweh's promise of blessing will be fulfilled. Brueggemann comments that 'right worship . . . is also an act of hope, a foretaste of the common abundance when there will be more than enough for all'.[33] This hope is not rooted in desire, wish, fantasy or dreaming but in the God of promise. Far from empty rituals, these costly acts are transformative, a means by which learning and growth come (Deut. 14:23). And lest this trust be thought grudging and reluctant, a kind of legalism, Deuteronomy stresses joy in worship and life. Not only was their worship to be characterized by joy when they came before Yahweh (12:7, 12, 18), but their whole life of service was to be characterized by joy. One of the grounds for the curses that will come is 'because you did not serve Yahweh your God *joyfully* and with gladness of heart for the abundance of everything' (Deut. 28:47). Faith and trust in the God who speaks is true in the Old Testament as well as the New.

Finally, they should be a people who *live justly*. As they live out what Moses has commanded them in full view of the nations, these nations will declare, 'Surely this great nation is a wise and discerning people!' (Deut. 4:6). Moses goes on to identify two distinctive characteristics of the 'great nation' they are. The first

---

32. Ibid., p. 17.

33. Brueggemann, *Deuteronomy*, p. 143.

is that they have a god, who is near to them when they pray (4:7). The second is that no other nation has statutes and ordinances as 'just' as the entire *tôrâ* he is setting before them in Moab (4:8). The adjective Moses uses to describe the *tôrâ* is 'just' or 'righteous' (*ṣaddîq*). Significantly, this is the only occasion on which this adjective modifies something impersonal. In Deuteronomy 32:4 Yahweh is *ṣaddîq*. Here Yahweh's *tôrâ* is. What is predicated of Yahweh is predicated of Yahweh's *tôrâ*, and will be predicated of Yahweh's people if they are obedient to *tôrâ* (6:25; cf. 24:13).

This is not partly about justice in a forensic sense. The judges are to judge justly, without showing partiality on the grounds of origin or status (Deut. 1:16; 16:16–18); there needs to be sufficient witnesses (19:15–21) and due thought needs to be given to the circumstances of the 'crime' (22:23–30) and exonerating evidence (22:13–21). But Deuteronomy's justice is more than the forensic justice. It is about the people living in a right relationship with those to whom they are bound in relational tie. Because they are all family members, 'brothers' as Deuteronomy expresses it, their life and laws are to reflect this. It is to shape their *governance*. When Deuteronomy sets out the structure of governance, there are four main roles identified: judge, king, priest and prophet (1:9–18; 16:18 – 18:22). Every single leadership role is defined with reference to the rest of the 'brothers' (1:16; 17:15, 20; 18:2, 7, 15, 18). Although there are distinctive roles and positions of authority, those in authority should recognize they are neither better nor above anyone else in the community. There are differences in how those in authority come to be there, with the judges being appointed democratically and meritocratically (1:9–18), while the priests are such by heredity. But in no case is the leader self-appointed. There is no place for grabbing power or authority and then suppressing opposition. The existence of 'distributed political authority'[34] may

34. McConville, 'Law and Monarchy', p. 76. Cf. Norbert Lohfink, 'Distribution of the Functions of Power: The Laws Concerning Public Offices in Deuteronomy 16:18–18:22', in Duane L. Christensen (ed.), *A Song of Power and the Power of Song* (Winona Lake, Ind.: Eisenbrauns, 1993), pp. 336–352.

well also serve as a check and a balance to ensure that there was 'no monopoly of public authority that could lead to abuses of power'.[35]

It is also to shape every other area. In an important article from the early 1960s Weinfeld outlined the distinctive 'humanism' of Deuteronomy and suggested that its origins lay in the wisdom tradition that produced the book of Proverbs.[36] Vogt has recently argued that Deuteronomy's concern for 'social justice' is more organically connected to Israel's relationship with Yahweh than Weinfeld allowed.[37] Nonetheless, Weinfeld's observations remain valid and are worth rehearsing. He examines Deuteronomy's laws in so far as they either modify those in the Book of the Covenant (Exod. 21 – 23) or are unique, and identifies three main groups.[38]

The first group are laws that 'emphasize the value of human life and dignity'. Examples include the attitude to women captives of war and to runaway slaves (21:10–14; 23:16); the warning against excessive flogging (25:1–3); the need to have appropriate safety measures in roof construction (22:8).

The second group are the laws 'dealing with interpersonal social relations'. Examples Weinfeld gives include the attitude to the poor (15:1–11); not discriminating against a less-favoured wife and her son (21:15–16); the commands to assist the stranger, the orphan and the widow (e.g. 14:29; 24:19–21); respecting the property of others by not putting a sickle to their grain (23:25). To these may be added many others: the newly married husband must stay at home for a year to 'bring joy' to his wife (not, incidentally, 'to be happy with his wife', as NRSV and ESV mistranslate); the male and female slaves should participate fully in the joy of the worshipping life; the slaves who are released are to be sent away with plenty (15:14); the wife of an Israelite who has died has recourse to the

---

35. Clements, 'Book of Deuteronomy', p. 416.

36. Moshe Weinfeld, 'The Origin of the Humanism in Deuteronomy', *JBL* 80 (1961), pp. 241–247.

37. Peter T. Vogt, 'Social Justice and the Vision of Deuteronomy', *JETS* 51 (2008), pp. 35–44.

38. Weinfeld, 'Origin', p. 241.

town gate and, by spitting in the face and removing the sandal of a reluctant brother-in-law, to the pressure of social stigma to enable the line of her husband to continue (25:5–10); handling loans and pledges requires due consideration for the pledge-giver (24:6, 10–13); kidnap is forbidden (24:7); wages should be paid on time (24:14–15).

The final group Weinfeld gives includes those concerned with animal welfare, such as not muzzling an ox when it is treading the grain (25:4) and not taking both mother and fledglings from a nest (22:6–7).

Deuteronomy's vision for Israel is rooted in what Israel *is*: a redeemed, chosen, loved, holy-to-Yahweh and familial people. As such, they *should be* a people that listens carefully, worships exclusively, trusts implicitly and lives justly. But how these laws that were to shape Israel should be interpreted and then appropriated by the Christian community is by no means straightforward. It is to these questions that we now turn.

5. DEAD ENDS IN INTERPRETING DEUTERONOMY'S LAWS

There are at least five dead ends in interpreting Deuteronomy's laws. For the most part I shall look at these from within Deuteronomy's own framework, rather than invoking the New Testament as the arbiter, though some of the points will dialogue with the New Testament. Before a word of protest is uttered about how too few Old Testament scholars give adequate place to the New Testament, it is important to point out that presumably the New Testament writers were not mistaken about the Old Testament. One part of Scripture is not repugnant to another. If it is true in the Old Testament within its own framework, then it remains true. It is 'essential to see the New Testament's insights in light of those of the Old' and not just the other way round.[1] After all, 'the New shows more signs of recognizing the authority of the Old than of reckoning it has authority over it'.[2] If there is a tension perceived with any of these 'dead ends' between Deuteronomy

1. Goldingay, *Israel's Gospel*, p. 21.
2. Ibid., p. 25.

and the New Testament, perhaps it is because the New Testament evidence needs to be revisited and reinterpreted.

Mechanistic

The first dead end is to see Deuteronomy and its laws as essentially *mechanistic*, operating within an inalienable retributive theology where human action determines divine conduct. It is an important observation that Deuteronomy connects obedience with blessing and disobedience with curse (Deut. 28). Further, at points there is a precision to the correspondence, such as with the rare word *ʿēqeb*, 'because': 'And *because* you listen to these rules and keep and do them, the LORD your God will keep with you the covenant and the steadfast love that he swore to your fathers' (7:12 ESV; cf. 8:20).[3] That is hardly surprising since Deuteronomy highlights Yahweh's justice and lack of partiality (32:4; 10:17). Yahweh is not arbitrary. At the same time, though, in the final analysis Deuteronomy does not operate with a mechanistic sense of 'cause' and inevitable 'effect' that could be seen to endorse a modern-day prosperity theology. A number of strands of evidence lead to this conclusion: Israel's election is a result not of human activity, but of Yahweh's love (Deut. 7:7–8);[4] Israel's possession of the land is ultimately not because of their obedience and righteousness but despite their disobedience and rebellion (9:4–7); when Israel does prosper in the land, they are not to think they have achieved this prosperity by their own actions (8:17–18); although Israel's wandering in the wilderness was Yahweh's judgment (ch. 1), there was also an educative dimension of suffering that transcended a retributive framework (8:3), showing that not all suffering is because of what was deserved; finally, there is a striking parallel between what Yahweh did with Balaam (Deut. 23:4–5) and the book of Deuteronomy as a whole.

---

3. JM §170g notes (on this, and similar instances) 'the special nuance of *in recompense for the fact that*' (emphasis original).

4. John G. Gammie, *Holiness in Israel*, OBT (Minneapolis: Fortress, 1989), p. 113.

Balaam had set out to curse Israel on Balak's instruction (Num. 22 – 24). However, Yahweh turned that curse to a blessing. In exactly the same way as with Balaam, Yahweh would turn round the curse of exile and bring about renewed blessing for his people (ch. 30). With Balaam, the reason for the change was Yahweh's love for his people (Deut. 23:5) rather than anything the people had done. The same is ultimately true of Deuteronomy's account of restoration. Although repentance is to be found, ultimately the priority and the initiative are with Yahweh.[5] The move from curse to blessing rests on the grace of God rather than on Israel's deserts. 'In the final analysis the book does not teach a so-called Deuteronomic view of retribution, that is, one that is rigorously anthropocentric, but rather one that is radically theocentric.'[6]

Meritorious

The second dead end is to see that Israel's *tôrâ*-governed relationship with Yahweh is essentially *meritorious*. This is, of course, related to the first dead end, but it warrants a treatment in its own right. Essentially it is to do with whether Israel's obedience is a means of acquiring or gaining merit. At first glance it seems obvious that this cannot be the case. Yahweh's choice of Israel was independent of Israel's numerical strength (Deut. 7:7); Israel's redemption from Egypt was not predicated on any merit on Israel's part, but on Yahweh's love (Deut. 7:8); the gift of land was not because of Israel's 'righteousness' (*ṣĕdāqâ*; 9:4–5). However, in Deuteronomy 6:25 some scholars *do* see a place for obedience as meritorious. The particular phrase occurs at the start of the verse: 'it/there will be righteousness to/for us' (*ûṣĕdāqâ tihyeh llānû*). Tigay translates it as 'It will be therefore to our merit' and explains further, 'that is, "it will be to our credit", implying that one accumulates credit for meritorious deeds'.[7] For Weinfeld there

---

5. See p. 53 above.

6. Gammie, *Holiness*, p. 114.

7. Tigay, *Deuteronomy*, p. 83. Cf. Weinfeld, *Deuteronomy 1–11*, p. 349.

is a sharp disjunction between the meaning of *ṣĕdāqâ* here and in
9:4–5. In 6:25 'the keeping of the law will be to the people's merit
or credit', while in 9:4–5 'the author speaks about unjustified feel-
ings of self-righteousness, not about merit'.[8] The sense of 'merit'
is paralleled in extrabiblical inscriptions and in subsequent Jewish
interpretation, such as the Targums.[9]

The phrase itself is a standard Hebrew way of expressing
someone's possession of something: the mode of expression we
have here, '*ṣĕdāqâ* will be to us' means 'we will *have ṣĕdāqâ*'.[10] This
sense of *ṣĕdāqâ* being possessed as the outcome of obedience is
reinforced by the immediate context, with the verse itself closely
connected to verse 24 by a chiastic ABB′A′ pattern:

A   Yahweh commanded (*ṣwh*) us to do ('*śh*) . . .
B   for our good (*ṭôb*), to keep us alive
B′   it will be righteousness (*ṣĕdāqâ*) for us
A′   if we . . . do ('*śh*) . . . just as Yahweh commanded (*ṣwh*)

There is a close nexus between obedience (A, A′) and the
ensuing blessings (B, B′). 'Righteousness' parallels 'good' and
'alive' (= life).[11] Together *ṣĕdāqâ*, 'good' and 'alive' are *consequences* of
obedience; *ṣĕdāqâ* is more than '*what God requires*, or *doing* what God
requires',[12] though it presupposes that. In questioning whether
'merit' is in view we should not lose sight of the significance of

---

8. Weinfeld, *Deuteronomy 1–11*, p. 406.

9. See Daniel I. Block, 'The Grace of Torah: The Mosaic Prescription for
    Life (Deut. 4:1–8; 6:20–25)', *BSac* 162 (2005), p. 18.

10. Cf. Christopher J. H. Wright, *Deuteronomy*, p. 106.

11. Cf. Georg Braulik, 'The Development of the Doctrine of Justification in
     the Redactional Strata of the Book of Deuteronomy', in Ulrika Lindblad
     (tr.), *The Theology of Deuteronomy: Collected Essays of Georg Braulik, O.S.B.*,
     BIBAL Collected Essays 2 (N. Richland Hills, Tex.: BIBAL, 1994), p. 155.

12. The proposal of Simon Gathercole, 'The Doctrine of Justification in Paul
     and Beyond: Some Proposals', in Bruce L. McCormack (ed.), *Justification
     in Perspective: Historical Developments and Contemporary Challenges* (Grand
     Rapids: Baker Academic, 2006), p. 237 (emphasis original).

obedience. The full enjoyment and blessings of a relationship with Yahweh require obedience. But is 'merit' the consequence of obedience?

These two verses form the end of an answer that Moses instructs a parent to say to a child who asks about the meaning of the laws (6:20, 21–25). The answer the parent gives makes it clear that redemption from slavery *precedes* an obligation to obey (cf. Deut. 5:6); this obedience is not the means of being redeemed from slavery, but a response to that redemption (6:21–23). Whatever may be meant by *ṣĕdāqâ*, it is not about 'earning' or 'meriting' redemption. But might it be about subsequent merit?

Further help in understanding comes from looking at the wider context, where it becomes clear that there is an organic continuity rather than arbitrary connection between action and outcome. Prior to this questioning, Moses instructs the people to 'do what is right (*yāšār*) and good (*ṭôb*) so that it may go well (*yṭb*, an alternative form of *ṭôb*) . . .' (6:18). What is 'right' (*yāšār*) is closely related to 'righteous' (*ṣaddîq*): in the song of Moses, Yahweh is described as 'righteous (*ṣaddîq*) and upright (*yāšār*)' (32:4b). The *ṣdq* root is parallel to and in a sense synonymous with the *yšr* root:

So in Deuteronomy 6:18–25 there is an organic continuity between action and outcome: doing what is 'good' (v. 18) leads to 'good' (v. 24; cf. v. 18); doing what is 'right' (√*yšr*, v. 18) leads to 'righteousness' (v. 25; √*ṣdq*, partially synonymous with √*yšr*); obedience leads to life. Yet none of these outcomes is arbitrarily connected with the action or is simply a consequence, let alone a reward. Obedience is not just the way to life; it is the way of life. In the same way, doing what is 'right' is not just the way to righteousness; it is the way of righteousness. As they perform the 'right' act, they are in right relationship with Yahweh (cf. Deut. 24:13; Gen. 15:6), and they receive the blessing of everything being right (note the parallel of *ṣĕdāqâ* and *bĕrākâ*, 'blessing', in Ps. 24:5). This 'righteousness' is no more meritorious than the 'good' or 'life' that verse 24 holds out for 'doing'.[13] 'Obedience, therefore, like faith, is

---

13. See further Block, 'Grace of Torah', pp. 17–19, and the brief summary in McConville, *Deuteronomy*, p. 145.

the means of *appropriating* God's grace and blessing, not the means of deserving it.'[14]

Malignant

A third dead end is to see the laws that Yahweh gave to Israel as essentially *malignant*, something of a poisoned chalice. A number of different factors coalesce to form a contemporary antipathy towards law more generally and Old Testament law in particular. In Western culture, laws, rules or 'red-tape' are sometimes said to 'cramp my style' and 'inhibit my freedom'. Sometimes lawyers seem to be the only or the biggest winners in situations of conflict. Within church history's attitudes to biblical law, first Marcion and then, more recently, certain strands of tradition owing a debt to Luther discern a strong contrast between the Old and New Testaments: the Old Testament speaks of works, the law and legalism; the New speaks of faith, gospel and grace. A particular reading of the apostle Paul's statements about the law features strongly, privileging the negative comments: 'For by works of the law no human being will be justified in his sight, since through the law comes knowledge of sin. But now the righteousness of God has been manifested *apart from the law* . . .' (Rom. 3:20–21 ESV); 'For sin will have no dominion over you, since you are not under law but under grace' (Rom. 6:14 ESV); 'But now we are released from the law, having died to that which held us captive, so that we serve in the new way of the Spirit and not in the old way of the written code' (Rom. 7:6 ESV); 'Now before faith came, we were held captive under the law, imprisoned until the coming faith would be revealed. So then, the law was our guardian until Christ came, in order that we might be justified by faith' (Gal. 3:23–24 ESV). Finally, 'the letter kills' and the ministry associated with it is a 'ministry of death' (2 Cor. 3:6–7 ESV). When these statements are put together, law goes with sin and death. It

---

14. Christopher J. H. Wright, *Deuteronomy*, pp. 280–281. Cf. Geerhardus Vos, *Biblical Theology: Old and New Testaments* (Grand Rapids: Eerdmans, 1948), p. 143.

is a burden, something that enslaves, something that brings death, not life; it is to do with Adam. Israel could not obey it, would not obey it. The unstated implication is that rather than being a gracious gift to a covenant people, it is something for which Israel should be pitied, a malignant gift.

There *is* a certain justification for a negative view of the law within the Old Testament itself, for, as we have seen, Deuteronomy does spell out a storyline that speaks of rebellion, judgment and exile as a certainty and not just a warning. Further, in Ezekiel 20:25, Ezekiel speaks in characteristically theocentric and shocking fashion as he characterizes the Deuteronomic laws: God gave them, yet they are 'not good' and by them Israel 'would/could not live'; the exile was somehow after all part of Yahweh's sovereign purposes so that they might come to know Yahweh (Ezek. 20:26).[15] Given that 'failure was part of the plan', Eslinger wonders 'whether Yahweh's foreknowledge predestined this outcome or was the ticking time-bomb of miscreant law only implanted in advance to prepare for a distant outcome'.[16] Yet this negative picture is far from the whole story, and if the rest of the narrative is left untold, a defective picture results.

The law was given to an already redeemed people, brought '*out of* the house of slavery' rather than *into* it (Deut. 5:6); the nations will look on in wonder because of Israel's privilege at having the law (Deut. 4:6–8); the words are words of life just as Yahweh himself is their 'life' (Deut. 32:47; cf. 30:20);[17] the parental response

---

15. See Scott W. Hahn and John S. Bergsma, 'What Laws Were 'Not Good?': A Canonical Approach to the Theological Problem of Ezekiel 20:25–26', *JBL* 123 (2004), pp. 201–218. Note in particular the timing of the giving of these laws, between wilderness wandering (Ezek. 20:23–24) and entry to the land (Ezek. 20:28). This is in some ways paralleled in Paul's language in Rom. 5:20 of the purpose (*not* the result, as NRSV has it) of giving the law to 'multiply the trespass' ultimately so that grace may abound.

16. Lyle M. Eslinger, 'Ezekiel 20 and the Metaphor of Historical Teleology: Concepts of Biblical History', *JSOT* 81 (1998), pp. 108–109.

17. Note how words predicated of Yahweh are also predicated of *tôrâ*. See p. 111, n. 96.

to their child's question about the purpose of the laws highlights
the immense privilege and blessing of having the laws: the laws are
for their 'good' so that they may 'live' and experience all the blessings of being rightly related (Deut. 6:24–25);[18] Yahweh is 'faithful'
and 'without injustice', providing for his people (Deut. 32:4,
7–14).

> How and why would God rescue the Israelites from the burdensome
> and death-dealing slavery of Egypt (Exod. 20:2) only to impose on them
> an even heavier burden of the Law, which they were unable to keep and
> which would sentence them to an even more horrible fate – damnation
> under His own wrath?[19]

The idea that the law was a malignant gift is mistaken.

Beyond Deuteronomy the Old Testament insists that Yahweh
is gracious and compassionate (Exod. 34:6); it was Pharaoh who
piled on the burdens, but Yahweh who removed them; the gift
of the law was enthusiastically welcomed by the people (Exod.
19:8; 24:3). This was not a case of heady initial enthusiasm, then
dawning anxiety and crestfallen dismay, for some of the psalms
extol the law's virtue (e.g. Pss 1; 19; 119) and even after the exile,
there is an astonishing hunger to listen and to obey (Neh. 8).

The New Testament picture confirms this. Jesus did not come
to 'abolish' the law but to 'fulfil' it. Controversies about precisely
what it means for Jesus to 'fulfil' the law must take account of
how Jesus continues: 'not one letter, not one stroke of a letter,
will pass from the law until all is accomplished' (Matt. 5:17–18).
There is not necessarily a sharp disjunction between 'law' and
'grace'. Although John 1:17 speaks of 'law' and 'grace and truth',
the grace of *both* is evident in verse 16.[20] For Paul the apparently
negative comments need to be held with his positive statements: in
Galatians 3:21 he writes, 'Is the law then contrary to the promises

---

18. See further Block, 'Grace of Torah'.

19. Ibid., p. 7.

20. D. A. Carson, *The Gospel According to John* (Leicester: Inter-Varsity Press,
    1991), pp. 131–134.

of God? Certainly not!';[21] in Romans 3:31, 'Do we then overthrow the law by this faith? By no means! On the contrary, we uphold the law'; in Romans 7:12, 'the law is holy, and the commandment is holy and righteous and good'. Finally, Paul speaks of *tôrâ* with all the *privileges* of his own people: 'to them belong the adoption, the glory, the covenants, *the giving of the law*, the worship, and the promises. To them belong the patriarchs, and from their race, according to the flesh, is the Christ who is God over all, blessed forever' (Rom. 9:4–5).

Ultimately, the tension between the law's offer of 'life' and the reality of 'curse' finds its resolution in the unfolding narrative of history and the gospel. As Paul puts it, 'the very commandment that promised life *proved to be* death to me' (Rom. 7:10 ESV). More literally, Paul says that 'the commandment that was for life was found for me, this for death'. With Adamic overtones Paul speaks of Israel's experience (not his own) of the law here.[22] And Paul uses the language of *the way things turned out*. It brought death instead of the life that it held out. The rest of Romans 7:1 – 8:11 spells out the gift of the Spirit and how life (what the law held out) is now available and secure in Christ. Whatever the complexities of the various statements on the law and its role within Israel's history, it is a dead end to see it as 'malignant'.

Moribund

A fourth dead end is that Deuteronomy's laws are *moribund*. That is, they are figuratively nearly 'dead', or over. However, Deuteronomy does not conceive of its laws as being temporary or provisional, for a season. Even the other side of exile they come to the penitent, heart-circumcised people with a renewed force

---

21. These quotations are taken from the ESV.

22. See Moo, *Epistle to the Romans*, pp. 438–439; N. T. Wright, 'The Letter to the Romans: Introduction, Commentary and Reflections', in Leander E. Keck (ed.), *New Interpreter's Bible*, vol. 10: *Acts, Introduction to Epistolary Literature, Romans, 1 Corinthians* (Nashville: Abingdon, 2002), pp. 562–564.

(Deut. 30:8). This shows that 'the function of the laws is not just
there to show that Israel cannot keep them. The commandment
has a real intent.'[23] Deuteronomy's storyline does not invalidate
the demand for obedience. The laws are about shaping the life of
the people of God and have a validity and relevance that endure
into Deuteronomy's future. *How* they are valid and relevant is a
matter for debate; *that* they are so is not. That is one reason why
continued reflection on Deuteronomy remains valuable, and why
dismissing the laws as a road map from a different era is not an
option.

Marginal

A fifth dead end is to see Deuteronomy's laws as *marginal*. There
are two different senses to marginal that come into play here. Both
of them are dead ends. Obviously they are not marginal to Israel's
life. The laws cover every area of life and are central for Israel's
seeking to relate rightly in love and loyalty to Yahweh. There is
another sense of marginal, that of being in some sense 'external'
to the Israelite believer, on the periphery rather than in the heart.
Perhaps the laws are statutory demands or obligations from the
outside to which they must conform? But Deuteronomy's vision is
of a 'heart' religion, of internal appropriation and response rather
than legalistic rule-keeping. It is of course true that the statutes and
commandments *are* external, for they are deposited beside the ark
containing the Decalogue (31:26), they are written on whitewashed
stones (Deut. 27) and are to be put on hands, heads, doorposts
and gates (6:8–9). But they are not *only* external. Just prior to this
latter passage stressing external placement Moses has insisted that
the words of the commands shall be 'on your heart' (Deut. 6:5). In
Deuteronomy the 'heart' (*lēb*, *lēbāb*) may speak of the seat of emo-
tions (rarely; e.g. 1:28; 28:45, 65), of understanding and knowledge,
approximating to 'mind' (e.g. 28:28; 30:1), and of moral will and
responsibility (e.g. 4:39; 17:17). To say that the 'words' shall be

---

23. McConville, 'Torah for the Church', p. 43.

'on your heart' is to insist that authentic Deuteronomic religion is internal to Israelite thinking and determination. One of the disadvantages of speaking of the central section of chapters 12–26 as a 'law code' is that it can conceal Deuteronomy's concern for internal attitudes that 'law' with enforceable sanctions strictly cannot touch (e.g. Deut. 15:9). Yet the presence within the Decalogue of an injunction against coveting 'shows that covenant loyalty in Israel went far deeper than external conformity to statute law'.[24] Wright sums this up admirably as he continues:

> Deuteronomy is concerned to inculcate a social ethos in which motives and desires, intentions and attitudes, matter greatly. All the rhetoric, the didactic, hortatory style, the urgent appeals, glowing promises, and dire warnings are directed precisely to the heart and mind, the inner world of will and purpose.[25]

Further, having 'words' on the heart is not the enemy of a profound emotional response but goes hand in hand with it, for they are to *love* the Yahweh who has revealed himself in word and action with all their heart (6:5), the very place where the 'words' are to be.

An emotional conception of 'love' language in Deuteronomy has not gone unchallenged, however. In an influential article Moran argued that language of love (*'hb*) in Deuteronomy is essentially non-affective. His main reasons include that love is commanded, that it is related to 'fear', that loyalty and obedience are the means of expression, and that such 'covenantal' language is evident both in the Old Testament (e.g. 1 Kgs 5:1) and in ancient Near Eastern treaties in a non-affective sense.[26] The covenantal dimension of love in Deuteronomy, a love expressed in obedience, is an important insight. Deuteronomic love entails obedience and action (cf. Lev. 19:18; John 14:15), but is not reducible to

---

24. Christopher J. H. Wright, *Deuteronomy*, p. 85.
25. Ibid.
26. William L. Moran, 'The Ancient Near Eastern Background of the Love of God in Deuteronomy', *CBQ* 25 (1963), pp. 77–87.

this.[27] Yahweh's 'love' for Israel clearly has an emotive content, as is evident from the verb *ḥšq*, 'love' (7:7; cf. 21:11); this suggests that other language of Yahweh's 'love' (*'hb*) should not be evacuated of emotive content and, therefore, nor should Israel's 'love' (*'hb*) for Yahweh.[28] In addition a denial of the affective leaves a gap between obedient action and motivation, where cynicism can flourish.[29] This is a far cry from Deuteronomy. In short, the laws are not marginal to Israel in any sense; in particular, Deuteronomy has a vision of their full-orbed internalization, which leads to a truly 'heartfelt' loving, obedient response.[30]

---

27. See most recently Bill T. Arnold, 'The Love–Fear Antinomy in Deuteronomy 5–11', *VT* 61 (2011), pp. 551–569.

28. See Jacqueline E. Lapsley, 'Feeling Our Way: Love for God in Deuteronomy', *CBQ* 65 (2003), p. 361.

29. See Moberly, 'Toward an Interpretation', p. 134, n. 19.

30. The propositional (words) is profoundly personal in terms of revelation (cf. Christopher J. H. Wright, *Old Testament Ethics for the People of God* [Leicester: Inter-Varsity Press, 2004], p. 464). In turn, it demands a personal (and 'passionate') response.

6. DEUTERONOMY'S LAWS: CHALLENGES FOR THE CHRISTIAN READER

Alongside dead ends in appropriating Deuteronomy's laws there are also significant challenges in doing so. This is not to raise difficulties for the sake of them. Rather, it is a way of exploring further the distinctive character of Deuteronomy. Broadly speaking, the contemporary Christian interpreter faces challenges arising from *diversity* within the Old Testament ethical material itself and from different kinds of *discontinuity* between Deuteronomy and the present.

Diversity within the Old Testament

First, and more briefly, there is diversity both in prescription and in standard in the Old Testament. In terms of prescription there are a number of laws in Deuteronomy that have counterparts elsewhere in the legal material of the Old Testament. Laws on the release of slaves are not just to be found in Deuteronomy 15:12–18; they are also in Exodus and Leviticus (Exod. 21:2–11; Lev. 25:39–46). Although there are many points of continuity between the laws in Exodus and Deuteronomy, for example, there are also some significant points of difference: the initiating agent is the poor person (Deut. 15:12: 'sells himself', or perhaps 'is sold') or the master (Exod. 21:2: 'buys'); the person sold is designated *'āḥ*, 'brother'/'kinsman' (Deut. 15:12) or 'slave' (Exod. 21:2). In Deuteronomy alone women are included equally (as *'āḥ*), there is generous giving on release, and motivation is rooted in the experience of Yahweh's blessing and Israel's slavery. Finally, in Exodus alone the decision of the slave to remain is also shaped by the desire to stay with his wife and his children born while a slave.[1]

In terms of standard, Deuteronomy 16:18–20 urges strict standards of justice on the judges. In particular, they are not to show partiality. Yet in other contexts a certain differentiation is endorsed, whether in permitting aliens and foreigners to eat what has died naturally, in excluding eunuchs, the deformed and the illegitimate from the assembly, or in charging interest to foreigners and not to Israelites (Deut. 14:21; 23:1–2, 19–20).[2] How should this diversity be handled in moral formation and in Christian appropriation?[3] To take the examples of the slave laws in Deuteronomy and Exodus, one point to make is that the law in Exodus is not the final word on the subject. Within the Old Testament itself there may be a development. The reader needs to interpret a text in the light of the wider Old Testament context. However, that does not mean the Exodus text has nothing to say because it has in a sense been superseded. One illustration of this is the importance of the phrase

---

1. For these, see McConville, *Deuteronomy*, pp. 261–264.

2. John Goldingay, *Approaches to Old Testament Interpretation*, 2nd ed. (Leicester: Inter-Varsity Press, 1990), p. 56.

3. For a book-length treatment on diversity, see John Goldingay, *Theological Diversity and the Authority of the Old Testament* (Grand Rapids: Eerdmans, 1987). For a specific focus on the laws on slave remission, see J. Gordon McConville, 'Old Testament Laws and Canonical Intentionality', in Craig G. Bartholomew, Scott W. Hahn, Robin Parry, Christopher R. Seitz and Al Wolters (eds.), *Canon and Biblical Interpretation*, SHS 7 (Grand Rapids: Zondervan, 2006), pp. 259–281; and Chris J. H. Wright's 'Response to Gordon McConville', in Bartholomew et al., *Canon and Biblical Interpretation*, pp. 282–290.

'Hebrew slave' (*'ebed 'ibrî*, Exod. 21:2). The noun *'ebed* (slave) is qualified by the adjective *'ibrî* (Hebrew) in only one other place, Genesis 39:17. The Exodus slave law in canonical context evokes memories of all that happened in the tragic slave-selling incident with Joseph and the distress that came to Potiphar's house as well as to Joseph. In doing so, slavery as an institution is discouraged.[4] An important corollary of this diversity is that we should not think the Old Testament gives a straightforward blueprint of praxis and penalties that should be directly reapplied.

Social/cultural discontinuity

One type of discontinuity is what we may term *social/cultural* discontinuity. Deuteronomy as a book does not work with the dualities, or either–or's, many Western Christians take for granted or accept without thinking. A first duality is *right versus left*.[5] In some ways Deuteronomy seems to be to the 'right' politically. There is no mandate for the government to extend its influence or expand its powers. The family plays a foundational role in society, with responsibility to inculcate the faith and morality right at the heart. Wealth is not a bad thing, but a good thing, something to be enjoyed. Obligatory contributions of the individual, or 'taxation', is limited to the tithe, at 10%; indeed, there is a clear warning against the king accruing too much wealth for himself, presumably by levies on the population (17:17). On the other hand Deuteronomy also seems to be to the 'left'. This is particularly evident in the egalitarian portrait of society. Deuteronomy speaks of 'all Israel': Israel is a unit, a whole.[6] This unity is reflected in the fact that the

---

4. See Victor P. Hamilton, *Exodus: An Exegetical Commentary* (Grand Rapids: Baker Academic, 2011), pp. 372–373.

5. A former student, Steffen Jenkins, highlighted the first two and provided some of the evidence.

6. This concern for 'integers', including 'all Israel', is one of the five distinctively Deuteronomic marks that Gordon J. Wenham, 'Deuteronomic Theology', identifies.

nation is a 'brotherhood': everyone from those in authority to the debtor, the slave or the poor is a 'brother', a family member of equal dignity and worth. The rest of the brotherhood has obligations to them. Presumably it was the role of the civil government to ensure that laws on loans and workers' pay, for example, were carried out (23:19–20; 24:10–15).[7]

A second duality, in some ways related to the first, is *libertarian versus authoritarian*. Deuteronomy is libertarian in the sense that the will of people is strongly endorsed and the individual is significant. The people are deputed to choose leaders for themselves (1:13) and they take the initiative in wanting to spy out the land (1:22). There is a certain suspicion of leadership structures, evident in the minimal powers that kings have and in the distributed power for the different leaders (16:18 – 18:22). Property ownership is expected, since there are houses that may be coveted (5:21). The responsibility for passing on the religious traditions is not the preserve of a professional elite, but that of every member.[8] Although the addressee in the call in 30:19 to 'choose life' is probably the nation as a whole, nonetheless there is the dignity of liberty in being both summoned and free to respond.

Alongside this is a certain authoritarianism. That is, submission to authority is not far from the surface and the claims Deuteronomy makes impinge on every area of life, not only in the apparently 'public' sphere. Children are to honour their father and mother (Deut. 5:16); the penalties for a son's being stubborn and rebellious are severe indeed (21:18–21); home life is further legislated upon with instructions for diet, weekly and annual routine (sabbath; festivals), and for treatment of those working within the home, that they may rest as well. If a family member veers towards idolatry, there are severe sanctions (13:6–11). Respecting and following the decision of the priest and judge who have been consulted is of the utmost importance; the penalty for failing to do so is death (17:1–13). Finally, there is even legislation covering nocturnal emissions and toiletry practice (23:10–14).

---

7. Christopher J. H. Wright, *Old Testament Ethics*, p. 408.

8. Christopher J. H. Wright, *Deuteronomy*, p. 100.

A third duality is *individualism versus collectivism*. In many ways Deuteronomy works with a collective identity. Israel as a whole is addressed as 'you' (e.g. Deut. 6:4–5); the destiny spoken of applies to the nation as a whole, whether blessing or curse, land or exile. Alongside this dominant perspective are places where individuals within the community are clearly differentiated: Caleb and Joshua alone are faithful and survive (1:36, 38); those who were unfaithful at Baal Peor experienced Yahweh's judgment, unlike those who held fast to him (4:3–4); any individual idolater is to be rooted out, whether prophet or family member (Deut. 13); the self-imprecations in 27:12–26 focus on an individual's conduct, often away from the public gaze, and proclaim a curse upon miscreant individuals; some of the covenant curses in chapter 28 deal at the level of the individual, and not just the nation (e.g. 28:30, 38–44); most strikingly, chapter 29 talks about 'a man or woman among you' who is in danger of turning away. The rhetoric moves beyond behaviour against which a law may legislate to the putative thinking of an individual person, 'I will be safe, even though I persist in going my own way' (29:18–19).[9]

A fourth duality is that of *sacred versus secular*. Deuteronomy knows of no split between the sacred and the secular, between the social and the spiritual, between the public marketplace and private sphere of spiritual experience. It is Yahweh who gives the land, so when they prosper in the land they are not to think that what they have is merely the product of their own strength and achievement (8:17–18). Rather, it is Yahweh who has given them the ability. Two of the three major festivals, of 'weeks' and 'booths', where all the people gather before Yahweh, relate to the harvest, which in turn is nothing other than the blessings they have received (16:9–17). Material abundance is Yahweh's blessing for which they should be grateful. In chapter 26 the people are to bring before Yahweh the produce of the land and, as they do so, are to recognize that Yahweh is the God who has rescued them. Governance too is rooted in *tôrâ*, with the king, in particular,

---

9. Cf. J. Gordon McConville, 'Singular Address in the Deuteronomic Law and the Politics of Legal Administration', *JSOT* 97 (2002), p. 28.

subject to and shaped by it (17:14–20). All areas of life belong to Yahweh.

A fifth and final duality, related to this, is *religious versus political*. Given the lack of gap between sacred and secular, it is no surprise that in Deuteronomy the religious is interwoven with the political. Whether the book of Deuteronomy ultimately aligns to one or the other has been a subject of scholarly discussion. In many ways Deuteronomy is a profoundly religious document. The bulk of the book comprises three sermons of Moses. Throughout, the style is very much one of preaching and persuasion. Even the 'central law-code', as it is often called,[10] is more than laws, though there is of course legal material. In particular, the laws are full of motivational clauses that go beyond what to do and sanctions for failing to do so. The code 'attains . . . power not through enforcement but through persuasion and conviction'.[11] Further, there is a great emphasis on teaching and learning, on passing on the faith from generation to generation. In many ways then it is a 'religious' book, designed to form and shape the people of God as a community under his rule.

But Deuteronomy is also profoundly political, indeed 'the OT's supreme political text'.[12] In one sense all literature is political, for it deals with questions of power and morality, and draws the reader into adopting a perspective on such questions. To say Deuteronomy is political is to say more than this, for many scholars see it as a 'constitution'.[13] They are not the first to do

10. E.g. Clements, *Deuteronomy*, p. 23.

11. Olson, *Deuteronomy*, p. 13.

12. McConville, 'Law and Monarchy', p. 69.

13. See Baruch Halpern, *The Constitution of the Monarchy in Israel*, HSM 25 (Chico, Calif.: Scholars Press, 1981), pp. 226–233; and esp. S. Dean McBride, Jr., 'Polity of the Covenant People: The Book of Deuteronomy', *Int* 41 (1987), pp. 229–244. Others have followed McBride to varying degrees, including Frank Crüsemann, *The Torah: Theology and Social History of Old Testament Law*, tr. Allan W. Mahnke (Minneapolis: Fortress, 1996), pp. 234–249; J. Gordon McConville, *God and Earthly Power: An Old Testament Political Theology, Genesis–Kings*, LHBOTS 454 (London: T. & T. Clark, 2006), pp. 74–98.

so, for Josephus speaks of Deuteronomy as *politeia* ('polity' or 'constitution').[14] It is given as the nation of Israel is constituted at Horeb and in Moab. Previously they were not a nation, now they are a nation (cf. Deut. 27:9–10). Deuteronomy ends the Pentateuch, and 'it is presented now as the polity for the community throughout its life in the land'.[15] It is written on whitewashed stones (27:1–8) and deposited by the ark (31:26). The king is to make a copy of it and live by it (17:19–20). There is, in other words, an emphasis on the written nature of *tôrâ*, covenantal law, reflected also in the fact that it is quoted elsewhere in the Old Testament.[16] Its very structure closely resembles ancient Near Eastern treaties between a suzerain, or overlord, and a vassal, or subject.[17] Although in its present form Deuteronomy does not precisely match a treaty structure, nonetheless the similarities are so strong that there is a clear depiction of Yahweh as the suzerain over the vassal, Israel. There is a formality to the relationship. Significant in this regard is the ratification ceremony with the swearing of oaths (26:16–19), along with blessings and curses.[18] Finally, chapters 16:18 – 18:22 outline the power structure, with the separating of powers and all ultimately subject to *tôrâ*. There is

---

14. McBride gives the following references: Josephus, *Ant.* 4.184, 193, 198, 302, 310, 312.

15. Patrick D. Miller, 'Constitution or Instruction? The Purpose of Deuteronomy', in John T. Strong and Steven S. Tuell (eds.), *Constituting the Community: Studies on the Polity of Ancient Israel in Honor of S. Dean McBride Jr.* (Winona Lake, Ind.: Eisenbrauns, 2005), p. 130.

16. McBride, 'Polity of the Covenant People', esp. pp. 231–236.

17. Whether Deuteronomy closely resembles Hittite treaties of the second millennium BC or Neo-Assyrian treaties of the seventh century BC has been hotly debated. For a recent detailed examination, see Markus Zehnder, 'Building on Stone? Deuteronomy and Esarhaddon's Loyalty Oaths (Part 1): Some Preliminary Observations', *BBR* 19 (2009), pp. 341–374; Markus Zehnder, 'Building on Stone? Deuteronomy and Esarhaddon's Loyalty Oaths (Part 2): Some Additional Observations', *BBR* 19 (2009), pp. 511–535.

18. McBride, 'Polity of the Covenant People', p. 234.

no need to choose between the religious and the political. Rather, 'it is precisely in the conjoining of the constitutional and catechetical aspects of the book of Deuteronomy that one may find its distinctive intention'.[19]

These dualities give an indicative illustration of the profound *social/cultural* discontinuity between Deuteronomy and the present that is everywhere apparent. The state envisaged is a theocracy. Laws cover agricultural practice, festival pilgrimages to Jerusalem and diet (22:9–10; 16:1–17; 14:1–29); they cover cities of refuge for manslaughter, exclusions from the assembly and marriage of a woman to her deceased husband's brother in order to perpetuate her husband's line and name (4:41–43; 19:1–13; 23:1–8; 25:5–10); they cover suspected lack of virginity in a wife, making atonement for an unsolved death by the slaughtering of a heifer and leaving parts of the harvest for the alien, the fatherless and the widow (22:13–21; 21:1–9; 24:19–22). There is something profoundly alien, strange and different about the laws that those familiar with them may forget.

Theological discontinuity

Alongside the social/cultural discontinuity is what may be termed *theological* discontinuity. Deuteronomy occupies a significant, but different, place in salvation history. Deuteronomy looks forward to exile, return and renewed obedience. The Christian looks back to the reality of restoration achieved in and through Jesus Christ, a restoration that is in fundamental continuity with Deuteronomy's vision, yet which bursts the banks of Deuteronomy's stated expectation. Deuteronomy does not have a 'messianic' theology, as such. The nearest it gets to this is to speak of a prophetic figure like Moses whom Yahweh will raise up (Deut. 18:15). At one level this is a declaration by Moses of a series of prophets, an ongoing prophetic office that will endure. In that sense the New Testament's speaking of Jesus as the prophet like

---

19. Miller, 'Constitution or Instruction', p. 141.

Moses might seem problematic (Acts 3:22–23; cf. John 6:14).[20]
Yet Deuteronomy *itself* envisages an individual 'Prophet'. In
Deuteronomy 34:10 the narrator looks back at a distance and says
that none has arisen like Moses, despite the fact that there *have*
been series of prophets. This tension is explicable in terms of a
Deuteronomic expectation of a singular prophet.[21] This 'prophet',
though, is not in essence a 'messianic' figure, for there are no royal
connections; yet it is readily apparent why such a figure should
coalesce with subsequent messianic expectations.

The theological discontinuity does not mean that it is impossible to speak of Christ from Deuteronomy. All of the Scriptures
have God's work in Christ, both Christ's person and work, as their
ultimate focus and reference point (cf. Luke 24:25–27), though
this needs to be understood carefully:

> To speak of the Bible being 'all about Christ' does not (or should not)
> mean that we try to find Jesus of Nazareth in every verse by some feat of
> imagination. Rather we mean that the person and work of Jesus become
> the central hermeneutical key by which we, as Christians, articulate the
> overall significance of these texts in both Testaments. Christ provides
> the hermeneutical matrix for our reading of the whole Bible.[22]

Thus, for example, Christ is the paradigm judge who judges
justly, the paradigm king who defies the cultural expectations of
kingship and embodies humble allegiance to *tôrâ*, the paradigm

---

20. Calvin in his commentary struggles with the 'great difficulty' evident in the
    fact that 'Peter applieth that unto the person of Christ which Moses spake
    generally of the prophets', and goes to great lengths to explain how it is
    feasible. See John Calvin, 'Commentary upon the Acts of the Apostles',
    in *Calvin's Commentaries*, vol. 18: *John 12–21; Acts 1–13* (Edinburgh: Calvin
    Translation Society, 1849; repr. Grand Rapids: Eerdmans, 1999),
    p. 154.

21. See Patrick D. Miller, 'Moses, My Servant: A Deuteronomic Portrayal of
    Moses', *Int* 41 (1987), p. 249.

22. Christopher J. H. Wright, *The Mission of God: Unlocking the Bible's Grand
    Narrative* (Nottingham: Inter-Varsity Press, 2006), p. 31.

priest who ministers before God, as well as the prophet par excellence (Deut. 16:18 – 18:22). But there are points of theological discontinuity here too. Christ embodies in himself, in one figure, the distributed leadership powers of Deuteronomy.

Theological discontinuity is also evident in other ways. In Deuteronomy Joshua was 'full of the Spirit of wisdom' (34:9); the Spirit is connected with leadership. In the New Testament the Spirit is poured out on the whole church. Finally, and perhaps most sharply, the church is no longer 'under *tôrâ*' (Rom. 6:14–15). The *tôrâ* is no longer the basis on which Yahweh and his people relate. This is a radical departure from Deuteronomy. For Paul circumcision of the heart is an alternative to circumcision in the flesh, while for Deuteronomy it was in addition.[23]

Ethical discontinuity

Alongside the sense of strangeness that comes from social/cultural discontinuity and the complexities that derive from theological discontinuity there is in many a sense of unease or something stronger at some of the laws. A major challenge in appropriating Deuteronomy is the sense of *ethical* discontinuity. Three areas illustrate this.

First, there is the question of *slavery*. Deuteronomy 15:12–18 envisages a situation where a fellow 'brother' (*'āḥ*), whether male or female, 'is sold' (or, perhaps, 'sells himself/herself') to another Israelite. The picture is of one person owning another member of the community. This 'debt' slavery was very different from the slavery associated with the slave trade of recent centuries. The slaves in Deuteronomy were fully involved with the worshipping life (5:12–15; 12:12; 16:1–17); their period of service was circumscribed to a maximum of seven years, so freedom was the goal (15:12); when they left their service, they were to be sent on their way with an abundance (15:13–14); the possibility that they might want to stay because they 'loved' their master (15:16) generates an

---

23. Lincicum, *Paul*, p. 150.

expectation that they were treated well; finally, if they ran away, they were not to be returned to their master (23:15–16). This is the 'best' slavery in Deuteronomy and in some ways gives a moving picture. After all, how many employees today 'love' their employer? Yet the concept of one person 'owning' another as an accepted norm remains in sharp ethical discontinuity with the present. The picture of perpetual servitude for those subjected to forced labour after capture in battle gives a bleaker picture (20:11), although even here freedom for those who ran away radically compromises the concept of slavery.

A second area is in some of the laws concerning *women*. This should be stated carefully, for Deuteronomy in many ways gives a dignified and emancipated role to women. The mother as well as the father is to be honoured (5:16); the mother is probably included in the teaching role in the home, given the danger of a stubborn rebellious son who obeys neither father *nor mother* (6:4–9; 11:18–21; 21:18–21); a wife can influence her husband's allegiance to Yahweh (13:6), so clearly has a significant role in the home; she plays a full part in the worshipping life, both in resting on the sabbath and in the festivals (5:14; 12:12, 18; 16:11, 14);[24] her happiness is in view in the law allowing a newly married man not to go to war for a year (24:5).

There are two main parts to a sense of ethical discontinuity.

1. There is a certain marginalization of women. The laws are for the most part addressed to men, who are expected to carry them out. In the Decalogue, for example, the prohibition against coveting is addressed to the man, not to covet his neighbour's wife. There is no corresponding commandment to the woman not to covet her neighbour's husband. When there has been inappropriate sexual conduct towards a woman and money is paid by way of recompense, it is paid to the woman's father, not to the woman herself (22:19, 29).

2. There are places where the treatment of women that

---

24. The wife is included within the 'you' in these commands, rather than
    being the sole exclusion (cf. 1 Sam. 1 and the participation of the whole
    family). See Weinfeld, *Deuteronomy 1–11*, pp. 307–308.

Deuteronomy sanctions differs substantially from modern views.[25] The fate meted out to a rapist depends on the status of the woman, whether she is betrothed or not (22:25–29). A young unbetrothed woman who is raped may well end up being married to the man who has raped her (Deut. 22:28–29).[26] In warfare against foreign cities it is permitted to take women as 'plunder' (20:14). After allowing a period of mourning of one month, the women may be taken as wives (21:10–14). The woman's will is not explicitly sought or recognized.

A third area of ethical discontinuity is seen in the conduct of *warfare*, and, in particular, in the *ḥērem* or 'ban'. As with slavery and women, an enormous amount has been written on the subject.[27] The main chapters are Deuteronomy 7 and 20, although there are other significant references (2:34; 3:6; 13:16, 18). The command to Israel is to *ḥrm* the inhabitants of the land and to 'show them no mercy' (7:2).

---

25. There are significant debates around the purposes of the laws, the construction of gender and whether the texts are irredeemable. See e.g. Eckart Otto, 'False Weights in the Scales of Biblical Justice? Different Views of Women from Patriarchal Hierarchy to Religious Equality in the Book of Deuteronomy', in Victor H. Matthews, Bernard M. Levinson and Tikva Frymer-Kensky (eds.), *Gender and Law in the Hebrew Bible and the Ancient Near East*, JSOTSup 262 (Sheffield: Sheffield Academic Press, 1998), pp. 128–146; Carolyn Pressler, *The View of Women Found in the Deuteronomic Family Laws*, BZAW 216 (Berlin: de Gruyter, 1993); Daniel I. Block, 'Marriage and Family in Ancient Israel', in Ken M. Campbell (ed.), *Marriage and Family in the Biblical World* (Downers Grove: InterVarsity Press, 2003), pp. 33–102. Block has a more positive perspective on biblical 'patricentrism' (a term preferred to 'patriarchy').

26. Jonathan R. Ziskind, 'The Treatment of Women in Deuteronomy: Moral Absolutism and Practicality – Part I', *JBQ* 27 (1999), p. 154, says this is a 'must'.

27. For an excellent recent summary of Christian responses, see Christian Hofreiter, 'Did God Command Genocide? Christian Responses Ancient and Modern', in Philip S. Johnston and David G. Firth (eds.), *Interpreting Deuteronomy: Issues and Approaches* (Nottingham: Apollos, 2012), pp. 240–262.

The narrative accounts illustrate what is typically involved with *ḥrm*: 'At that time we captured all his [Sihon's] towns, and in each town we utterly destroyed (*ḥrm*) men, women and children. We left not a single survivor' (2:34). This is what Yahweh subsequently endorses as Israel undertakes the campaign against Og (3:2).[28] There are many ways in which a response may be constructed. Wright helpfully identifies and then rejects three mistaken approaches.

The first is to say that the New Testament puts right an Old Testament problem. But this fails because the Old Testament is full of the love of Yahweh, the New Testament speaks of the wrath of God, and the New Testament accepts, rather than sets aside the Old Testament stories.[29] A second mistaken response is to say that God did not command it, but that the Israelites mistakenly thought he did.[30] But in Deuteronomy 'the nature of Israel's love for YHWH is particularly expressed in the *ḥērem* command';[31] the command is organically connected to the central thrust of the book and can hardly be a peripheral error. Further, throughout the Old Testament the conquest is not a mistake but is the fulfilment of Yahweh's promises.[32] A third mistaken response is to see

---

28. Sometimes animals and plunder were taken for spoil (e.g. Deut. 2:35; 3:7); sometimes they too were subject to *ḥrm* (Josh. 6:21). Note in particular Achan's sin (Josh. 6:17–19; 7:1, 10–25).

29. Christopher J. H. Wright, *The God I Don't Understand: Reflections on Tough Questions of Faith* (Grand Rapids: Zondervan, 2008), pp. 76–81.

30. This seems to me to be the position taken in Kenton L. Sparks, *God's Word in Human Words: An Evangelical Appropriation of Critical Biblical Scholarship* (Grand Rapids: Baker Academic, 2008), p. 297: 'Is it only in Israel's case that divine sanction legitimizes the extermination of pagans? Or is it more likely that the biblical text has simply assumed standard but erroneous Near Eastern ideas about the relationship between ethnicity, religion, and war? Theologically speaking, the latter possibility seems more likely to me than the former. The Israelite massacre of Canaanites is no more compatible with a gospel of love than was European imperialism or the crusades.'

31. Nathan MacDonald, *Deuteronomy and the Meaning of 'Monotheism'*, FAT 2.1 (Tübingen: Mohr Siebeck, 2003), p. 3.

32. Christopher J. H. Wright, *God I Don't Understand*, pp. 82–83.

it as allegorical, a fictional account that illustrates spiritual truths. Certainly, spiritual truths may be drawn from the account, but *'it was not allegorical Israelites who attacked or allegorical Canaanites who died'*.[33]

There are many other points that may have or have been made. Some more than others contribute positively to reflection on Yahweh's command as recorded in Deuteronomy. (1) The term *ḥērem* does not always speak of destruction; it may designate irrevocable giving over to Yahweh; this is apparent from commands not to make covenants and intermarry (7:2–3). Certainly, in other contexts the word may be used of inanimate objects such as fields (Lev. 27:21), but in Deuteronomy's context of war, destruction of people is in view (2:34; 20:16–17). (2) It was Yahweh's punishment of the wickedness of the inhabitants (9:4–5). This is an important point, and Yahweh had been patient (cf. Gen. 15:16), but was *everyone* wicked, including the children? (3) It was not about ethnic cleansing, but religious purity. True, but is destruction of the idolater an acceptable norm today? (4) There were chances for the inhabitants to align themselves with Yahweh, as is clear from Rahab. The others in Jericho had clear knowledge of what Yahweh had done already (Josh. 2:10) and significant opportunity afforded by seven days of Israelite marching round the city, yet they chose not to respond. True, but is forced conversion on pain of death a good thing? (5) The language is hyperbolic, as 'theological preaching'.[34] But this is hard to prove. (6) There was something particular and distinctive about the conquest that serves to limit it to a time and place. It is not a blueprint for subsequent wars that Israel fought.[35] Jesus was not being inconsistent nor overthrowing Old Testament authority when he stopped his disciples in midstream with 'it is enough' when they said they had two swords (Luke 22:38), nor when he stopped the use of swords with 'no more of this' and a touch that healed the slave's ear (Luke 22:49–51). (7) It is a metaphor rooted in the historical memory of warfare (e.g.

---

33. Ibid., p. 84 (emphasis original).
34. So Millar, *Now Choose Life*, p. 156.
35. Christopher J. H. Wright, *God I Don't Understand*, p. 90.

1 Sam. 15), but not mandated as a literal practice.[36] Certainly, there
are hints of this, evident in the contrastive clauses indicating what
they *should* do (7:5) as opposed to what they should not do (7:3–4).
The commands are all to do with religious iconoclasm. Further, a
later historical context for the book of Deuteronomy in its final
form encourages metaphorical implementation (cf. Ezra 9:1).
But other places in Deuteronomy indicate that literal execution is
chiefly in view (e.g. 2:34; 3:2; 20:16–17). (8) Yahweh commanded
it to enable this fulfilment of the promises made to the patriarchs, so the action must be right. This is the 'divine command'
approach to ethics and owes a lot to Calvin.[37] Moral sensitivity at
this point is evidence of failing to share Yahweh's abhorrence of
human wickedness. Again, although this point is important, it is
expressed too starkly. It needs nuancing significantly, as I shall do
below. (9) Yahweh's action is consistent. When he sees recurring
wickedness within his own people when they enter the land, they
face the same *ḥrm* that the Canaanites faced (7:26; 13:12–18).[38]
(10) In similar vein Yahweh's action through Israel is in principle
no different (albeit without the same explicit divine mandate)
from that of other nations taking possession of the land of others
(e.g. Deut. 2:10–12, 18–23) or using the Assyrians, Babylonians
or Persians for his purposes (Habakkuk; Isa. 45:1). (11) It is not
a case of arrested ethics but of anticipated eschatology. This is
an extension of the point that speaks of the destruction of the
Canaanites as Yahweh's punishment, but it draws on the future,
not the past. One day God will vindicate his people. On that day
there will be judgment for those who have not willingly submitted
to God in Christ. This is an important perspective, but here again

36. Cf. Moberly, 'Election'; Douglas S. Earl, *Reading Joshua as Christian
    Scripture*, JTISup 2 (Winona Lake, Ind.: Eisenbrauns, 2010).
37. For a helpful brief summary, see J. Gordon McConville and Stephen
    Williams, *Joshua*, Two Horizons Old Testament Commentary (Grand
    Rapids: Eerdmans, 2010), pp. 116–120.
38. In addition to *ḥrm* being threatened for Israel, the same verbs of
    destruction that indicate the fate of the nations are also threatened
    for Israel (*'bd*, 7:10, 24; *šmd*, 7:4, 23–24).

there needs to be caution. Justice *will* be done and will be seen to be done, but the Judge is none other than the Lamb who was slain, and that must shape the eschatological picture.[39] (12) Israel as a people were Yahweh's instrument for fulfilling his purpose of rec-reation and restoration. Blessing for the nations was a part of this. There was a significant danger that the redemptive plan would be shipwrecked by Israel's indulging in Canaanite idolatry (7:4, 16; 12:29–31; 20:18). A potentially catastrophic impact on Yahweh's rescue plan demanded a drastic, uncompromising response that would never be acceptable in another context.

Many of the observations above fit with each other, so they should not be treated in isolation and 'refuted'. But when all these have been said, there still remains (at least for this reader) a sense of moral puzzle, struggle and repulsion. I shall return again below to this area. For the moment, though, I want to highlight the ethical discontinuity such a command highlights.

Reflections

Faced with such discontinuities, whether social and cultural, theological or ethical, perhaps Deuteronomy's laws and vision for Israel should be left to one side. Even if Deuteronomy expects that its laws endure the other side of exile and are not moribund (Deut. 30:8), maybe that expectation should be overriden. Perhaps no enduring authority should be granted to them. That, at any rate, was the view of Marcion in the second century AD, and of Harnack in his book on Marcion:

> To discard the Old Testament in the C2nd was a mistake which the Church rightly rejected; to have maintained it in the C16th was a fate which the Reformation was not yet able to escape; but still to preserve it as a canonical document in Protestantism after the C19th is the consequence of religious and ecclesiastical paralysis.[40]

---

39. McConville and Williams, *Joshua*, pp. 123–124.
40. Adolf von Harnack, *Marcion: Das Evangelium vom fremden Gott: Eine*

More recently, Rodd has argued that the Old Testament should
not be seen as an 'external authority'.[41] But such views are problematic. The Christian reader of the Old Testament draws his or
her attitude to the Old Testament from the one in whom they have
put their trust, Jesus Christ.[42] And Jesus treated the Old Testament
as God's word. He submitted to it, whether as a baby being circumcised and dedicated (Luke 2:21, 23), or as an adult, studying
it, praying in the temple and celebrating the Passover. He defined
his mission and identity by it (e.g. Dan. 7; Isa. 53; 61:1–3; cf. Luke
4:18–21). He used it for himself, in his temptations (quoting from
Deuteronomy on each occasion) and on the cross. He regarded
it as authoritative in debate (Matt. 22:37–40) and, most strikingly
of all, he regarded it as inspired. In John 5:37–39 it is the Father's
testimony about him. In Matthew 19:4–5, in a debate on divorce,
Jesus talks of the 'one who made them male and female and said
. . .'. The subject of the two verbs is the same: the God who 'made'
is also the God who 'said'. But in Genesis the words Jesus insists
God 'said' are in fact spoken not by God but by the narrator (Gen.
2:24). The implication is clear. For Jesus what the narrator said
in Genesis God in fact said. God's words are not limited to the
words on his lips.

In similar vein Paul insists on the inspiration and authority
of the Old Testament. In 2 Timothy 3:15–17 he declares that
'all Scripture is God-breathed' and goes on to maintain that it is

---

Footnote 40 (*cont.*)

> *Monographie zur Geschichte der Grundlegung der katholischen Kirche*, 2nd ed.,
> TUGAL 3.15 (Leipzig: J. C. Hinrichs, 1924), p. 217 (my tr.).

41. Cyril S. Rodd, *Glimpses of a Strange Land: Studies in Old Testament Ethics*
    (Edinburgh: T. & T. Clark, 2001), p. 327. The only 'assistance' in
    constructing a moral vision that it can still offer consists in 'opening our
    eyes to completely different assumptions and presuppositions, motives
    and aims' (p. 329). Part of this is because in his view Israel's concerns
    are very different from modern ones.

42. For Jesus' attitude, see John W. Wenham, *Christ and the Bible* (London:
    Tyndale, 1972), pp. 11–37. Many of the following points derive from
    there.

'useful for teaching, rebuking, correcting and training in right-eousness'. Paul's Scriptures, of which Deuteronomy was a part, have an ongoing validity. 'This statement not only affirms the reliability of the Old Testament as divinely breathed Scripture, but especially that it is ethically relevant and through its application God creates a transformed people.'[43] It is theoretically possible from the language of 'useful' that the Old Testament is illustrative, rather than authoritative. But elsewhere Paul himself recognizes the authority of Deuteronomy for his ethics. The laws are 'in some sense, commands reflecting the will of God', not 'suggestions under the loose guidance of the Spirit'.[44] In Romans 13 he quotes part of the Decalogue, following the order found in the LXX of Deuteronomy. The way he does so demonstrates 'Deuteronomy's Decalogue . . . expresses for Paul the basic moral commandments in a manner that is still *unproblematically valid*.'[45] That authority is also recognized in Paul's command to purge the evil from their midst (1 Cor. 5, esp. v. 13; cf. Deut. 23; 17:7), the command not to muzzle the ox (1 Cor. 9:9; cf. Deut. 25:4), the insistence on the testimony of two or three witness (2 Cor. 13:1; cf. Deut. 19:15) and the claim that vengeance belongs properly to the Lord (Rom. 12:19; cf. Deut. 32:35 LXX). Paul's letter Galatians, which empha-sizes most strongly that the Christian is no longer 'under law' (cf. Gal. 3:23; 4:5, 21; 5:18; also Rom. 6:14–15), ends by insisting that the Christian led by the Spirit should behave in ways that the law looked to regulate. It is not the law's 'content', but its 'incapacity' that is the problem.[46] Calvin is right to emphasize the so-called 'third use' of the (moral) law as a guide for Christian living: 'The third and principal use, which pertains more closely to the proper purpose of the law, finds its place among believers in whose hearts

---

43. Daniel I. Block, 'Preaching Old Testament Law to New Testament Christians', *Hiphil* 3 <http://www.see-j.net/hiphil> (2006), accessed 2 Aug. 2012.

44. Lincicum, *Paul*, p. 7.

45. Ibid., p. 127 (my emphasis).

46. Christopher R. Seitz, *Word Without End: The Old Testament as Abiding Theological Witness* (Grand Rapids: Eerdmans, 1998), p. 326.

the Spirit of God already lives and reigns.' Although Christians already have the law written on their heart by the action of the Spirit so 'they long to obey God', yet the law is still of 'profit' to the believer in two ways. First, it brings 'understanding': 'Here is the best instrument for them to learn more thoroughly each day the nature of the Lord's will to which they aspire, and to confirm them in the understanding of it.' Secondly, it brings 'exhortation' so that 'the servant of God' will, 'by frequent meditation upon it . . . be aroused to obedience, be strengthened in it, and be drawn back from the slippery path of transgression'.[47]

Further, the negative conclusions drawn from discontinuities are too often overblown. From a theological point of view, I take it that the Scriptures are flawless, precisely as God wanted them to be. Their inspiration entails this. Their strangeness and difference is not a 'problem' to be 'overcome' but the means by which God reveals himself. God's revelation of himself is always enculturated, always in a context, never acultural or acontextual. That the laws are rooted in a place and time is just as much true of the New Testament as it is of the Old Testament. The prophets' vision of the future, for example, is always couched in the language and thought forms of their own day. The same is true of Jesus' words. That means interpretation is always necessary. The task of appropriating the message of Scripture requires a constant (re)hearing of the unchanging words in Scripture in ever-changing contexts.

From another angle, some of the strangeness of Deuteronomy, as seen in the discontinuities, is valuable precisely as a word from the outside that can cause a questioning of contemporary paradigms or frameworks of thinking, whatever they might be. The very process of (re)hearing and discerning how the authority of the text functions in a particular context is precious, provided that it is carried out without a hermeneutical arrogance that assumes right lies only with the interpreter and not with the text. That is, Deuteronomy

---

47. *Institutes* 2.7.12. His other two uses are to reveal God's righteousness (*Institutes* 2.7.6) and to restrain sin (*Institutes* 2.7.10). For cogent and more detailed reflections on the Old Testament's enduring authority, see Christopher J. H. Wright, *Old Testament Ethics*, pp. 454–470.

is not a text that can simply be picked up and followed as if it were addressed to the contemporary context. The discontinuities invalidate that approach. But nor is Deuteronomy simply a text that furnishes illustrations of what the New Testament (or the modern context) has already decided. To pick up the language and imagery of Fishbane, Deuteronomy is the *traditum*, the given, the 'continuity'; it stands over and against every untethered interpretation; but *traditio* is essential, *traditio* that is about reappropriation in new contexts, 'a matter of "challenge and innovation" – a challenge to each generation to confront its religious situation and mundane needs, to reform its values and heritage, and to renovate its ideas and history'.[48] To give a more concrete example, Deuteronomy's place *beyond* the simple binary of left versus right or libertarian versus authoritarian provides the means whereby fresh light may be shed on sterile or weary contemporary discussions.

Finally, the discontinuities are not necessarily always as sharp as the analysis above might suggest. If we look, for example, at the dualities of sacred versus secular and religious versus political, there is a common suspicion in the West, both inside and outside the church, of any attempt to connect God with politics. Religion and politics do not mix.[49] On this reading Israel was religious, so there is a sharp discontinuity between Israel and the modern Western secular democracies (and governments more generally). Israel was political, so there is a sharp discontinuity between Israel and the church, especially if the church is not established. By way of response, there *are* discontinuities – the line from Israel in Deuteronomy to the church or to the secular nation state is not a straight one, such that laws or commands can simply be reimposed – but they require nuancing.

On the one hand the church is *political*. The word that designates a church in the New Testament, *ekklēsia*, has political connotations. It is the word used in the LXX of Deuteronomy for Israel as they

---

48. Fishbane, *Biblical Interpretation*, p. 428.

49. In some ways Islam's holding them together and the 'God-talk' on both sides of the Atlantic in connection with the war in Iraq have fuelled this sentiment.

are gathered around Horeb. That day at Horeb was the 'day of the *ekklēsia*' (Deut 9:10; 10:4; 18:16), and those who gathered were in the 'congregation' ('church'?, *ekklēsia*; Acts 7:38). According to Hebrews 12, every Christian is now gathered around a mountain to hear the voice of God. The danger is that they will refuse him who speaks (Heb. 12:25). There is then a direct *continuity* between Israel at Horeb (Sinai) and the church, although the mountain now has Christological focus as Mount Zion. Further, the language of *ekklēsia* has a broader domain than the ecclesiastical. In Acts 19 Luke uses the word to describe the political assembly of the citizens, the formal council, and the mob who have gathered and shout, 'Great is Artemis of the Ephesians!' (Acts 19:32, 39–40). In other words language of 'church' can beguile us into having a religious conception as opposed to a political one. In the New Testament the *ekklēsia* found in Galatia or Corinth (Gal. 1:2; 1 Cor. 1:2) corresponds in some senses with both (the political) Israel at Horeb and the political gatherings that were part of ordinary 'secular' life.

This political nature of the church is also apparent in other ways. Just as there were twelve tribes in Israel, Jesus chose twelve apostles, reconstituting the nation. Jesus spoke of a 'kingdom' and of himself as Son of Man' (Dan. 7), profoundly political language. All of his actions, culminating in his death, were 'political', involving as they did Israel's national renewal.[50] Paul berates the Corinthian church for going to court 'before the unrighteous' rather than 'before the saints' (1 Cor. 6:1–3). This was a serious mistake in part because 'the saints will judge the world' and angels too, so are thoroughly qualified to judge ordinary matters. These notions of a reconstituted community of twelve tribes, of a kingdom and of sitting on thrones judging, all coalesce in Luke 22:28–30: 'You are those who have stood by me in my trials; and I confer on you, just as my Father has conferred on me, a kingdom, so that you may eat and drink at my table in my kingdom, and you will sit on thrones judging the twelve tribes of Israel.' Finally, in Philippians 3, Paul declares to the church in Philippi that 'our citizenship is in heaven'

---

50. See further e.g. N. T. Wright, *New Testament; Jesus*.

(Phil. 3:20). Philippi was a Roman colony and justifiably proud of its status. A Roman colony was an extension of Rome, established to avoid overcrowding in the capital and to expand Roman influence.[51] To be a Roman citizen in a colony like Philippi was not to expect to live in Rome, but it was to have a new political status. When Paul says the citizenship of the Philippian Christians is in heaven, he is not making the point that the Philippian Christians will one day end up in heaven, or that heaven is their true 'home'. Paul goes on to say 'it is from there [heaven] that we are expecting a Saviour, the Lord Jesus Christ'. The movement is from heaven to earth, not from earth to heaven. What Jesus does when he comes is to 'transform' our bodies so that they are like his by the same power that he exercises in his rule as the true human (Phil. 3:21; cf. Ps. 8:6; 1 Cor. 15:27; Eph. 1:22; Heb. 2:8). The titles Paul uses, of Saviour, Lord and King (Christ), are all 'imperial'.[52] He brings true transformation, exercises a global rule as the true human and brings true peace (Phil. 4:7), unlike the *pax romana*. In other words the Christian's identity is found in relation not to Rome but to Jesus Christ in heaven; the Christian's allegiance is ultimately not to Caesar, but to Jesus Christ; the Christian's hope is not of a *pax romana* and Roman rule, but of God's peace and of Jesus Christ's rule. The church is not a social or country club; it is a new humanity, a new society. This is all avowedly *political*.

On the other hand the state is not *areligious*. With Jesus' announcement of the kingdom of God there are no longer two kingdoms but one. The enduring duality of Israel in Babylon, under Yahweh's and Babylon's rule, was over:

> Jesus . . . unsettled the Two Kingdoms conception, which had, in one way or another, shaped Israel's understanding of its political position since the exile. He announced the coming of God's Kingdom to sweep away existing orders of government. Those orders were of a passing age . . .[53]

---

51. Tom Wright, *Surprised by Hope*, p. 111.

52. Ibid., p. 112.

53. Oliver O'Donovan, *The Desire of the Nations: Rediscovering the Roots of Political Theology* (Cambridge: Cambridge University Press, 1996), p. 137.

Jesus has been declared both Lord and Christ by the resurrection (Rom. 1:1–4). As God's Son and anointed king, every nation and state are to come before Jesus the king and bow before him (Ps. 2). Not only is government instituted by God (Rom. 13:1–7; 1 Pet. 2:13–14), but everything any government is and does is ultimately answerable to Jesus Christ.

In short, notwithstanding the dead ends and the challenges that certain discontinuities brought about, the church and the individual Christian need to appropriate Deuteronomy's laws. But how? It is to this that we now turn, first to some principles, and then to a worked example.

7. DEUTERONOMY'S LAWS FOR THE CHRISTIAN

Principles for appropriating Deuteronomy's laws

An extraordinary amount has been written on how the Old Testament laws relate to the Christian, both through church history and in contemporary scholarship.[1] One traditional way of doing so is to separate the laws into different categories, and maintain that while some categories endure in their ethical authority, others do not. The most famous is the threefold distinction of moral, civil and ceremonial law. Moral laws are said to be timeless and universal, civil laws govern Israel's life as a nation state, so do not endure in their authority, and ceremonial laws have been fulfilled in Christ, so illuminate his work but do not have enduring authority for the Christian. This classification is sometimes criticized as being an alien imposition on the text rather than something that arises organically from it. Certainly, taking Israel's

---

1. Note the helpful summary in Christopher J. H. Wright, *Old Testament Ethics*, pp. 387–440.

laws on their own terms, this classification is both 'too sharp' and
'too blunt'.[2] It is 'too blunt' because Israel's laws are more diverse,
including both social and family legislation. It is 'too sharp'
because many of the laws do not fit neatly into one of the three
classifications. The sabbath commandment is ceremonial, to do
with Israel's worshipping life, yet it has moral, social and familial
dimensions (Deut. 5:12–15). Laws on slavery are civil, to do with
the organization of society, yet are concerned with a slave's well-
being and are rooted in Israel's experience of slavery and Yahweh's
action. The Ten Commandments are by no means straightforwardly all enduring moral laws (esp. commandments 1–4).
Nonetheless, there is value in classifying the constituent elements
from an external perspective different from Israel's own, rather
like recognizing literary genres.[3] Further, it is a laudable Christian
attempt to make sense of what has happened with the arrival of
Jesus and a recognition that, as we shall see below, the demand of
different laws for the Christian *does* vary. My main concern with
the threefold classification is not that it is an alien imposition, but
that it fails to deal with the organic interconnections between the
laws and in practice leads to the marginalization of some of the
laws.

There are three principles that are for me most helpful and
determinative.

Humbly and thoughtfully heed the demand of each law

In a perceptive analysis of what it means to ask of the laws,
'Do they apply to us?', O'Donovan notes the ambiguity of that
question:

> It may be a question about *authority*, or it may be a question about
> prescriptive *claim*. A prescription . . . instructs somebody to do, or not
> to do, something. We may ask in each case who is instructed and who
> instructs. If, as I walk down the street, somebody in a blue coat says,

---

2. Goldingay, *Approaches*, pp. 64–65.

3. Cf. Oliver O'Donovan, 'Towards an Interpretation of Biblical Ethics',
   TynB 27 (1976), p. 60.

'Stop!', I shall have to ask, first, 'Is he speaking to me?' – the question of claim – and, then, 'Is he a policeman?' – the question of authority. And so it is with the commands of the Old Testament: we must ask, 'Do they purport to include people like us in their scope?' – the question of claim – and, 'If so, ought we to heed them?' – the question of authority.[4]

The distinction between authority and claim is important. A thief may say 'stop' to me and thus have a 'claim' in the sense that they are speaking to me, but they are doing so without authority. O'Donovan observes that whereas early in church history the focus was on the question of claim, more recent (at his time of writing) attention was restricted to questions of authority; claim had receded. I have argued above that, by virtue of inspiration, authority *does* reside in the one making the claims in the text and in the text itself. But we need to think further about the question of claim. Some further distinctions are important.

First, there is a distinction between addressee, audience and intended audience that bears on the question of 'claim'.[5] The question 'Is he speaking to me?' does not have a simple 'yes' or 'no' answer.[6] Presumably in this example there is a primary *addressee* (a thief?). But there may well be others, a wider *audience*, who will hear what the police officer is saying. Within that wider audience there could be at least one *intended audience*, people whom the police officer desires should heed in some way what he is saying. While the thief should heed the officer's authority and claim and stop, others walking along the pavement should also heed the officer's authority in an appropriate way, whether by getting out of the way or by assisting.

Although the words within Deuteronomy's laws were addressed

---

4. Ibid., pp. 58–59 (my emphases).

5. See further Nicholas Wolterstorff, *Divine Discourse: Philosophical Reflections on the Claim That God Speaks* (Cambridge: Cambridge University Press, 1995), pp. 54–57.

6. As indeed is hinted at in O'Donovan's broadening out, without explanation, of the question 'Is he speaking to me?' to 'Do they purport to include people like us in their scope?'

to a particular group of Israelites at a point in time, Deuteronomy envisages future generations of Israelites as an intended audience (cf. Deut. 29:14–15). Deuteronomy also envisages, as we shall see, the nations round about as another intended audience (Deut. 4:6–8). Theologically, there is a strong case for saying that the church, made up of both Jewish and Gentile believers, is also in one sense an *intended audience* of Deuteronomy. From one point of view this is because God had them in mind as hearers from the very beginning. From another point of view they stand in a certain continuity with those envisaged as the (future) *intended audience*. Note that the church is not the *addressee*. This is evident from the discontinuities and particularities discussed above. But it still is an intended audience.[7] And the authority of the one speaking, albeit to a different addressee, still needs to be heeded. There remains in some sense a 'claim'.

A second distinction is that a person may intentionally say different things to different people with the *same* words. What the police officer is saying to the addressee and the intended audience(s) by the same words may in fact be different.[8] While the

---

7. In the New Testament there are a number of places where the Old Testament is said to speak directly to the present church situation (e.g. 1 Cor. 9:9–10; 10:11; Heb. 3:7; 1 Pet. 1:12). Lincicum (*Paul*, p. 133) speaks of the instance in 1 Cor. 9 as 'a sort of eschatologically-determined halakhic reasoning, that is, the formulation of ethical decisions based on the conviction that the text must address the present age and should be interpreted to do so'. Some interpret the example in 1 Cor. 9 as evidence of complete lack of concern for 'oxen' and for the original context, and translate with 'entirely' (e.g. ESV, NRSV). NIV prefers 'surely', reflecting God's greater concern for humans than for oxen. This is possible lexically and preferable given v. 11, where there is another comparison between lesser and greater. See Brian S. Rosner, 'Deuteronomy in 1 and 2 Corinthians', in Steve Moyise and Maarten J. J. Menken (eds.), *Deuteronomy in the New Testament: The New Testament and the Scriptures of Israel*, LNTS 358 (London: T. & T. Clark International, 2007), pp. 129–130.

8. This illustrates the difference between *locutionary* acts, 'acts of uttering or inscribing words', and *illocutionary* acts, 'acts performed *by way of*

thief should heed the officer's authority and claim and stop, others walking along the pavement should heed the officer's authority in a different way. The *demand* that the officer is making may be different.

To think what the demand might be we need to bring in a third distinction, between 'direct' and 'indirect' speech acts. An indirect speech act is one where there is 'an indirect relationship' between the 'structure' of the speech act and its 'function'.[9] If my wife says to me, 'The bin is full,' it may be a 'direct' or 'indirect' speech act. It is a 'direct' speech act if she is making the statement 'I hereby tell you there is no space in the bin.' The structure of the utterance matches the function. It is an 'indirect' speech act if she is making the request 'I hereby request of you that you take it outside and empty it.' Though the structure is that of a statement, the function is to make a request.

In the case of the police officer saying, 'Stop,' it is a command to the *addressee* to 'stop'. It has authority (a police officer says it); it has claim on the thief; the demand comes from the fact it is a direct speech act. The thief is to stop. For certain passers-by the word comes with authority (a police officer says it). It has a claim, in so far as the passers-by are within the intended audience. The demand may be different from that which comes to the addressee, though it should be recognizable and defensible. As an indirect speech act, with a particular intended audience in mind, 'stop' could mean anything from 'I hereby request that you get out of the way' to 'I hereby request that you assist me in apprehending the thief' to 'I hereby request that you stop.' The latter is a possible, but not the only, demand. An act of imagination, of interpretation, is required on the part of the hearer or reader to discern the *demand.*

When it comes to appropriating Deuteronomy, the commands come with authority (it is God who says them); they have a claim on the church, not as addressee but as intended audience. Given

locutionary acts, acts such as asking, asserting, commanding, promising, and so forth'. See Wolterstorff, *Divine Discourse*, p. 13 (emphasis original).

9. George Yule, *Pragmatics* (Oxford: Oxford University Press, 1996), p. 55.

that there are strong lines of continuity between addressee and intended audience, as the people of God, the demand is likely to be similar. An interpreter's attitude and approach are critical. The attitude should be one of humility, and thoughtfulness should characterize the approach.

In my judgment the most cogent way of discerning the 'demand' has been articulated by Chris Wright in his paradigmatic approach to using Old Testament law. For Wright

> a paradigm is a model or pattern that enables you to explain or critique many different and varying situations by means of some single concept or set of governing principles. To use a paradigm you work by analogy from a specific known reality (the paradigm) to a wider or different context in which there are problems to be solved or answers to be found, or choices to be made.[10]

The Old Testament Scriptures 'render to us a paradigm, in one single culture and slice of history, of the kinds of social values God looks for in human life generally'.[11] In other words there is respect for the particularity, while recognizing a universal relevance.

Warrant for this way of reading Deuteronomy, in particular, comes from two quarters.

First, from biblical theology, we have seen how Israel in Deuteronomy is the vehicle by which Yahweh's purposes for creation as a whole are continued. Israel in the Promised Land mirrors Adam in Eden. Thus Israel embodies in space and time what it means to live in relationship with the creator God. This is not narrowly parochial, but reflects Yahweh's wider purpose for humanity.

The second source of warrant is that of exegesis of Deuteronomy 4:5–8. In Deuteronomy 4 Moses turns from rehearsal of history (chs. 1–3) to exhortation (cf. 'and now' in v. 1). Moses' words in this chapter are framed by two sections that have prominent interconnections (4:1–8, 32–40). Both have as their theme the

---

10. Christopher J. H. Wright, *Old Testament Ethics*, pp. 63–64.
11. Ibid., p. 65.

first commandment, 'no other gods', rooted in the uniqueness of Israel's historical experience of Yahweh ('I am Yahweh your God, who brought you out of Egypt') and the particularity of the law given to them (cf. Deut. 5:6–7). Both sections are marked by rhetorical questions and universalism of outlook (Deut. 4:7–8, 32–34). Finally, both speak of what is 'great' (*gādôl*) and of their eyes seeing (Deut. 4:3, 34).[12] The central section (4:9–31) deals with the polar opposite of having Yahweh alone (cf. 5:8–10): the repeated 'be careful' (vv. 9, 15, 23) shapes the warnings against idolatry.

The opening eight verses split neatly in two (vv. 1–4, 5–8). Both units, as with the other parts of the chapter, start with a call to obey, and then give a historical reference.[13] Both also have motivations for obedience. In verses 1–4 the motivation is that they might enjoy life in the Promised Land (4:1). In verses 5–8, although language of purpose is not explicitly used, the motivation is that the nations may look on and declare, 'Surely this great nation is a wise and understanding people' (4:6). The verdict the nations have arises from Israel's obedience: 'you shall observe and do them [i.e. what Moses has taught at Yahweh's command (v. 5)], for *this* [i.e. *their obedience*] is your wisdom and understanding in the sight of the nations, who will hear all these statutes and say, "this great nation is a wise and understanding people"' (v. 6).

What is so significant is the language the nations use to describe the people. They *are* a great nation, but they are great in a way somewhat different from the military might of other nations: they are a 'wise and understanding' people (cf. the judges in 1:13). In the ancient world, wisdom was something international, something universal. It was not restricted to Israel, but reflected a common quest rooted in creation and observations drawn from it. Job was not an Israelite, nor were his three friends. Eliphaz, for example, was from Teman in Edom, a country renowned for its wisdom (Jer. 49:7; Obad. 8). Within this wisdom quest, moral and

12. See A. D. H. Mayes, 'Deuteronomy 4 and the Literary Criticism of Deuteronomy', *JBL* 100 (1981), p. 26.

13. Ibid., p. 25.

natural law corresponded at a deep level. Across the ancient Near East and in Israel the themes of creation and conduct, whether human (wise living) or divine (theodicy) dominated. In Job 28 the question comes twice over, 'Where can wisdom be found?' (Job 28:12, 20). Deuteronomy answers in a way that particularizes and narrows: wisdom is not in the common, not in the general, not in the universally available, but in the particular, in the covenantal, in the revealed words of Yahweh. Wisdom is obedience to *tôrâ*.

But there is another side to this particularizing. These very specific laws, these particular, at-one-point-in-time, covenantal, revealed words have a universal grammar that anyone from any nation will recognize and affirm as something good. There is something universal and recognizable about the nature of the laws and of the society created by such laws that any nation looking in will say, 'This is wise, this is understanding.' As Chris Wright highlights, 'Old Testament law explicitly invites, even welcomes, public inspection and comparison.'[14] In other words *tôrâ* may be particular to Israel, but its values are universal. Obedience to *tôrâ* is wisdom.[15] In other words Deuteronomy's *tôrâ* transcends nationalistic boundaries, and connects with creation and the nations. This is of course not surprising, for Israel is the vehicle by which Yahweh's re-creative purposes are carried forward. Here, then, redemption and the shape of life of the redeemed people is in a profound sense in continuity with creation. This all means that Deuteronomy can speak to those outside the covenant community. It also means that Deuteronomy is not locked to a particular point and place in time. Naturally Yahweh's word and values are embodied and enculturated in Israel, as they always are. But they are not imprisoned there.

What this looks like in practice is spelled out in more detail as Wright indicates four 'ethical steps towards the contemporary context':[16]

---

14. Christopher J. H. Wright, *Deuteronomy*, p. 48.

15. Cf. Sirach 24.23, where God's word that created the world is embodied in *tôrâ*.

16. Christopher J. H. Wright, *Old Testament Ethics*, pp. 321–323.

1. 'Distinguish the different kinds of law in the text.' This is not a categorization from the outside, but from 'within Israel's own social perspective'.

2. 'Analyse the social function and relative status of particular laws and institutions.' In particular this recognizes that there is a scale of values within Israel's laws, of which more below.

3. 'Define the objective(s) of the law in Israelite society.' This asks the question why the law was there, and a number of questions guide the interpreter towards an answer:

   • What kind of situation was this law trying to promote, or prevent?
   • Whose interests was this law aiming to protect?
   • Who would have benefited from this law and why?
   • Whose power was this law trying to restrict and how did it do so?
   • What rights and responsibilities were embodied in this law?
   • What kind of behavior did this law encourage or discourage?
   • What vision of society motivated this law?
   • What moral principles, values or priorities did this law embody or instantiate?
   • What motivation did this law appeal to?
   • What sanction or penalty (if any) was attached to this law, and what does that show regarding its relative seriousness or moral priority?

4. Preserve the objective but change the context. There is, in other words, a transposition of the particular law to a new situation. The authority of the speaker remains, the claim comes to church and world as intended audience, and the demand may be expected to stand closely allied with the original.

This approach of discerning the 'demand', a term I prefer as it retains the sense of authority and claim in a way that 'principle' or 'middle axiom' does not, does have certain potential pitfalls. It can acquire a quasi-objectivity and an independent life of its own. Or it can lose something of the illustrative power and the specificity of being rooted in a real context and situation. For both of these the solution lies in constantly revisiting the biblical text itself and being ready to revise the demand. There is also the danger of isolation of one demand from others, when in Israel's life the laws form an interlocking web. This is one reason why Chris Wright's 'paradigm' is so helpful, for at its best it acknowledges the integrated nature of the laws and how they functioned together within one context.[17]

Remember the difference between the ideal and the real

Deuteronomy's laws indicate an ideal but also reflect the practical realities of life in a particular cultural context. We noticed above that Deuteronomy is *both* religious *and* political. That is to say, it is both catechetical, giving religious instruction, and constitutional, giving laws for the governance of society. This means, as O'Donovan insightfully articulates it, that the laws 'have a *task* to perform within the community institutions which is other than that of moral education'.[18] The legislative dimension as it governs the order of society is not identical to the moral instruction, though it will overlap to varying degrees. This does not suddenly mean that there is no moral principle to be found in the societal legislation; rather, 'moral principle is expressed, but hypothetically, all the time under the control of a particular social task'.[19] There is a '*compromise* which distinguishes legislation from morality'.[20] What is ethically desirable as God's ultimate good may not actually be viable given the particular social and political context of Israel. Coexisting together, then, is the 'ideal' of what God ultimately desires, and the 'real' of what is commanded for *that* people in *that* place at *that* point in time.

This view is found early on within church history. In a dialogue purported to have taken place in AD 135 in Ephesus, Justin Martyr

---

17. Another helpful work is J. Daniel Hays, 'Applying the Old Testament Law Today', *BSac* 158 (2001), pp. 21–35.

18. O'Donovan, 'Towards', p. 66 (emphasis original).

19. Ibid., p. 67.

20. Ibid., p. 76 (my emphasis).

explains to the Hellenized Jew Trypho why Christians would not follow some of the Jewish rituals.[21] This was part of his 'apologia for Christian nonobservance of Torah':[22]

> For we too would observe the fleshly circumcision, and the Sabbaths, and in short all the feasts, if we did not know for what reason they were enjoined you, – namely, on account of your transgressions and the hardness of your hearts.[23]

For Justin the sacrifices were also instances of God's 'accommodating' to the people so that they did not fall into idolatry, given that they had been 'unrighteous and ungrateful to God, making a calf in the wilderness'.[24] This was part of a wider approach whereby Justin divided the Old Testament into three parts, 'ethical teachings, prophetic – Christological – teachings, and historical accommodations'.[25] Not every part has equal claim for the Christian. This is evident particularly in the following quotation from Justin:

> Some injunctions were laid on you in reference to the worship of God and practice of righteousness; but some injunctions and acts were likewise mentioned in reference to the mystery of Christ, [or] on account of the hardness of your people's hearts.[26]

In short, Justin recognizes that some of the Old Testament laws are rooted in God's accommodating himself to a particular people at a particular point in time. But Justin is not an innovator in

---

21. I follow the basic outline of analysis as found in Sparks, *God's Word*, pp. 236–237.
22. Stephen D. Benin, *The Footprints of God: Divine Accommodation in Jewish and Christian Thought*, SUNY Series in Judaica (Albany: State University of New York Press, 1993), p. 2.
23. Justin, *Dialogue with Trypho*, p. 18 (*ANF* 1.203).
24. Ibid., p. 19 (*ANF* 1.204).
25. Benin, *Footprints of God*, p. 3.
26. Justin, *Dialogue with Trypho*, p. 44 (*ANF* 1.217).

drawing distinctions within Old Testament laws and recognizing divine accommodation.

This is in fact nothing other than what Jesus himself recognizes and validates. At the start of Mark 10 Jesus is involved in a discussion with the Pharisees about divorce. The Pharisees acknowledge Moses' perspective, taken from Deuteronomy 24:1–4, 'Moses allowed a man to write a certificate of dismissal and to divorce her' (Mark 10:4). Jesus responds neither by endorsing Moses' words, nor by innovating, as Jesus does in Matthew 5:21–48 with 'you have heard it said . . . but I say to you . . .'. Instead, he justifies them, explaining how Moses could say something on which Jesus was going to differ. Jesus gives two grounds for why his view differs from that of Moses and why Moses' words were nonetheless right and appropriate. First, God's purpose 'from the beginning of creation' was different (Mark 10:6; cf. vv. 6–9). God's initial purpose was not for divorce. Divorce is not a good thing. Secondly, God gave through Moses a permission for divorce 'because of your hardness of heart'. There was a right reason at that point in time for Moses' command. O'Donovan identifies two possible grounds for the contrast. This permission could be taken to validate different ethical standards for different groups of people, a 'pastorally-oriented double-standard ethic, offering a milder demand to meet the needs of the weak'.[27] The alternative, which he (and Aquinas and the Reformers) prefers, is the 'legislative' one. That is, 'the social legislator . . . has to modify principle to suit practicability, he has to be content to control what he cannot eradicate'.[28]

This insight is of the greatest importance. Some of the laws are about controlling and working with the reality of life and culture. They need to be set against the ideals that the very same text expounds. We shall look at two concrete examples, those of slavery and war. Deuteronomy insists on the 'brotherhood' of every member of the community. Equality is taken for granted. The laws on slavery within the Israelite community are not neces-

---

27. O'Donovan, 'Towards', p. 66.
28. Ibid.

sarily, then, an ultimate 'ideal' but make provision for the reality of falling on troubled times and into debt. The aim of the laws is ultimate release and restoration, economic productivity, not the permanently enshrined ownership of one Israelite by another. In similar vein war is not an ultimate good. God's goal is peace, *šālôm*, not war. The prophets look forward to the day when swords will be beaten into ploughshares and 'nation shall not lift up sword against nation, neither shall they learn war any more' (Isa. 2:4). Soldiers become unclean through slaughter and David was forbidden from building the temple because he had shed so much blood (Num. 31:19; 1 Chr. 22:8). This is a critical perspective on the treatment of the Canaanites and on any understanding that Yahweh *commanded* the destruction.

> If and where God ever commands what he abhors, we may be sure that he does so with a heavy heart . . . If God commands violence, it is part of a whole concessionary scheme of operation, an accommodation to the fact of rampant evil which he detests but has not [yet] abolished.[29]

In other words the law does not ban what it disapproves of in its values, for that would be 'unrealistic'; instead, 'Deuteronomy's policy is to circumscribe them by, and to harness them to, the values and the theology it propounds.'[30] There are potential misunderstandings and dangers that can arise once this important perspective is granted. A first misunderstanding is to think that perhaps *all* the laws are like this. In reply it is true that *every* word is addressed to a particular social and cultural context. But some of its commands, such as the Decalogue, transcend the grid of social regulation. Further, alongside the specific laws, Deuteronomy expounds and extols values such as justice and 'brotherhood', which serve to relativize, even undermine, some of its injunctions. These values underpin to varying degrees the different commands, but are not identical with them. They may not be confounded with and should not be interpreted as if they were 'accommodating'

---

29. McConville and Williams, *Joshua*, p. 121.
30. Goldingay, *Theological Diversity*, p. 156.

laws. In other words Deuteronomy *itself* gives an interpretative framework within which to evaluate the individual laws.

> Deuteronomy . . . both undergirds and subverts the social order it
> presupposes . . . Formally, it accepts many features of that social order,
> yet its 'creative, egalitarian, and liberating dynamic' explicitly undermines
> other aspects that it formally leaves untouched.[31]

A second misunderstanding is to think this is a way of privileging the moral perspective of the interpreter over that of the text itself. For some contemporary readers that would be a good thing! But for this reader that would be a profound mistake, and it is *not* what is in view here. It is Scripture itself, read thoughtfully and in both local and canonical context, that encourages a distinction between the 'real' and the 'ideal', not contemporary moral superciliousness.

One danger is to dismiss the accommodating law, given that it is less than the ideal.[32] Yet to be less than the ideal does not mean that it has *no* moral or enduring value. The laws were still instances of *divine* accommodation. They were God's way of controlling, circumscribing or maintaining something as close to the ideal as was practical, and much may be gleaned.

A second danger is to settle for second best. If God is willing to give a law accommodated to 'real life', then perhaps the 'ideal' should be consigned to the naive or the 'super-spiritual'. But that is to misunderstand the nature of God and his dealing with his people.[33] The gap that is found in the *tôrâ* between the 'ideal' and the 'real' is an expression of God's patience and grace, on the one hand, and of the character that God looks to inculcate, on the other. What God *desires* is not simply defined negatively, by what his people should *not* do. Nor is what God desires law-keeping

---

31. Ibid., p. 165.

32. For this and the following, see Goldingay, *Approaches*, p. 60.

33. The stimulating reflections of Gordon J. Wenham ('The Gap Between Law and Ethics in the Bible', *JJS* 48 [1997], pp. 17–29; *Story as Torah*, pp. 73–108) provide the springboard for my thoughts here.

per se. The laws in many ways mark not the ethical 'ceiling' but the 'floor'. Sanctions come not for failing to live up to the ideal, the ethical 'ceiling', but for flouting the ethical 'floor'. The ethical 'ceiling' God desires of his people is a character expressed *positively*. So alongside the negative command to avoid idols is the positive one, to love, serve and fear Yahweh (Deut. 6:4–5; 10:12). Loving God is not the same as, and cannot be reduced to, not making graven images or bowing down to them. 'The ethico-religious goal was far deeper and more embracing: it involved both loyalty to God and an enjoyment of his presence.'[34] In similar vein marital ethics should not be reduced to certain laws, such as 'do not commit adultery', particularly since, 'crudely' put, the law 'discriminated harshly against women'. Evidence elsewhere indicates both a social and customary pressure on the man (cf. Deut. 25:5–10) and an ideal of monogamous faithfulness and mutuality (Gen. 2:24; Job and the prophetic marital metaphor with God as the faithful husband).[35] In Exodus God declares that he is gracious and compassionate, slow to anger and abounding in love. God's patience and grace are seen in that he puts up with much less than he desires. This is obviously true in the narrative texts of Genesis and Judges, where God works with the reality of sin and failure. It is also true in the law. But that is no ground for settling for second best, even more so now that Christ has come (cf. the Sermon on the Mount).

A further benefit of recognizing the distinction between the ideal and the real is that it provides a backdrop for the observation, important both for the prophets in the Old Testament and for Jesus and Paul in the New, that there is a hierarchy to the laws. The prophets castigated Israel for tolerating injustice alongside thriving religion (e.g. Amos 4:4–5; 5:21–24). Jesus denounced the Pharisees for tithing herbs and 'neglecting' the 'weightier matters: justice, mercy and faith(fulness)' (Matt. 23:23).[36] In debate he summarized the law with Deuteronomy 6:5 and Leviticus 19:18,

---

34. Gordon J. Wenham, *Story as Torah*, p. 82.

35. Ibid., pp. 84–87.

36. Note that Jesus *did* insist they should have tithed the herbs, though.

and went on to say, 'on these two commands hang all the law and the prophets' (Matt. 22:40). Paul speaks of 'love' as the 'fulfilment of the law' (Rom. 13:8–10) and insists that 'in Christ Jesus neither circumcision nor uncircumcision counts for anything, but [the only thing that counts is] faith working through love' (Gal. 5:6).

Read them through the lenses of what God has done in Jesus Christ

For the Christian, Jesus – his person and work, his life, death, resurrection, ascension, pouring out of the Spirit and return in glory – is the climax of all that the Old Testament, including Deuteronomy, anticipated. At the risk of oversimplification, there are two opposite perspectives from which to approach Deuteronomy's laws and Jesus Christ.

The first is to see how the laws prefigure Christ, and how they can illuminate his person and work. It is to start with the laws and look forward. Before we go any further, a danger and a mistake should be acknowledged.

The danger is that connections made to Christ are somehow seen as an end in themselves, without our dwelling either on how Christ's person and work are illuminated or on how the 'demand' applies to the Christian.

The mistake is to treat the laws as prophecies 'about' Christ, especially if by 'prophecy' 'prediction' is in fact meant.[37] We have already seen how Deuteronomy's story of the future ends with what God in Christ has done. That is some distance from a prediction giving a blueprint of the future. Deuteronomy – and Old Testament prophecy more generally – does not contain Nostradamus-like predictions. Such a view implies the announcement beforehand of something that will happen in the (distant) future and that once it has happened, that is the end of the matter. But that fails to account for either the purpose of prophecies or their enduring nature.

Old Testament prophecy is not concerned to inform present or

---

37. Note the discussion above on Jesus as 'The Prophet' like Moses.

future generations about the future, but to transform the hearer.[38] Further, those same words come with renewed force and claim to subsequent generations beyond the original rhetorical context – there are, after all, prophetic books. The words are not exhausted once the events envisaged have passed.

Having made that clarification, it is entirely appropriate, indeed necessary, to emphasize that the laws illuminate the person and work of Christ. In thinking about the laws on slavery, it is necessary to remember Jesus Christ as the one who came to 'serve' and give his life as a ransom for many. Just as a servant is not greater than his master, so too the disciple of Christ is not greater than Christ. The Christian remains one who has been 'bought with a price'. The Passover celebrates God's great deliverance of his people from Egypt and the preservation of Israelite life through the death of a lamb. It anticipates Jesus the Passover Lamb, slain for the sins of the world (cf. John 1:35; 1 Cor. 5:7).[39] The joyful celebration that marked the Passover should be expected to characterize the redemption won in Christ. When considering Deuteronomy's laws on warfare, and on *ḥērem*, they anticipate Jesus the conquering king, akin to the commander of Yahweh's army in Joshua 5, come to destroy the works of the evil one, fighting the spiritual enemies of God (Mark 1:24; 3:27; 1 John 3:8). But he is not just that.

Quickly, however, the second perspective comes into view, as we turn the telescope round and look through the other end, thinking about the laws from the perspective of Christ. As we think of war, Jesus is not just the conqueror; he is also the slain.

---

38. See esp. Richard L. Pratt, Jr., 'Historical Contingencies and Biblical Predictions', in James I. Packer and Sven K. Soderlund (eds.), *In the Way of Wisdom: Essays in Honor of Bruce K. Waltke* (Grand Rapids: Zondervan, 2000), pp. 180–203, though the use of the word 'predictions' rather than 'prophecies' may confuse.

39. Although in Exodus the slaying of the Passover lamb is not connected with Israel's sin, but with God's claim on the newborn more generally, by the New Testament the sacrificial system more generally focused on atonement and sin-bearing.

He is the one who willingly experiences in himself God's holy hatred of sin, though not of course as a third party, for God was *in Christ* reconciling the world to himself (2 Cor. 5:19). He became the one 'devoted to destruction', as he experienced his Father's hatred of sin, a hatred expressed in *ḥērem*. God in Jesus is victim, the 'other', enabling God's enemies to become his friends (Rom. 5:10). 'God the warrior became the Crucified God.'[40]

In thinking about women in Deuteronomy, we need to remember Jesus Christ as the bridegroom who loved his bride and gave himself up for her in self-sacrifice. We should also recall his willingness to cross the social and cultural boundaries laid out for women. He spoke with a Samaritan woman (John 4:27); he let his feet be wetted with a prostitute's tears, anointed with her oil, kissed with her lips and wiped with her hair (Luke 7:38); he delighted that Mary sat at his feet, learning (Luke 10:39; cf. Acts 22:3).

Jesus brings something radically new that in some cases transforms the shape of the 'demand' that Deuteronomy's laws articulated. One particularly striking example is the food laws (Deut. 14). There the distinction between 'clean' and 'unclean' determines what animals may or may not be eaten. Jesus transcends these boundaries. In Mark 7 he declares all food clean (7:21–22); in Mark 1 he touches the leper (Mark 1:40–45), but makes the leper clean rather than himself unclean. In Luke 7 he touches the funeral bier (Luke 7:14), but removes the uncleanness by raising the widow's son to life. He associates with Samaritans (John 4) and even heals Gentiles, amazed at the faith he finds (Matt. 8:5–10). In the Old Testament, uncleanness related to death and disorder. Animals and birds were designated clean or unclean because of Israel's consecration to Yahweh and separation from the nations (Lev. 20:24–26). In Acts, Peter sees a vision of animals being let down from heaven and hears a voice saying 'Get up, Peter! Kill and eat' (Acts 10:13). The removal of dietary restrictions goes hand in hand with taking the gospel to the Gentiles (Acts 11:4–12).

---

40. Peter C. Craigie, *The Problem of War in the Old Testament* (Grand Rapids: Eerdmans, 1978), p. 100. Cf. McConville and Williams, *Joshua*, pp. 123–124.

Initially it might seem that there is a contrast between the New Testament's handling of some of Deuteronomy's laws and Deuteronomy itself. That may be true at the surface level. But at a deeper level there is a fundamental continuity. God's kingdom has broken in: the dawn of redemption, which in fact is nothing other than recreation. Because God's purposes for creation were carried forward in and through Israel, restoration of Israel goes together with renewal of creation. Salvation is present. In that sense the people of God are not bound contractually to the law of Moses as Israel was (1 Cor. 9:20–21; Gal. 3:24–25). We are no longer 'under law' in the sense that it provides the framework for governing our relationship with God. We are, rather, under the 'law of Christ' (1 Cor. 9:21). But the laws are neither overthrown, nor obsolete, nor abrogated, though their demand may be transformed.[41]

A worked example of appropriating Deuteronomy's laws: Deuteronomy 15:1–11

Analysis

Deuteronomy 15:1–11 covers two related social issues, the release of debts (vv. 1–6) and the potential unwillingness to lend to the poor because of the release (vv. 7–11). The technical term *šĕmiṭṭâ* unites the two sections (vv. 1, 2, 9). The verbal root (*šmṭ*) is used literally for to 'fling down' or 'let drop' (2 Kgs 9:33). In Exodus 23:11 it is used figuratively for letting land lie fallow in the seventh year; here the metaphorical sense extends to 'releasing' debts.

There are three main ways in which these verses connect with the wider context.

First, these verses are introduced by what is to happen at the end of every period of seven years.[42] This fits with a number of other laws in the context that deal with the question of *time*

---

41. See further N. T. Wright, *Jesus*; Gordon J. Wenham, *Story as Torah*.

42. This is more likely than 'at the end of every seven years'; see Deut. 31:10; Jer. 34:14.

(14:22 – 16:17).[43] A number of scholars regard the laws in chapters 12–26 as broadly following the order of the commands in the Decalogue.[44] If so, the concern for time more generally, and 'seven' in particular, fits in well with the sabbath command. The sabbath is not merely religious, but also social, concerned with community life and alleviation of poverty.

Secondly, the whole section from 12:1 to 16:17 is concerned for *place*, the place where Yahweh shall choose to place his name.[45] Chapter 12 relates this very closely with right worship of Yahweh and avoidance of Canaanite deities. It is in the context of distinguishing Israelite and Canaanite worship that Deuteronomy's social and humanitarian concerns are so evident.[46] True worship of Yahweh goes together with care for the poor.

The third significant link to the surrounding content is the rooting of the commands in the promise of Yahweh's blessing (15:4–6, 10).[47] Israel's obedience brings Yahweh's blessing and, in turn, renewed opportunity for obedience.

The opening section (vv. 1–6) starts with a general heading on 'debt remission' (v. 1), verses 2–3 explain what remission should look like and verses 4–6 give the ideal, spelled out as a restriction. The structure of verses 2–3 may be analysed as a chiasm. This emphasizes the centrality of Yahweh's involvement (D). It is *Yahweh's remission*:[48]

---

43. Cf. Deut. 14:22, 28; 15:12, 20; 16:16. The subsequent law on the releasing of slaves is connected with 15:1–11 in many ways, including the themes of debt, the seventh year and letting someone bound go free.

44. So esp. Stephen A. Kaufman, 'The Structure of the Deuteronomic Law', *Maarav* 1.2 (1978–9), pp. 105–158; Georg Braulik, 'The Sequence of the Laws in Deuteronomy 12–26', in Duane L. Christensen (ed.), *A Song of Power and the Power of Song* (Winona Lake, Ind.: Eisenbrauns, 1993), pp. 313–335.

45. See Deut. 12:5, 11, 14, 18, 21, 26; 14:23, 24, 25; 15:20; 16:2, 6, 7, 11, 15, 16.

46. Cf. also 14:28–29.

47. Cf. Deut. 14:29; 15:14, 18; 16:15.

48. Cf. Martin J. Oosthuizen, 'Deuteronomy 15:1–18 in Socio-Rhetorical Perspective', *ZABR* 3 (1997), p. 67.

A   Every creditor . . . should remit (*šmṭ, yād*) (v. 2aβ)

B   what (*'ăšer*) he loans his neighbour

C   He should not press claim against (*ngś*) his neighbour, that is, his brother

D   for Yahweh's remission (*šĕmiṭṭâ*) has been proclaimed (*qr'*; cf. v. 9)

C'   The foreigner you may press claim against (*ngś*) (v. 3)

B'   (but) what (*'ăšer*) is yours with your brother . . .

A'   you shall remit (*šmṭ, yād*)

From another perspective, there is a linear flow to these verses. Verse 2aβ gives the basic injunction that a creditor should remit debts. The subsequent verses then explain this further with three main clauses. The main clauses in 2b and 3a (C, C') are introduced without the coordinating conjunction waw, 'and'/'but'. This is a characteristic way of giving further explanation or qualification to what precedes. The first (C) indicates what the creditor should *not* do. The second (C') gives a permission, what they *may* do, while the third (A') gives a command, what they *must* do. This movement is reinforced by the move from the third person, 'he', to the second person, 'you', in verse 3.

Probably what is in view here is not remission of the pledge taken on the debt, whether temporary or permanent,[49] but the remission of the whole loan. One problem with this view is whether lending would ever be feasible, especially if the debtor has prospered significantly as a result of the loan. Three reasons, though, make this more likely: the term suggests the dropping of the whole loan, rather than merely ability to recall it in the seventh year;[50] there is a different word for pledge that could easily have been used (*'ăbōṭ*; cf. Deut. 24:10); further, verse 9 makes more sense if the loan itself is in view.[51]

---

49. So e.g. Christopher J. H. Wright, *God's People in God's Land*, pp. 171–172.

50. See S. R. Driver, *A Critical and Exegetical Commentary on Deuteronomy*, ICC (Edinburgh: T. & T. Clark, 1895), pp. 179–180.

51. Gregory C. Chirichigno, *Debt-Slavery in Israel and the Ancient Near East*, JSOTSup 141 (Sheffield: JSOT Press, 1993), p. 273.

The following three verses (vv. 4–6) articulate the ideal, that there 'should be no needy' because of Yahweh's blessing, as long as they obey. The flow of the argument runs

4a	However there should be no needy among you
4b	for Yahweh shall surely bless you . . .
5a	only if you are sure to obey Yahweh's voice
5b	by doing carefully the commandment I am commanding today
6a	When Yahweh has blessed . . .
6bα	. . . then you shall lend
6bβ	but you shall not be lent to (i.e. 'borrow')
6bγ	you shall rule
6bδ	but you they shall not rule

There are five points to make here.

First, although almost every English version seems to regard the start of verse 4 as a prediction, albeit conditional ('there will be no poor . . ., if . . .), it is a prohibition: 'there *should* be no poor among you'. This is clear from the opening conjunction (*'epes kî*, 'however') that continues what precedes, while restricting or qualifying it. Given that the preceding clause is volitional, expressing Moses' desire or will, that same force remains here.[52] It is not what 'will' be but what 'should' be. Explicitly Moses spells out the *ideal* of no poverty, having given a law that deals with its *reality*.

Secondly, in the flow of the argument it is the blessing (v. 4b) that is dependent on Israel's obedience ('if you are sure to obey', v. 5a), not the absence of needy people (v. 4a). This is likely because of the parallel syntax of Hebrew infinitives absolute (expressed here by 'sure[ly]') in verses 4b and 5a, because of the link between obedience and blessing elsewhere in Deuteronomy, and because of the backward link in verse 4a ('however'). The difference is subtle. To say 'there should be no needy among you for Yahweh

---

52. See William S. Morrow, *Scribing the Center: Organization and Redaction in Deuteronomy 14:1–17:13*, SBLMS 49 (Atlanta, Ga.: Scholars Press, 1995), p. 93; Oosthuizen, 'Deuteronomy 15:1–18', p. 68.

shall bless you . . ., if you obey' leaves the means of poverty alleviation vague; it could just be general experience of blessing in the
community. Instead, Moses says, 'there should be no needy among
you, for Yahweh shall bless you if you obey . . .'. Though the link
is not stated between their experience of blessing and poverty
alleviation, it is obvious: it is precisely *their blessing* that is to be the
means of preventing need.

Thirdly, there is a window into Yahweh's economy. Obedience
is costly, for *they* are to be the means of alleviating poverty. Yet
in Yahweh's economy, obedience is the route to abundance:
there will be more than enough, so there is no need for anxiety
about obedience here (cf. 2 Cor. 9:5–8). This dynamic has trust in
Yahweh's word as the a priori.

Fourthly, given Israel's track record, the ideal of absence of
poverty seems a distant utopia. The close link between obedience,
blessing and the lack of poverty does not hold out great promise
for those who are poor.

Finally, a lender is powerful while a debtor is powerless. The
parallel structure of verse 6 indicates that to lend is to rule, to
borrow is to be ruled: 'a loan relationship unavoidably entails
dependency in either the personal or political realm'.[53] This fits
with the language of verse 2, where language used there of a
creditor ('exact', 'press'; *ngś*) is used elsewhere of more general
oppression or extortion and even of tyrannical rule (e.g. Isa. 9:4;
14:2; 53:7). It also fits with the perceptive proverb 'The rich rules
over the poor, and the borrower is the slave of the lender' (Prov.
22:7).

Moses then turns to tackle a plausible scenario in verses 7–11.
Someone in a position to lend and perhaps otherwise willing might
be reluctant given the potential financial loss that might arise
due to remission. With tightly structured and powerfully crafted
rhetoric, Moses confronts attitude and action directly:

7   If there is a needy (*'ebyōn*) person, one of your brothers (*'āḥ*)
       Do not harden your heart (*lēbāb*) and   (A)

---

53. Nelson, *Deuteronomy*, p. 195.

do not shut your hand (*yād*) to your needy (*'ebyôn*) brother

(*'āḥ*)   (B)

8 But be sure to open your hand (*yād*) to him and   (B')

be sure to lend what he needs   (A')

9 Be careful lest

there is a base word (*dābār*) in your heart (*lēbāb*)

which says 'remission approaching'

so your eye (*'ayin*) is evil against your needy (*'ebyôn*)

brother (*'āḥ*) and

you do not give and

he cries out (*qr'*; cf. v. 2) to Yahweh and

it is a sin for you

10 Be sure to give to him and

do not have an evil heart (*lēbāb*)

for

because of this action (*dābār*)

Yahweh will bless you . . . in all the undertaking of your

hand (*yād*)

11 Because the needy (*'ebyôn*) will not cease . . .

therefore I command you,

'Be sure to open your hand (*yād*) to your brother (*'āḥ*), to your

poor and your needy (*'ebyôn*)'

Again, a number of points may be made.

First, there is a clear distinction between the ideal and the real. Although most of the clauses are commands, they are rooted in two situations: in verse 7, '*if* there is a needy person', and in verse 11, '*because* the needy will not cease'. There is movement on poverty's presence through the chapter from 'there should not be' (v. 4) to 'if there is' (v. 7) to 'because there will be' (v. 11). Alongside the *ideal* of poverty elimination is the realism about Israel's sinfulness. Poverty will be present given the anticipated lack of obedience, so it is important to speak to that reality.

Secondly, there is an integration of thought and action. Structurally, this is seen in verses 7–8, where there is a chiastic ABB'A' pattern, except that whereas A deals with the heart ('do not harden your heart'), A' deals with the action ('be sure to lend what he needs'). The counterpart to a hard heart is lending what is needed.[54] That integration is also seen in the presence of language speaking of different parts of the body, whether hand (7–8, 10–11; cf. 2–3), heart (7, 9, 10) or eye (9). 'The actions of opening and closing the hand, the inner will of the heart, and the visible glance of the jealous eye combine to express a unity of action and attitude.'[55]

Thirdly, the commands here are about ethics, not social legislation.[56] Lending is not compelled by the sanction of the law. Moses appeals to the heart and the motivation, not to the court. Failure to comply is not a matter for human courts; rather, it is a sin before God. The poor cannot appeal to the court, but only to God (v. 9b). Deuteronomy 12 – 26 is not simply legislative, a 'law code', but is also catechetical. The concern of the *tôrâ* in Deuteronomy is not merely with external behaviour, but with the heart and with attitudes.[57] It is concerned to inculcate character.

Fourthly, there are some critical insights about poverty. The lending in view here is not a commercial transaction to make money or exploit a debtor, but a means of helping the poor 'brother'. Further, the one who is 'poor' is not part of a category of 'the poor' as if they were a detached, nameless and faceless group. Although many modern translations dilute the translation of verse 11 (e.g. ESV, NIV, NRSV), the pronoun 'your' is found with 'brother' *and* with 'poor' and 'needy'. They are '*your* poor' and '*your* needy'. 'Your brother' expresses unity; 'your poor' expresses responsibility. They are not someone else's problem. This is part of a wider picture where 'the law typically addresses not the poor themselves but *those who wield economic or social power*'.[58]

Finally, those in view here are different from the orphan, the

54. That Sihon had a hard heart does not bode well for any that do (cf. Deut. 2:30).

55. Nelson, *Deuteronomy*, p. 193.

56. Tigay, *Deuteronomy*, p. 146.

57. In v. 9 there are eighteen words in Hebrew to describe the bad attitude, and only three for the resultant negative action. See Jeffries M. Hamilton, *Social Justice and Deuteronomy: The Case of Deuteronomy 15*, SBLDS 136 (Atlanta, Ga.: Scholars Press, 1992), p. 33.

58. Christopher J. H. Wright, *Old Testament Ethics*, p. 174.

widow and the resident alien, the long-term poor who were regular
beneficiaries of ongoing charity (e.g. 14:29). While there was no
straightforward means of those participating in economic life, the
'poor' person in view here is one who would normally be able to
participate, but for whatever reason has fallen on hard times. The
goal is to restore such a person to economic productivity. This
simply highlights that those who are needy were not a homoge-
neous group; there was not one strategy for provision.[59]

Appropriation

Regardless of whether a person views the Old Testament as
authoritative for ethical formulation or not, there are many ways in
which these verses in Deuteronomy are informative and provoke
further thought. They highlight graphically the damaging nature of
debt and the power relationships that go with it. In a culture where
personal debt is normalized and portrayed almost as the sine
qua non of a happy consumerist lifestyle, Deuteronomy's sober-
ing voice of the debtor being 'ruled' arrests attention. Further,
Deuteronomy recognizes that economic productivity is important
and that poverty is neither desirable nor homogenous.

Deuteronomy is also suggestive of possible strategies for handling poverty. For example, it mandates a process of tiered
assistance, with loans to help return the 'poor' to productivity and,
as a second stage, cancellation of debts. As I write, there is substantial frustration in the UK towards banks which have received
the benefit of substantial tax-payer bail-outs, yet are reluctant to
make loans to those trying to become productive again in new
businesses.

However, these insights are different from Deuteronomy's
demand today. How should we understand and frame Deuteronomy
15:1–11 as authoritative word? The demand for the church will
be the main focus, but there remains a demand for the world, a
demand rooted in the paradigmatic nature of Israel's *tôrâ*.

---

59. The existence of the 'resident alien' as a beneficiary of charity makes it
     clearer that the foreigner from whom it is permissible to exact interest
     is a merchant (15:3).

If we use the New Testament as one set of interpretative lenses, these verses plausibly lie behind at least four places.[60]

First, and most obviously, when a woman anoints Jesus' head with expensive oil from an alabaster jar, the disciples criticize her, saying that the ointment could have been sold and given to the poor. Jesus defends her action, saying she has done a wonderful thing by anointing him for burial. He concludes by saying, 'For you always have the poor with you, but you will not always have me' (Matt. 26:11; cf. Mark 14:7; John 12:8; Deut. 15:11). At first glance Jesus might seem to be giving the disciples an excuse not to care for the poor. But the opposite is the case, as is evident from Deuteronomy 15:11. The fact that the poor will always be with them in Deuteronomy is not a reason for ignoring poverty but for continuing to open their hand to the poor.

Secondly, in Matthew 6:21–24 Jesus talks about the location of a person's treasure and the impossibility of serving two masters. In the middle of this he speaks of two kinds of 'eye', 'healthy', 'clear' or 'single' (*haplous*), and 'unhealthy' or 'bad' (*ponēros*). The latter comes as part of a phrase, 'if your eye is bad' (*ean de ho ophthalmos sou ponēros ē*). Although Jesus might seem to be talking about hygiene, a different background is preferable. The LXX of Deuteronomy 15:9 warns of the danger that 'your eye is evil' (*ponēreusētai ho ophthalmos sou*) such that you see the poverty of your 'brother' and fail to 'give'. In other words Jesus is talking about *generosity* at this point; serving God and not mammon is evident in and through generosity to the poor. Not to do so is to have an 'evil eye' for Jesus and Deuteronomy.

Thirdly, in Acts 4:34 Luke observes that with the outpouring of the Holy Spirit and the renewed generosity in the community 'there was not a needy person among them' (cf. Deut. 15:4). The word for 'needy' (*endeēs*) is found nowhere else in the New Testament. Barrett concludes, 'it may be inferred that the clause is intended as a fulfilment of Deut. 15.4'.[61] In Deuteronomy such a

---

60. The list in Moyise and Menken, *Deuteronomy*, p. 191, gives only one: Deut. 15:11 in Mark 14:7.

61. C. K. Barrett, *A Critical and Exegetical Commentary on the Acts of the Apostles*, 2 vols., ICC (London: T. & T. Clark, 1994), vol. 1, p. 254.

situation is dependent both on the people's obedience and on their generous distribution of Yahweh's blessings. There is a breaking in of the age-to-come, of the 'ideal' even in the midst of Jesus' recognition that the 'reality' of poverty will continue (Matt. 26:11).

Finally, when Jesus confronted the rich young man, he told him to sell what he had, to give to the poor and then come and follow Jesus (Matt. 19:21; Mark 10:21) if he wanted to be 'perfect' (*teleios*; cf. Deut. 18:13 LXX). His response, according to many commentators and translations, was to go away 'sad'.[62] However, there may be a darker side here. In Mark 10 there are two verbs to describe his demeanour. The first is *stygnazō*, a rare verb which elsewhere has the connotation of anger, extending to a 'threatening angry sky' (Matt. 16:3). The second is the verb *lypeō*. Within its field of meaning as found in the New Testament it typically denotes sorrow and grief. Strikingly, though, it appears in the LXX of Deuteronomy 15:10. Moses instructs an Israelite confronted with a needy 'brother', 'you shall give freely to him ... and you shall not be grudging (*lypeō*) in your heart when you give to him'. Now the situation in Deuteronomy is slightly different, for Jesus is talking about a grudging attitude *in giving*, and what is in view in Deuteronomy is *lending*, not simply giving to the poor. Nonetheless, perhaps the overlap in handing over money and the connotations of *stygnazō* suggest that the demeanour of the rich young man is a grudging simmering rather than a more endearing sadness.

From all of these a generosity with possessions and a heart for the poor are characteristics of these verses' ongoing demand. These New Testament connections do not confer an authority on Deuteronomy, but recognize and confirm Deuteronomy's enduring authority and claim. The demand is broader than this, covering understanding, attitude and action.

In terms of understanding, the church should recognize that all its dealings, indeed all of life, are *coram deo* (in the presence of God). It was *Yahweh*'s release of debts that was proclaimed (15:2); it is before *Yahweh* that the cry of the poor goes up if generosity

---

62. E.g. 'in distress', R. T. France, *The Gospel of Matthew*, NICNT (Grand Rapids: Eerdmans, 2007), p. 728.

is not forthcoming (15:9); God will surely vindicate such a poor believer (cf. Luke 16:19–31). The church should also recognize the familial nature of the relationship with other believers. Every other believer is a family member, equal with them. The church should also recognize that although there may be distinctions between different types of poor, the notion of 'deserving' and 'undeserving' poor is not one of them. Why the 'brother' had fallen on hard times is never mentioned. Finally, it should recognize that the abundance a person may have is only ever a gift from God and that in God's economy the one who gives generously finds blessing (Deut. 15:4–6, 10). This is something endorsed in the New Testament (e.g. Acts 20:35; 2 Cor. 9:8).

In terms of attitude and action, these go together (cf. 15:8–9). There should be a generosity rather than a withholding. This generosity should be willing and liberal, rather than grudging and niggardly. That it is to meet 'need' (15:9) guards against a naive implementation, for a person's real need may not be for money, even if that is what they may want. The priority in context is for the people of God; the 'brother' in Deuteronomy 15 is the fellow Israelite. Practical love for one another is, as Jesus says, the way the world will know we are his disciples (John 13:35). But it does not end there (cf. Gal. 6:10).

The demand of this passage for the world derives from the paradigmatic nature of *tôrâ*. It is not that the world is under *tôrâ* any more than the church is. But what God desires of humanity more broadly, as evidenced in the demands of Israel, is a society where there is no poverty, where those who have more are concerned for those who are poor; where that concern is not detached but is rooted in an awareness of a common humanity; where they are willing to take action to alleviate that poverty. But none of this should mask the necessity of recognizing all belongs to Yahweh, including their own wealth. This is not an ethic detached from relationship to God, but one that in its profoundest sense should be rooted in that relationship.

Moving towards a sermon

Although this book is not a primer on how to preach Deuteronomy, many readers will be preachers, and it is one of the aims of this book that readers will be more motivated and confident to preach Deuteronomy. So some reflections are appropriate on the move from text to sermon for Deuteronomy 15:1–11. Three more general reflections on preaching provide an important backdrop to the reflections that follow.

First, a premature focus on preaching can end up producing worse preachers, who are more boring, more predictable and more superficial. Being too quick to jump to preaching or teaching a text ends up treating the text as a commodity to be packaged rather than a word to be cherished, loved, meditated upon, obeyed, assimilated – shaping who I am, what I believe and what I do. Given that caution, how should Deuteronomy's demand here be preached?

Secondly, preacher and context make a profound difference. Sometimes I come across the view that 'outline of book' + 'biblical theology' = 'sermon series', and 'exegesis of passage' + 'biblical theology' = 'sermon outline'. What is missing here is due reflection on the personality, style or gifting of the preacher and the context in which the message is to be delivered. Personality and gifting make a great difference. The great expository preachers and teachers of the Bible have very different styles and approaches. What unites them all is a deep love for the Bible, and a deep desire for hearers to listen carefully to the text, not an identical sermon outline. The context also makes a great difference. Contemporary relevance and major lines of application may differ significantly, depending on those listening. Are those listening a group of largely non-Christian teenagers on a run-down estate in London or a group of civic leaders, some of whom may be Christians, or a largely retired rural congregation or a relatively affluent, suburban professional congregation. Just how different depends in part on one's view of homiletics. My own view is that awareness of one's audience should impact the heart of one's sermons, not only the tone of voice and examples used. Application is part of the message. In other words there is something unique about every sermon that resists being packaged and preserved.

Thirdly, a sermon that is accessible, memorable and powerful to generate change should have a unitary aim. That aim will depend on the context, but will be an outworking of the exegetical idea.

With those convictions about preaching, what of a sermon on Deuteronomy 15:1–11? The main exegetical idea that should form the heart of a sermon is something like this: right worship of the Lord involves generous provision for your poor. The aim will relate to that. What follows is one suggestion.

Opening: ask every person listening to get their wallet or purse out of their pocket or bag and pass it to their neighbour – it engages the attention and relates directly to the aim. Then there might follow brief portraits of individuals (anonymized) who are either rich or poor.

Main section: set out the situation envisaged in Deuteronomy; context of 12:1 – 16:17 shows that care for the poor is about right worship; introduce and illustrate some of the points above (under 'understanding') not as isolated or separate items, but as ones serving the main aim. These should include God's blessing of his people with abundance; God's concern for the poor; the obligation to other members of the Christian family; the fact that this is not a church subcommittee's responsibility; the goal of such generosity, which is not to foster a dependency culture, but to restore productivity. Move towards the main insight.

Application: give adequate space here to how this insight impacts, focusing on the merging of attitude and action as found in Deuteronomy 15. Illustrate what this insight might mean for the different individuals introduced in the opening. This will involve exploring the dynamic of the heart's inclination to rationalize and justify lack of generosity; it will also explore what generosity actually looks like, given that it is possible to think our actions are generous, when they are not. The challenge is to embed and earth what a response might look like, without prescribing inappropriately, engendering false guilt or self-righteousness.

Response: give opportunity for writing down (1) a person who might be helped; (2) what to do to help. Encourage the congregation to be specific.

EPILOGUE

It has been the aim of this work to enable the reader to taste 'honey from the rock', to savour something sweet and nourishing from the words of God found in the book of Deuteronomy. In that sense it is a book that points beyond itself, and may be judged a success or a failure in so far as it its readers do indeed take delight in and find sustenance from Deuteronomy. It has not held out the possibility of mastering that book, for it has been written with the conviction that Deuteronomy is to master us. But for Deuteronomy to master us, it is important that it is read thoughtfully and carefully, with insight as well as enthusiasm.

There are two main highways from Deuteronomy to the contemporary Christian and the church. Both pass through the life, death and resurrection of Jesus Christ. The Christian should not read Deuteronomy independently of Jesus Christ. The first highway is that of story – both the story Deuteronomy tells and the larger story of which Deuteronomy itself is a part. That story speaks of God's faithfulness and generosity, of Israel's unfaithfulness, of God's judgment and restoration. It speaks of promises held out, of rescue and redemption, of rebellion and wandering, of the urgent day of decision that is 'today', of life lived in the land, of ejection from the land and of transformation and restoration. The story Deuteronomy tells and is part of has of course moved on. What it foresaw has happened, though with a newness that characterizes the God of surprises who is not constrained by the possibilities of the present. That flow of history under God's grace is testimony to his faithfulness. And yet, alongside this, there is a sense in which this story remains ever true, ever present, as the church and every person faces the call 'today' to 'choose life'.

The second highway is that of demand – the demand that Deuteronomy continues to make on the life of the Christian believer, the church and, in some senses, on the watching world. How to frame that demand and to engage with it is not straight-forward, but it is a task that must be done. That word of demand comes to a redeemed people, insisting that obedience to the living God is rooted in a when – a point in time – and a where – a place, in the public arena and in the heart of every believer (cf. Deut. 27:1–8; 6:5–6). It is to be an embodied word that testifies to a watching world that there is a God who is just and righteous, loving and good, demanding and uncompromising. It is an urgent word, a contemporary word, seen in the repeated 'today' and the persuasive rhetoric that marks even the laws themselves. And this word holds out life, life as it is meant to be, lived under God's rule. In Jesus Christ that life becomes a joy-filled reality.

BIBLIOGRAPHY

Ackroyd, Peter R., *Exile and Restoration*, OTL (London: SCM, 1968).

Alexander, T. Desmond, *From Paradise to the Promised Land*, 2nd ed. (Carlisle: Paternoster, 2002).

Allen, David M., *Deuteronomy and Exhortation in Hebrews: A Study in Narrative Re-Presentation*, WUNT 238.2 (Tübingen: Mohr Siebeck, 2008).

Allen, Leslie C., *1, 2 Chronicles*, Mastering the Old Testament 10 (Dallas: Word, 1987).

Alter, Robert, and Frank Kermode (eds.), *The Literary Guide to the Bible* (London: Fontana, 1987).

Arnold, Bill T., 'The Love–Fear Antinomy in Deuteronomy 5–11', *VT* 61 (2011), pp. 551–569.

Ash, Christopher, *Remaking a Broken World: A Fresh Look at the Bible Storyline* (Milton Keynes, UK: Authentic Media, 2010).

Barker, Paul A., 'The Theology of Deuteronomy 27', *TynB* 49 (1998), pp. 277–304.

——, *The Triumph of Grace in Deuteronomy: Faithless Israel, Faithful Yahweh in Deuteronomy*, PBM (Carlisle: Paternoster, 2004).

Barrett, C. K., *A Critical and Exegetical Commentary on the Acts of the Apostles*, 2 vols., ICC (London: T. & T. Clark, 1994).

Bauckham, Richard J., *Bible and Ecology: Rediscovering the Community of Creation*, Sarum Theological Lectures (Waco: Baylor University Press, 2010).

——, 'Biblical Theology and the Problems of Monotheism', in Craig Bartholomew, Mary Healy, Karl Möller and Robin Parry (eds.), *Out of Egypt: Biblical Theology and Biblical Interpretation*, SHS 5 (Bletchley, UK: Paternoster, 2004), pp. 187–232.

Benin, Stephen D., *The Footprints of God: Divine Accommodation in Jewish and*

Christian Thought, SUNY Series in Judaica (Albany: State University of New York Press, 1993).

Biddle, Mark E., *Deuteronomy*, Smyth & Helwys Bible Commentary 4 (Macon, Ga.: Smyth & Helwys, 2003).

Blenkinsopp, Joseph, *Creation, Un-Creation, Re-Creation: A Discursive Commentary on Genesis 1–11* (London: T. & T. Clark, 2011).

Block, Daniel I., 'Bringing Back David: Ezekiel's Messianic Hope', in P. E. Satterthwaite, R. S. Hess and G. J. Wenham (eds.), *The Lord's Anointed: Interpretation of Old Testament Messianic Texts* (Grand Rapids: Baker, 1995), pp. 167–188.

——, 'The Grace of Torah: The Mosaic Prescription for Life (Deut. 4:1–8; 6:20–25)', *BSac* 162 (2005), pp. 3–22.

——, 'Marriage and Family in Ancient Israel', in Ken M. Campbell (ed.), *Marriage and Family in the Biblical World* (Downers Grove: InterVarsity Press, 2003), pp. 33–102.

——, 'Preaching Old Testament Law to New Testament Christians', *Hiphil* 3 <http://www.see-j.net/hiphil> (2006), accessed 2 Aug. 2012.

Bock, Darrell L., *Luke*, 2 vols., BECNT (Grand Rapids: Baker, 1994–6).

Bonhoeffer, Dietrich, *Life Together*, tr. John W. Doberstein (London: SCM, 1954).

Boston, James R., 'Wisdom Influence upon the Song of Moses', *JBL* 87 (1968), pp. 198–202.

Braulik, Georg, 'Deuteronomy and Human Rights', in Ulrika Lindblad (tr.), *The Theology of Deuteronomy: Collected Essays of Georg Braulik, O.S.B.*, BIBAL Collected Essays 2 (N. Richland Hills, Tex.: BIBAL, 1994), pp. 131–150.

——, 'The Development of the Doctrine of Justification in the Redactional Strata of the Book of Deuteronomy', in Ulrika Lindblad (tr.), *The Theology of Deuteronomy: Collected Essays of Georg Braulik, O.S.B.*, BIBAL Collected Essays 2 (N. Richland Hills, Tex.: BIBAL, 1994), pp. 151–164.

——, 'The Sequence of the Laws in Deuteronomy 12–26', in Duane L. Christensen (ed.), *A Song of Power and the Power of Song* (Winona Lake, Ind.: Eisenbrauns, 1993), pp. 313–335.

Brueggemann, Walter, *Deuteronomy*, Abingdon Old Testament Commentaries (Nashville: Abingdon, 2001).

——, *Theology of the Old Testament: Testimony, Dispute, Advocacy* (Minneapolis: Fortress, 1997).

Cairns, Ian, *Word and Presence: A Commentary on the Book of Deuteronomy*, ITC (Grand Rapids: Eerdmans, 1992).

Calvin, John, 'Commentary upon the Acts of the Apostles', in *Calvin's Commentaries*, vol. 18. *John 12–21; Acts 1–13* (Edinburgh: Calvin Translation Society, 1849; repr. Grand Rapids: Eerdmans, 1999).

——, *Institutes of the Christian Religion*, 2 vols., ed. John T. McNeill, tr. Ford Lewis Battles, LCC 20–21 (Philadelphia: Westminster, 1960).

Came, Daniel, 'Richard Dawkins's Refusal to Debate Is Cynical and Anti-Intellectualist', 22 Oct. 2011.

Carasik, Michael, 'To See a Sound: A Deuteronomic Rereading of Exodus 20:15', *Proof* 19 (1999), pp. 257–265.

Carson, D. A., *The Gospel According to John* (Leicester: Inter-Varsity Press, 1991).

Carson, D. A., and Greg K. Beale (eds.), *Commentary on the New Testament Use of the Old Testament: An Exploration of Old Testament Quotations, Allusions, and Echoes Occurring from Matthew Through Revelation* (Grand Rapids: Baker; Nottingham: Apollos, 2007).

Childs, Brevard S., *Introduction to the Old Testament as Scripture* (London: SCM, 1979).

Chirichigno, Gregory C., *Debt-Slavery in Israel and the Ancient Near East*, JSOTSup 141 (Sheffield: JSOT Press, 1993).

Clements, Ronald E., 'The Book of Deuteronomy: Introduction, Commentary, and Reflections', in Leander E. Keck (ed.), *The New Interpreter's Bible* (Nashville: Abingdon, 1998), vol. 2, pp. 269–538.

——, *Deuteronomy*, OTG (Sheffield: JSOT Press, 1989).

——, *God's Chosen People: A Theological Interpretation of the Book of Deuteronomy* (London: SCM, 1968).

Clines, David J. A., 'The Old Testament Histories: A Reader's Guide', in *What Does Eve Do to Help? And Other Readerly Questions to the Old Testament*, JSOTSup 94 (Sheffield: JSOT Press, 1990), pp. 85–105.

——, *The Theme of the Pentateuch*, 2nd ed., JSOTSup 10 (Sheffield: Sheffield Academic Press, 1997).

Craigie, Peter C., *The Book of Deuteronomy*, NICOT (Grand Rapids: Eerdmans, 1976).

——, *The Problem of War in the Old Testament* (Grand Rapids: Eerdmans, 1978).

Cranfield, C. E. B., *Romans*, 2 vols., ICC (Edinburgh: T. & T. Clark, 1975–9).

Crüsemann, Frank, *The Torah: Theology and Social History of Old Testament Law*, tr. Allan W. Mahnke (Minneapolis: Fortress, 1996).

Dawkins, Richard, 'Why I Refuse to Debate with William Lane Craig', *The Guardian*, 20 Oct. 2011.

Dozeman, Thomas B., Konrad Schmid and Thomas Römer, 'Introduction', in Thomas B. Dozeman, Konrad Schmid and Thomas Römer (eds.), *Pentateuch, Hexateuch, or Enneateuch? Identifying Literary Works in Genesis Through Kings*, Ancient Israel and Its Literature 8 (Atlanta, Ga.: Society of Biblical Literature, 2011), pp. 1–10.

—— (eds.), *Pentateuch, Hexateuch, or Enneateuch? Identifying Literary Works in Genesis Through Kings*, Ancient Israel and Its Literature 8 (Atlanta, Ga.: Society of Biblical Literature, 2011).

Driver, S. R., *A Critical and Exegetical Commentary on Deuteronomy*, ICC (Edinburgh: T. & T. Clark, 1895).

Duggan, Michael W., *The Covenant Renewal in Ezra-Nehemiah (Neh. 7:72b–10:40): An Exegetical, Literary, and Theological Study*, SBLDS 164 (Atlanta, Ga.: Society of Biblical Literature, 2001).

Dumbrell, William J., *The Faith of Israel: Its Expression in the Books of the Old Testament* (Leicester: Apollos, 1988).

Earl, Douglas S., *Reading Joshua as Christian Scripture*, JTISup 2 (Winona Lake, Ind.: Eisenbrauns, 2010).

Eichrodt, Walther, 'The Holy One in Your Midst: The Theology of Hosea', *Int* 15 (1961), pp. 259–273.

Eslinger, Lyle M., 'Ezekiel 20 and the Metaphor of Historical Teleology: Concepts of Biblical History', *JSOT* 81 (1998), pp. 98–125.

Evans, Craig A., 'Jesus & the Continuing Exile of Israel', in Carey C. Newman (ed.), *Jesus & the Restoration of Israel: A Critical Assessment of N.T. Wright's* Jesus and the Victory of God (Downers Grove: InterVarsity Press, 1999), pp. 77–100.

Fishbane, Michael, *Biblical Interpretation in Ancient Israel* (Oxford: Clarendon, 1985).

Fokkelman, J. P., *Major Poems of the Hebrew Bible at the Interface of Hermeneutics and Structural Analysis*, vol. 1: *Exodus 15, Deuteronomy 32 and Job 3*, SSN (Assen, The Netherlands: Van Gorcum, 1998).

France, R. T., *The Gospel of Matthew*, NICNT (Grand Rapids: Eerdmans, 2007).

Fretheim, Terence E., 'The Book of Genesis: Introduction, Commentary, and Reflections', in Leander E. Keck (ed.), *New Interpreter's Bible* (Nashville: Abingdon, 1994), vol. 1, pp. 319–674.

Gammie, John G., *Holiness in Israel*, OBT (Minneapolis: Fortress, 1989).

Gathercole, Simon, 'The Doctrine of Justification in Paul and Beyond: Some Proposals', in Bruce L. McCormack (ed.), *Justification in Perspective:*

Historical Developments and Contemporary Challenges (Grand Rapids: Baker Academic, 2006), pp. 217–241.

Geller, Stephen A., 'Fiery Wisdom: Logos and Lexis in Deuteronomy 4', *Proof* 14 (1994), pp. 103–139.

Goldingay, John, *Approaches to Old Testament Interpretation*, 2nd ed. (Leicester: Inter-Varsity Press, 1990).

——, *Old Testament Theology*, vol. 1: *Israel's Gospel* (Downers Grove: InterVarsity Press, 2003).

——, *The Message of Isaiah 40–55: A Literary-Theological Commentary* (London: T. & T. Clark, 2005).

——, *Theological Diversity and the Authority of the Old Testament* (Grand Rapids: Eerdmans, 1987).

Goldsworthy, Graeme, *According to Plan: The Unfolding Revelation of God in the Bible* (Leicester: Inter-Varsity Press, 1991).

——, *Gospel & Kingdom: A Christian Interpretation of the Old Testament* (Homebush West, NSW: Lancer, 1981).

——, *Preaching the Whole Bible as Christian Scripture* (Leicester: Inter-Varsity Press, 2000).

Goudoever, Jan van, 'The Liturgical Significance of the Date in Dt 1, 3', in Norbert Lohfink (ed.), *Das Deuteronomium: Entstehung, Gestalt und Botschaft*, BETL 68 (Leuven: Leuven University Press, 1985), pp. 145–148.

Gowan, Donald E., 'The Exile in Jewish Apocalyptic', in Arthur L. Merrill and Thomas W. Overholt (eds.), *Scripture in History and Theology: Essays in Honor of J. Coert Rylaarsdam*, PTMS 17 (Pittsburgh, Pa.: Pickwick, 1977), pp. 195–213.

——, *Theology of the Prophetic Books: The Death and Resurrection of Israel* (Louisville: Westminster John Knox, 1998).

Green, Douglas J., 'Ezra-Nehemiah', in Leland Ryken and Tremper Longman III (eds.), *The Complete Literary Guide to the Bible* (Grand Rapids: Zondervan, 1993), pp. 206–215.

Hahn, Scott W., *Kinship by Covenant: A Canonical Approach to the Fulfillment of God's Saving Promises*, Anchor Yale Bible Reference Library (New Haven: Yale University Press, 2009).

Hahn, Scott W., and John S. Bergsma, 'What Laws Were "Not Good?": A Canonical Approach to the Theological Problem of Ezekiel 20:25–26', *JBL* 123 (2004), pp. 201–218.

Halpern, Baruch, *The Constitution of the Monarchy in Israel*, HSM 25 (Chico, Calif.: Scholars Press, 1981).

Hamilton, Jeffries M., *Social Justice and Deuteronomy: The Case of Deuteronomy 15*, SBLDS 136 (Atlanta, Ga.: Scholars Press, 1992).

Hamilton, Victor P., *Exodus: An Exegetical Commentary* (Grand Rapids: Baker Academic, 2011).

Harnack, Adolf von, *Marcion: Das Evangelium vom fremden Gott: Eine Monographie zur Geschichte der Grundlegung der katholischen Kirche*, 2nd ed., TUGAL 3.15 (Leipzig: J. C. Hinrichs, 1924).

Hatina, Thomas R., 'Exile', in Craig A. Evans and Stanley E. Porter (eds.), *Dictionary of New Testament Background* (Leicester: Inter-Varsity Press, 2000), pp. 348–351.

Hays, J. Daniel, 'Applying the Old Testament Law Today', *BSac* 158 (2001), pp. 21–35.

Hays, Richard B., *Echoes of Scripture in the Letters of Paul* (New Haven, Conn.: Yale University Press, 1989).

Hofreiter, Christian, 'Did God Command Genocide? Christian Responses Ancient and Modern', in Philip S. Johnston and David G. Firth (eds.), *Interpreting Deuteronomy: Issues and Approaches* (Nottingham: Apollos, 2012), pp. 240–262.

Hwang, Jerry, *The Rhetoric of Remembrance: An Investigation of the 'Fathers' in Deuteronomy*, Siphrut: Literature and Theology of the Hebrew Scriptures 8 (Winona Lake, Ind.: Eisenbrauns, 2012).

Japhet, Sara, *The Ideology of the Book of Chronicles and Its Place in Biblical Thought*, BEATAJ 9 (Frankfurt am Main: Peter Lang, 1989).

Johnston, Philip S., and David G. Firth (eds.), *Interpreting Deuteronomy: Issues and Approaches* (Nottingham: Apollos, 2012).

Joyce, Paul M., *Divine Initiative and Human Response in Ezekiel*, JSOTSup 51 (Sheffield: JSOT Press, 1989).

——, 'King and Messiah in Ezekiel', in John Day (ed.), *King and Messiah in Israel and the Ancient Near East: Proceedings of the Oxford Old Testament Seminar*, JSOTSup 270 (Sheffield: Sheffield Academic Press, 1998), pp. 323–337.

Kaminsky, Joel S., 'Election Theology and the Problem of Universalism', *HBT* 33.1 (2011), pp. 34–44.

Kaufman, Stephen A., 'The Structure of the Deuteronomic Law', *Maarav* 1.2 (1978–9), pp. 105–158.

Kelly, Brian E., 'Ezra-Nehemiah', in T. Desmond Alexander and Brian S. Rosner (eds.), *New Dictionary of Biblical Theology* (Leicester: Inter-Varsity Press, 2000), pp. 195–198.

Lapsley, Jacqueline E., 'Feeling Our Way: Love for God in Deuteronomy', *CBQ* 65 (2003), pp. 350–369.

Levinson, Bernard M., *Deuteronomy and the Hermeneutics of Legal Innovation* (Oxford: Oxford University Press, 1998).

Lim, Timothy H., 'Deuteronomy in the Judaism of the Second Temple Period', in Steve Moyise and Maarten J. J. Menken (eds.), *Deuteronomy in the New Testament: The New Testament and the Scriptures of Israel*, LNTS 358 (London: T. & T. Clark International, 2007), pp. 6–26.

Lincicum, David, *Paul and the Early Jewish Encounter with Deuteronomy*, WUNT 2.284 (Tübingen: Mohr Siebeck, 2010).

——, 'Paul's Engagement with Deuteronomy: Snapshots and Signposts', *CBR* 7 (2008), pp. 37–67.

Lohfink, Norbert, 'Distribution of the Functions of Power: The Laws Concerning Public Offices in Deuteronomy 16:18–18:22', in Duane L. Christensen (ed.), *A Song of Power and the Power of Song* (Winona Lake, Ind.: Eisenbrauns, 1993), pp. 336–352.

Long, V. Philips, *The Art of Biblical History*, Foundations of Contemporary Interpretation 5 (Grand Rapids: Zondervan, 1994).

Lyons, Michael A., *From Law to Prophecy: Ezekiel's Use of the Holiness Code*, LHBOTS 507 (New York: T. & T. Clark, 2009).

McBride, S. Dean, Jr., 'Polity of the Covenant People: The Book of Deuteronomy', *Int* 41 (1987), pp. 229–244.

McConville, J. Gordon, *Deuteronomy*, AOTC 5 (Leicester: Apollos, 2002).

——, 'Deuteronomy: Torah for the Church of Christ', *EuroJTh* 9 (2000), pp. 33–47.

——, 'Deuteronomy, Book of', in T. Desmond Alexander and David W. Baker (eds.), *Dictionary of the Old Testament: Pentateuch* (Leicester: Inter-Varsity Press, 2003), pp. 182–193.

——, *Exploring the Old Testament*, vol. 4: *Prophets* (London: SPCK, 2002).

——, *God and Earthly Power: An Old Testament Political Theology, Genesis–Kings*, LHBOTS 454 (London: T. & T. Clark, 2006).

——, *Grace in the End: A Study in Deuteronomic Theology*, Studies in Old Testament Biblical Theology (Carlisle: Paternoster, 1993).

——, *Judgment and Promise: An Interpretation of the Book of Jeremiah* (Leicester: Apollos, 1993).

——, 'Law and Monarchy in the Old Testament', in Craig Bartholomew, Jonathan Chaplin, Robert Song and Al Wolters (eds.), *A Royal Priesthood?*

The Use of the Bible Ethically and Politically, SHS 3 (Carlisle: Paternoster, 2002), pp. 69–88.

——, *Law and Theology in Deuteronomy*, JSOTSup 33 (Sheffield: JSOT Press, 1984).

——, 'Old Testament Laws and Canonical Intentionality', in Craig G. Bartholomew, Scott W. Hahn, Robin Parry, Christopher R. Seitz and Al Wolters (eds.), *Canon and Biblical Interpretation*, SHS 7 (Grand Rapids: Zondervan, 2006), pp. 259–281.

——, 'Singular Address in the Deuteronomic Law and the Politics of Legal Administration', *JSOT* 97 (2002), pp. 19–36.

McConville, J. Gordon, and Stephen Williams, *Joshua*, Two Horizons Old Testament Commentary (Grand Rapids: Eerdmans, 2010).

MacDonald, Nathan, *Deuteronomy and the Meaning of 'Monotheism'*, FAT 2.1 (Tübingen: Mohr Siebeck, 2003).

Martens, Elmer A., *God's Design: A Focus on Old Testament Theology*, 2nd ed. (Grand Rapids: Baker; Leicester: Apollos, 1994).

Mayes, A. D. H., *Deuteronomy*, NCBC (London: Marshall, Morgan & Scott, 1979).

——, 'Deuteronomy 4 and the Literary Criticism of Deuteronomy', *JBL* 100 (1981), pp. 23–51.

Michener, James A., *The Source* (London: Mandarin, 1993).

Millar, J. Gary, 'Living at the Place of Decision: Time and Place in the Framework of Deuteronomy', in J. Gordon McConville and J. Gary Millar, *Time and Place in Deuteronomy*, JSOTSup 179 (Sheffield: Sheffield Academic Press, 1994), pp. 15–88.

——, *Now Choose Life: Theology and Ethics in Deuteronomy*, NSBT 6 (Leicester: Apollos, 1998).

Miller, Patrick D., 'Constitution or Instruction? The Purpose of Deuteronomy', in John T. Strong and Steven S. Tuell (eds.), *Constituting the Community: Studies on the Polity of Ancient Israel in Honor of S. Dean McBride Jr.* (Winona Lake, Ind.: Eisenbrauns, 2005), pp. 127–146.

——, 'Moses, My Servant: A Deuteronomic Portrayal of Moses', *Int* 41 (1987), pp. 245–255.

——, 'The Theological Significance of Biblical Poetry', in Samuel E. Balentine and John Barton (eds.), *Language, Theology and the Bible: Essays in Honour of James Barr* (Oxford: Clarendon, 1994), pp. 213–230.

Moberly, R. W. L., 'Is Election Bad for You?', in Jill Middlemas, David J. A. Clines and Else K. Holt (eds.), *The Centre and the Periphery: A European*

Tribute to Walter Brueggemann, Hebrew Bible Monographs 27 (Sheffield: Sheffield Phoenix Press, 2010), pp. 95–111.

——, *The Theology of the Book of Genesis*, Old Testament Theology (Cambridge: Cambridge University Press, 2009).

——, 'Toward an Interpretation of the Shema', in Christopher R. Seitz and Kathryn Greene-McCreight (eds.), *Theological Exegesis: Essays in Honor of Brevard A. Childs* (Grand Rapids: Eerdmans, 1999), pp. 124–144.

Moo, Douglas J., *The Epistle to the Romans*, NICNT (Grand Rapids: Eerdmans, 1996).

Moran, William L., 'The Ancient Near Eastern Background of the Love of God in Deuteronomy', *CBQ* 25 (1963), pp. 77–87.

——, 'The End of the Unholy War and the Anti-Exodus', *Bib* 44 (1963), pp. 333–342.

Morrow, William S., *Scribing the Center: Organization and Redaction in Deuteronomy 14:1–17:13*, SBLMS 49 (Atlanta, Ga.: Scholars Press, 1995).

Moyise, Steve, and Maarten J. J. Menken (eds.), *Deuteronomy in the New Testament: The New Testament and the Scriptures of Israel*, LNTS 358 (London: T. & T. Clark International, 2007).

Najman, Hindy, *Seconding Sinai: The Development of Mosaic Discourse in Second Temple Judaism*, JSJSup 77 (Leiden: Brill, 2003).

Nelson, Richard D., *Deuteronomy*, OTL (Louisville: Westminster John Knox, 2002).

Newman, Carey C. (ed.), *Jesus & the Restoration of Israel: A Critical Assessment of N. T. Wright's Jesus and the Victory of God* (Downers Grove: InterVarsity Press, 1999).

Noonan, Benjamin J., 'Abraham, Blessing, and the Nations: A Reexamination of the Niphal and Hitpael of ברך in the Patriarchal Narratives', *HS* 51 (2010), pp. 73–94.

Noth, Martin, *The Deuteronomistic History*, tr. D. Orton, JSOTSup 15 (Sheffield: JSOT Press, 1981, 2nd ed. [German original 1957]).

O'Donovan, Oliver, *The Desire of the Nations: Rediscovering the Roots of Political Theology* (Cambridge: Cambridge University Press, 1996).

——, 'Towards an Interpretation of Biblical Ethics', *TynB* 27 (1976), pp. 54–78.

Olson, Dennis T., *Deuteronomy and the Death of Moses: A Theological Reading*, OBT (Minneapolis: Fortress, 1994).

Oosthuizen, Martin J., 'Deuteronomy 15:1–18 in Socio-Rhetorical Perspective', *ZABR* 3 (1997), pp. 64–91.

Otto, Eckart, 'False Weights in the Scales of Biblical Justice? Different Views of Women from Patriarchal Hierarchy to Religious Equality in the Book of Deuteronomy', in Victor H. Matthews, Bernard M. Levinson and Tikva Frymer-Kensky (eds.), *Gender and Law in the Hebrew Bible and the Ancient Near East*, JSOTSup 262 (Sheffield: Sheffield Academic Press, 1998), pp. 128–146.

Pate, C. Marvin, J. Scott Duvall, J. Daniel Hays, E. Randolph Richards, W. Dennis Tucker, Jr., and Preben Vang, *The Story of Israel: A Biblical Theology* (Leicester: Apollos, 2004).

Patrick, Dale, 'Election', in *ABD*, vol. 2, pp. 434–441.

Polzin, Robert, 'Deuteronomy', in Robert Alter and Frank Kermode (eds.), *The Literary Guide to the Bible* (London: Fontana, 1987), pp. 92–101.

Porter, Stanley E., 'Allusions and Echoes', in Stanley E. Porter and Christopher D. Stanley (eds.), *As It Is Written: Studying Paul's Use of Scripture*, SBLSS 50 (Atlanta, Ga.: Society of Biblical Literature, 2008), pp. 29–40.

Pratt, Richard L., Jr., 'Historical Contingencies and Biblical Predictions', in James I. Packer and Sven K. Soderlund (eds.), *In the Way of Wisdom: Essays in Honor of Bruce K. Waltke* (Grand Rapids: Zondervan, 2000), pp. 180–203.

Pressler, Carolyn, *The View of Women Found in the Deuteronomic Family Laws*, BZAW 216 (Berlin: de Gruyter, 1993).

Rad, Gerhard von, 'The Form-Critical Problem of the Hexateuch', in E. W. Trueman Dicken (tr.), *The Problem of the Hexateuch and Other Essays* (London: Oliver & Boyd, 1966), pp. 1–78.

——, *Old Testament Theology*, tr. D. M. G. Stalker, 2 vols. (Edinburgh: Oliver & Boyd, 1962–5).

——, *The Problem of the Hexateuch and Other Essays*, tr. E. W. Trueman Dicken (New York: McGraw-Hill, 1966).

Raitt, Thomas M., *A Theology of Exile: Judgment/Deliverance in Jeremiah and Ezekiel* (Philadelphia: Fortress, 1977).

Rendtorff, Rolf, 'Is It Possible to Read Leviticus as a Separate Book?', in John F. A. Sawyer (ed.), *Reading Leviticus: A Conversation with Mary Douglas*, JSOTSup (Sheffield: Sheffield Academic Press, 1996), vol. 227, pp. 22–35.

Roberts, Vaughan, *God's Big Picture: Tracing the Story-Line of the Bible* (Leicester: Inter-Varsity Press, 2003).

Robson, James E., 'Forgotten Dimensions in Holiness', *HBT* 33 (2011), pp. 121–146.

——, 'The Literary Composition of Deuteronomy', in Philip S. Johnston and David G. Firth (eds.), *Interpreting Deuteronomy: Issues and Approaches* (Nottingham: Apollos, 2012), pp. 19–59.

——, *Word and Spirit in Ezekiel*, LHBOTS 447 (New York: T. & T. Clark, 2006).

Rodd, Cyril S., *Glimpses of a Strange Land: Studies in Old Testament Ethics* (Edinburgh: T. & T. Clark, 2001).

Rofé, Alexander, *Deuteronomy: Issues and Interpretation*, OTS (Edinburgh: T. & T. Clark, 2002).

——, 'The Monotheistic Argumentation in Deut. 4:32–40: Contents, Composition and Text', *VT* 35 (1985), pp. 434–445.

Römer, Thomas C., 'Deuteronomy in Search of Origins', in Gary N. Knoppers and J. Gordon McConville (eds.), *Reconsidering Israel and Judah: Recent Studies on the Deuteronomistic History*, Sources for Biblical and Theological Study (Winona Lake, Ind.: Eisenbrauns, 2000), vol. 8, pp. 112–138.

Rosner, Brian S., 'Deuteronomy in 1 and 2 Corinthians', in Steve Moyise and Maarten J. J. Menken (eds.), *Deuteronomy in the New Testament: The New Testament and the Scriptures of Israel*, LNTS 358 (London: T. & T. Clark International, 2007), pp. 118–135.

——, *Paul, Scripture and Ethics: A Study of 1 Corinthians 5–7*, AGJU 22 (Leiden: Brill, 1994).

Ryken, Leland, and Tremper Longman III (eds.), *The Complete Literary Guide to the Bible* (Grand Rapids: Zondervan, 1993).

Sarna, Nahum M., *Exodus*, JPS Torah Commentary (Philadelphia: Jewish Publication Society, 1991).

Scott, James M., 'Restoration of Israel', in Gerald F. Hawthorne and Ralph P. Martin (eds.), *Dictionary of Paul and His Letters* (Leicester: Inter-Varsity Press, 1993), pp. 796–805.

—— (ed.), *Exile: Old Testament, Jewish, and Christian Conceptions*, JSJSup 56 (Leiden: Brill, 1997).

Seitz, Christopher R., *Word Without End: The Old Testament as Abiding Theological Witness* (Grand Rapids: Eerdmans, 1998).

Sleeman, Matthew, *Geography and the Ascension Narrative in Acts*, SNTSMS 146 (Cambridge: Cambridge University Press, 2009).

Smith-Christopher, Daniel L., *A Biblical Theology of Exile* (Minneapolis: Fortress, 2002).

Snodgrass, Klyne R., 'Reading & Overreading the Parables in *Jesus and the Victory of God*', in Carey C. Newman (ed.), *Jesus & the Restoration of Israel: A*

Critical Assessment of N. T. Wright's Jesus and the Victory of God (Downers Grove: InterVarsity Press, 1999), pp. 61–76.

Sparks, Kenton L., *God's Word in Human Words: An Evangelical Appropriation of Critical Biblical Scholarship* (Grand Rapids: Baker Academic, 2008).

Steck, Odil H., *Israel und das gewaltsame Geschick der Propheten: Untersuchungen zur Überlieferung des deuteronomistischen Geschichtsbildes im Alten Testament, Spätjudentum und Urchristentum*, WMANT 23 (Neukirchen-Vluyn: Neukirchener, 1967).

Tiemeyer, Lena-Sofia, 'To Read – Or Not to Read – Ezekiel as Christian Scripture', *ExpTim* 121 (2010), pp. 481–488.

Tigay, Jeffrey H., *Deuteronomy*, JPS Torah Commentary (New York: Jewish Publication Society, 1996).

Turner, Kenneth J., *Death of Deaths in the Death of Israel: Deuteronomy's Theology of Exile* (Eugene, Or.: Wipf & Stock, 2010).

VanderKam, James C., *The Dead Sea Scrolls Today*, 2nd ed. (Grand Rapids: Eerdmans, 2010).

Vang, Karsten, 'God's Love According to Hosea and Deuteronomy: A Prophetic Reworking of a Deuteronomic Concept?', *TynB* 62 (2011), pp. 173–194.

Vogt, Peter T., 'Social Justice and the Vision of Deuteronomy', *JETS* 51 (2008), pp. 35–44.

Vos, Geerhardus, *Biblical Theology: Old and New Testaments* (Grand Rapids: Eerdmans, 1948).

Ware, Bruce A., *God's Lesser Glory: A Critique of Open Theism* (Leicester: Apollos, 2001).

Weinfeld, Moshe, *Deuteronomy 1–11*, AB 5 (New York: Doubleday, 1991).

——, *Deuteronomy and the Deuteronomic School* (Oxford: Oxford University Press, 1972).

——, 'The Origin of the Humanism in Deuteronomy', *JBL* 80 (1961), pp. 241–247.

Wellhausen, Julius, *Prolegomena to the History of Ancient Israel: With a Reprint of the Article 'Israel' from the Encyclopaedia Britannica* (Gloucester, Mass.: Peter Smith, 1983 [German original 1878]).

Wenham, Gordon J., 'The Deuteronomic Theology of the Book of Joshua', *JBL* 90 (1971), pp. 140–148.

——, *Exploring the Old Testament*, vol. 1: *The Pentateuch* (London: SPCK, 2003).

——, 'The Gap Between Law and Ethics in the Bible', *JJS* 48 (1997), pp. 17–29.

——, *Genesis 1–15*, WBC 1 (Dallas: Word, 1987).

——, *Story as Torah: Reading the Old Testament Ethically*, OTS (Edinburgh: T. & T. Clark, 2000).

Wenham, John W., *Christ and the Bible* (London: Tyndale, 1972).

Williamson, H. G. M., *Ezra, Nehemiah*, WBC 16 (Waco: Word, 1985).

——, *Variations on a Theme: King, Messiah and Servant in the Book of Isaiah* (Carlisle: Paternoster, 1998).

Willis, Timothy M., "'Eat and Rejoice Before the Lord": The Optimism of Worship in the Deuteronomic Code', in Rick R. Marrs (ed.), *Worship and the Hebrew Bible*, JSOTSup 284 (Sheffield: JSOT Press, 1999), 276–294.

Wilson, Ian, *Out of the Midst of the Fire: Divine Presence in Deuteronomy*, SBLDS 151 (Atlanta, Ga.: Scholars Press, 1995).

Wolff, Hans W., *Anthropology of the Old Testament*, tr. M. Kohl (London: SCM, 1974).

Wolterstorff, Nicholas, *Divine Discourse: Philosophical Reflections on the Claim That God Speaks* (Cambridge: Cambridge University Press, 1995).

Wright, Christopher J. H., *Deuteronomy*, NIBC (Peabody, Mass.: Hendrickson, 1996).

——, *The God I Don't Understand: Reflections on Tough Questions of Faith* (Grand Rapids: Zondervan, 2008).

——, *God's People in God's Land: Family, Land and Property in the Old Testament* (Grand Rapids: Eerdmans, 1990).

——, *The Mission of God: Unlocking the Bible's Grand Narrative* (Nottingham: Inter-Varsity Press, 2006).

——, *Old Testament Ethics for the People of God* (Leicester: Inter-Varsity Press, 2004).

——, 'Response to Gordon McConville', in Craig G. Bartholomew, Scott W. Hahn, Robin Parry, Christopher R. Seitz and Al Wolters (eds.), *Canon and Biblical Interpretation*, SHS 7 (Grand Rapids: Zondervan, 2006), pp. 282–290.

Wright, N. T., *The Climax of the Covenant: Christ and the Law in Pauline Theology* (Edinburgh: T. & T. Clark, 1991).

——, 'In Grateful Dialogue: A Response', in Carey C. Newman (ed.), *Jesus & the Restoration of Israel: A Critical Assessment of N. T. Wright's* Jesus and the Victory of God (Downers Grove: InterVarsity Press, 1999), pp. 244–280.

——, *Christian Origins and the Question of God*, vol. 1: *The New Testament and the People of God* (London: SPCK, 1992).

——, *Christian Origins and the Question of God*, vol. 2: *Jesus and the Victory of God* (London: SPCK, 1996).

——, *Christian Origins and the Question of God*, vol. 3: *The Resurrection of the Son of God* (London: SPCK, 2003).

——, 'The Letter to the Romans: Introduction, Commentary and Reflections', in Leander E. Keck (ed.), *New Interpreter's Bible*, vol. 10: *Acts, Introduction to Epistolary Literature, Romans, 1 Corinthians* (Nashville: Abingdon, 2002), pp. 393–770.

——, *Christian Origins and the Question of God*, vol. 3: *The Resurrection of the Son of God* (London: SPCK, 2003).

Wright, Tom, *Surprised by Hope* (London: SPCK, 2007).

Yule, George, *Pragmatics* (Oxford: Oxford University Press, 1996).

Zehnder, Markus, 'Building on Stone? Deuteronomy and Esarhaddon's Loyalty Oaths (Part 1): Some Preliminary Observations', *BBR* 19 (2009), pp. 341–374.

——, 'Building on Stone? Deuteronomy and Esarhaddon's Loyalty Oaths (Part 2): Some Additional Observations', *BBR* 19 (2009), pp. 511–535.

Zimmerli, Walther, 'Promise and Fulfillment', in Claus Westermann (ed.), James Luther Mays (tr.), *Essays on Old Testament Hermeneutics* (Richmond: John Knox Press, 1963), pp. 89–122.

Ziskind, Jonathan R., 'The Treatment of Women in Deuteronomy: Moral Absolutism and Practicality – Part I', *JBQ* 27 (1999), pp. 152–158.

INDEX OF AUTHORS

INDEX OF SUBJECTS

love
  Yahweh's for Israel
    118
  Israel's for Yahweh
    146–147

merit 138–141
monarchy See under
  kingship
monotheism 36, 65, 126
Moses, death of 15,
    44–45, 71

nations 75, 94, 98–99
nationalism 78–79, 121,
    176–178

obedience
  Israel 80, 92,
    122–123, 131–132
  church 196–199

Paul 107–108, 110–112,
    141–142, 143–144
Pentateuch 80–82

politics 48, 153–155,
    167–170
poverty 189–201
preaching 199–201
Primary History 69, 82
promises, Abrahamic /
    Patriarchal 32–35,
    51, 52, 66, 73–76,
    79, 90–91, 95,
    162
prophet 155–156
prophecy 186–187
prosperity 137–138

recreation 78
redemption 36, 77, 117,
    119
remembering (or
    memory) 15–17,
    40–42, 49–50, 57,
    123
repentance 52–54, 94,
    95
restoration 52–54,
    60–62, 91–101

retribution 137–138
seeing 122–123
Shema 126–127
slavery
  institution of
    148–150, 157–158,
    182–183, 187
  Israel's 36, 37, 52
  Song of Moses 44,
    54–64

teaching 39, 125–126
temple 97
today 15–17, 31,
    43–46
Torah 49, 54–56, 64,
    82, 133

unbelief See under faith

war, holy/Yahweh See
    under *ḥērem*
wilderness 40–42
women 158–159, 185,
    188

INDEX OF SCRIPTURE REFERENCES

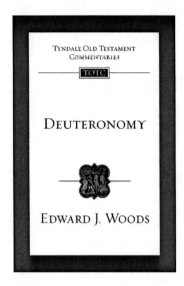

related titles from Apollos

APOLLOS OLD TESTAMENT COMMENTARIES

Deuteronomy
J. G. McConville

ISBN: 978-0-85111-779-9
544 pages, hardback

In this outstanding commentary Gordon McConville offers a theological interpretation of the Old Testament book of Deuteronomy in the context of the biblical canon. He gives due attention to historical issues where these bear on what can be known about the settings in which the text emerged. His dominant method is one that approaches Deuteronomy as a finished work.

Professor McConville argues that, in the context of the ancient world, Deuteronomy should be understood as the radical blueprint for the life of a people, at the same time both spiritual and political, and profoundly different from every other social, political and religious programme. The book incorporates the tension between an open-ended vision of a perfectly ordered society under God and practical provisions for dealing with the frailty and imperfections of real people. Hence, it is capable of informing our thinking about the organization of societies, while maintaining a vision of the kingdom of God.

Available from your local Christian bookshop or **www.thinkivp.com**

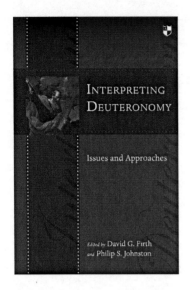

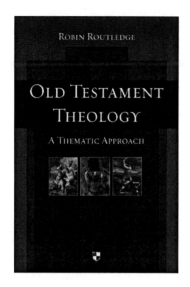

related titles from Apollos

Old Testament Theology
A thematic approach
Robin Routledge

ISBN: 978-1-84474-286-8
384 pages, hardback

Numerous useful books on Old Testament theology are now available. However, they often give too much information – or too little. Some can seem large, and daunting to the ordinary student or pastor, and because of their layout, information may be hard to access. Others take a more introductory approach and do not deal with many of the theological issues and questions that the Old Testament raises.

Robin Routledge's aim is to bridge this gap. He provides a substantial overview of the central issues and themes in Old Testament theology in the main body of the text, with more detailed discussion and references for further reading in the footnotes. His purpose is to examine the theological significance of the various texts in their wider canonical context, noting unity and coherence within the Old Testament, whilst also being aware of diversity. A brief outline of the relationship between exegesis and biblical theology within the overall task of interpreting and applying biblical material is given in the first chapter.

His hope is that, while this volume has grown out of a teaching context, and is intended for students, it will also be of benefit to others who want to take the theological content of the Old Testament seriously, and to apply its message to the life and ministry of the church today.

Available from your local Christian bookshop or **www.thinkivp.com**

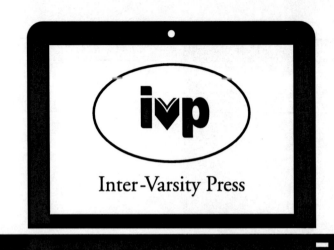

Inter-Varsity Press

For more information about IVP
and our publications visit
www.ivpbooks.com

Get regular updates at **ivpbooks.com/signup**
Find us on **facebook.com/ivpbooks**
Follow us on **twitter.com/ivpbookcentre**

Inter-Varsity Press, a company limited by guarantee registered in England and Wales, number 05202650. Registered
office IVP Bookcentre, Norton Street, Nottingham NG7 3HR, United Kingdom. Registered charity number 1105757.